An Encyclopedia of
Assholes

An Encyclopedia of
Assholes

Kristoffer Darlington and Diane Law

Magpie Books, London

Constable & Robinson Ltd
3 The Lanchesters
162 Fulham Palace Road
London W6 9ER
www.constablerobinson.com

This edition published by Magpie Books,
an imprint of Constable & Robinson Ltd, 2008

A copy of the British Library Cataloguing in Publication Data
is available from the British Library

ISBN: 978-1-84529-794-7

Printed and bound in the EU

Contents

Introduction

A Definition of the Term Asshole

"Opinions," goes the lowbrow adage, "are like assholes. Everyone's got one, and everyone thinks everyone else's stinks but their own." While this may be at least partially true, as most clichés are, what of our opinions of the people we label *as* assholes? Are they just one person's reaction to another, at a given, unpleasant moment, and therefore *totally* subjective? Or are these judgments based on more generally accepted criteria, whereby certain individuals are exclusively and almost universally recognized as assholes by just about everybody who encounters them? This needs to be understood, if only because one should try to be accurate with insults, or their power is greatly limited.

And "asshole" *is* a powerful insult. Its reductive and metaphorical nature makes it clear that those described as such – in the eyes of the person doing the describing at least – are nothing more than a human-sized sphincter muscle, the common anus, a mindless portal for shit to enter the world. Who, one has to ask, *truly* warrants this humbling description?

Usually, when the term "asshole" is used to describe someone, it stems from that person's actions toward us, or toward those around him or her, in a particular moment. Someone cuts you off in traffic, takes the last piece of pizza, runs over your puppy, or does any number of other inconsiderate or horrible things, and you think, "What an asshole!" almost as a knee-jerk reaction, a reflex. But something more is required than simply this kind of rude, destructive and/or hurtful action for someone to be really deserving of the term. That something is *intent*.

For example, if the guy who cut you off in traffic was trying to get his pregnant wife, who'd just gone into labor, to a hospital, very few people would consider him an asshole; he'd simply be someone trying to do the right thing, just not very well. Likewise, if the woman who took the last piece of pizza were a recently arrived refugee from a country in the grip of a severe famine, most people would actually feel a great deal of sympathy her, and might even inquire if she'd like more to eat. And while most people would never *consciously* run over a puppy, someone might very well do so if the puppy and his or her vehicle were both on a large patch of black ice. Obviously, these are *not* the people we are attempting to define, and scrutinize, in this book.

The people we are concerned with are far more *deliberate* in their behavior than we (and probably anyone within fifty feet of them) are comfortable with. They are the kind of people who *intentionally* cut you off, who eat that last slice, and/or kill your puppy for two simple reasons: the opportunity was there, and they felt like taking it. When we know we are dealing with *this* kind of individual, we return to that knee-jerk reaction mentioned earlier, with unsurprisingly, near universal agreement that we are in the presence of an asshole. Sickeningly enough though, there is more going on than these immediate perceptions, at least when it comes to *true* assholes.

For the worst examples of the term do *more* than just behave selfishly in ways which hurt or inconvenience us; they also make it perfectly clear that they couldn't care less what we think of them. If we honk our horn, the true asshole responds with an insult or an unconcerned shrug, thereby making his or her "world view" painfully obvious to us as well as to any onlookers. Likewise, if we protest at the last piece of pizza being eaten, or the demise of our puppy, and get the same reaction, we can safely assume that we are dealing with a true asshole. The situation, or the scope of it, really doesn't matter with such people, and neither does our opinion of their actions. The *only* thing that matters to them is getting what they want, when they want it, as quickly and easily as possible.

It is these remorselessly destructive egocentrists whom we are exposing to public attention in this book. If we were to attempt to include every individual who fits this rather specific criterion in a single collection, this would be a multi-volume set of books which would make the *Encyclopedia Britannica* or the *Oxford Unabridged Dictionary* seem insubstantial by comparison. With this in mind, we have concerned ourselves with some of the worst, most notorious, and/or most up-to-the-minute examples, as a cautionary service to the public, for a problem cannot be solved if it is not thoroughly understood by those affected by it.

A caveat at this stage is that there are some subjects included here, who, while they may be widely perceived to be assholes, may, in the end, be exonerated of the charge. For example, Michael Moore may be fairly castigated for twisting the truth, but, in doing so as a necessary antidote to mainstream media distortions, is probably guilty of a lesser evil. Or George Lucas, while undoubtedly an exceptional film-maker, deserves censure for his role in making the blockbuster the dominant force in cinema, thereby damaging it, perhaps irreparably. (He is also to be condemned for messing up his own legacy with his late-in-life tinkering with his *Star Wars* trilogy.) And Madonna is a partial asshole – for her appalling films, rather than for her music. Likewise, the Catholic Church is asshole-like for sheltering child-abusing priests.

In short, an organization or individual's inclusion in the encyclopedia does not necessarily mean that he, she, or it deserves to be branded an out-and-out asshole. KD

The Encyclopedia

Political and Religious Assholes

Mahmoud Ahmadinejad

Seeking Hostility

Born in 1956, Iran's President Mahmoud Ahmadinejad is an enigma in some respects. He is belligerent yet naïve, a fundamentalist but also a nationalist. He is clearly highly skilled at mobilizing Iranian public opinion. In his first year as president, he moved from obscurity to be one of the most prominent and controversial leaders in the world. His uncompromising insistence on Iran's right to enrich uranium, which he insists is for a nuclear power program, together with his uncompromising hostility toward Israel, has increased the threat of further turmoil in the Middle East, and perhaps edged the United States and Iran ever closer to military confrontation. His comments about Israel being "wiped from the map" seem to have been misreported, but he has made other belligerent comments on the situation and his state continues to support armed groups that threaten to destabilize the region even further.

Ahmadinejad was elected with the mandate to improve the economic situation of the Iranian people. His campaign slogan, "We can do it," was a reference to tackling corruption, rather than building nuclear weapons, but the United States was nonetheless uneasy from the start, in a period when it was keen to identify the "axis of evil" in the world. Previously a commander in the Revolutionary Guards and mayor of Tehran, Ahmadinejad's message, which went down well with ordinary Iranians, was that Iran should become strong again; enriching uranium became a point of national pride in pursuit of that end. His message to the United States seemed to be that they could do nothing to stop him, but many saw his provocations as a dangerous gamble, fearing that the United States might flex its military muscle, if only to prove him wrong. Unsurprisingly, Ahmadinejad's posturing – poking sticks at the United States, while making friendly overtures to Russia – made the international community somewhat uneasy. Ahmadinejad has also been accused of stifling free speech, supporting religious tyranny, and of suppressing academia and opposition groups.

When he took office in August 2005, Ahmadinejad was the first non-clerical president to lead Iran in 24 years. His public image was that of a straightforward man, who lived a simple life with his family in a modest apartment. His populist platform, which included a proposed monthly stipend to citizens, won votes from people concerned about the economy and unemployment. But Ahmadinejad's main advertisement was a film depicting him praying and wearing military fatigues, while addressing war veterans. The military is supposed to steer clear of politics in Iran, but it has always played a crucial role. But the election won by Ahmadinejad placed an unprecedented prominence on the military.

Ahmadinejad is seen differently abroad. President George W. Bush has asserted that the Iranian presidential elections are designed to keep power in the hands of rulers who suppress freedoms at home and who will spread terror around the world. According to the US State Department, the Iranian election didn't meet minimum democratic standards. The United States has its own historical problems with Iran, but many other nations view Ahmadinejad as an asshole for playing dangerous games with a twitchy, trigger-happy US administration.

Ahmadinejad's tact has been in doubt since his early career. After the 1979 Islamic Revolution, he was a member the ultra-conservative Office for Strengthening Unity between Universities and Theological Seminaries (OSU). Apparently when the idea of storming the US embassy in Tehran was raised by the OSU, he suggested storming the Soviet embassy at the same time. Some of the US hostages who were held in the Tehran embassy have alleged that Ahmadinejad was one of their captors, but Iranians known to have been involved in the incident have denied that he was involved.

Appointed mayor of Tehran in April 2003, Ahmadinejad started "cleaning up" the city by reversing many of the reforms of his moderate predecessors. He closed fast-food restaurants and required male city employees to grow beards and wear long sleeves. He instituted separate elevators for men and women in the municipal offices and asked for the martyrs of the Iran–Iraq War to be buried in Tehran's major squares. On 26 April 2005, he decreed a plaque would be installed in honor of the victims of Iraqi chemical warfare, citing "major" crimes that had been committed against the Iranian nation.

In an interview in June 2005, on state TV, Ahmadinejad claimed Iran was the target of a Western cultural onslaught. He said that the West aimed to undermine the self-confidence of Iranian managers and influence the young generation. He told a news conference that he would not improve ties with any country that "seeks hostility" against Iran. "The US administration cut off ties unilaterally to lay waste to the Islamic republic," he argued. Rather illogically, he continued, "They want to restore them today for the same reason."

He also accused Iran's nuclear negotiators, on 20 June 2005, of bowing to European pressure. According to Ahmadinejad, "those who are handling the talks are terrified, and before they even sit down at the negotiating table they retreat 500 kilometers . . . A popular and fundamentalist government will quickly change that."

His campaign issued a statement saying that it "would be suicidal for a country to attack Iran . . . so we must not bend to threats." Meanwhile, during the run-off election in June 2005, Ahmadinejad said he would continue to talk to Europe over Iran's nuclear program: "We will continue the current policies of the Islamic Republic. In principle, dialogue with Europe, Asia, and Africa is within the framework of our foreign policy. And of course, in order to defend the rights of our nation, we will continue the [nuclear] dialogue [with Europe]." Commenting on Iran's foreign policy, Ahmadinejad said Iran was interested in friendly ties with all nations. He claimed Tehran would co-operate with any government that did not have a hostile attitude towards Iran. However, he seems unwilling to include the United States in this friendly attitude, now or at any time in the future. He simply doesn't want to mend the broken bridges with the United States.

In September 2005, in a speech at the UN General Assembly, Ahmadinejad accused the United States of proliferating weapons of mass destruction and also of having created a "climate of intimidation and injustice." In September 2005, the International Atomic Energy Agency (IAEA) announced that Iran wasn't in compliance with the Non-Proliferation Treaty (NPT), and recommended sanctions. Ahmadinejad threatened to continue enriching uranium if the IAEA kept pursuing sanctions against Iran. In response to the sanctions, Ahmadinejad announced to the West, "I want you to know that the Iranian nation has humiliated you many times, and it will humiliate you in the future."

Ahmadinejad seems to react to any outside pressure to change his ways with the stubborn selfishness of a small child, though one with the power to be very dangerous. He continues to do as he likes and thumb his nose at those who vainly hope for a more reasonable approach to a job that has the capacity to be a crucial one in the passage of the Middle East and the Gulf States toward eventual war or peace. DL

Idi Amin

Ugandan Madman

Idi Amin was not merely an asshole; he was, quite literally, a madman. After his death in 2003, his doctor released information which corroborated the theory that Amin was clinically insane. He was being treated with anti-psychotic drugs, and was also receiving drugs for syphilis.

Having been obsessed with the military from an early age, he joined the King's African Rifles in 1946, at the age of 18, although he never learned to read or write. One story originating from Amin's time in the British Army draws attention to just how mentally unstable he was, even then. When his Commanding Officer persuaded him to open a bank account, Amin deposited $20, but then spent $4,000 in the next few hours, buying new suits, a car, and a huge amount of food and drink. He then posed around town in his uniform, acting like a king. Tales of rapes and captives being tied up and bayoneted were consistently linked to the presence of an unusually large, happy, laughing officer.

After being made Deputy Commander of the Army, Amin launched a military coup against President Milton Obote. Beginning at 3 a.m., Amin's army stormed the parliament, the airport (where two priests were killed), and the radio station. All telephone lines were cut, and Amin himself watched it all from his heavily fortified luxury home. In the days following the coup there was an almost carnival atmosphere. Anti-Obote protestors took to the streets, hailing Major-General Amin as their savior and hero. The protestors were mainly from the Buganda tribe, which had resented Obote for expelling its king.

Amin then declared himself president, dissolved parliament, and amended the constitution to give himself absolute power. Within three weeks of Amin's coup, 2,000 army officers and men had been killed on his orders, and 10,000 civilians were murdered within three months. These murders were carried out secretly and systematically, by Amin's "Killer Squads." At first, the main targets were people belonging to other tribes. As time went on though, many people were killed simply for their possessions. Some civilians were taken off the street, killed, and their relatives were then charged for the return of their often badly mutilated bodies.

When Amin discovered that there were 36 officers in his army from the targeted tribes, they were summoned to Mackindye for "training in internal security." They were all locked in cells, and subsequently murdered with bayonets. Amin also ordered the death of the former Army Chief of Staff, Brigadier Hussein Suleiman, whom he had resented since Obote had appointed him. Amin had him slowly beaten to death with wrenches, before having his head cut off and frozen. Brigadier Suleiman's head formed the beginning of what was to become a large collection, which would eventually require its own room and refrigerator. A year later, Amin is said to have brought out Suleiman's frozen head to show it off proudly to his guests at a dinner party. Next, without any apparent reason, he began to destroy his own army.

At first the outside world didn't know what was going on in Uganda. On Amin's first official visit to the United Kingdom, he had dinners with Conservative prime minister Edward Heath, and also with Queen Elizabeth and Prince Philip. His official reception in Scotland impressed him so much that he acquired a fetish for all things Scottish, believing that the Scots wanted him as their king, a position he said he would be delighted to accept.

Incoherent messages were sent to many world leaders whenever Amin thought it necessary, often giving them "advice" on various problems, and sometimes just taunting them. Amin also made a request to the United Kingdom for Harrier jets so that he could bomb

South Africa, Tanzania, and Sudan. Leaders across the globe began to realize that all was not well with Idi Amin, but they had no idea of the atrocities being committed inside Uganda.

Back in Uganda, inflation soared to 700 per cent, with a bar of soap costing about two weeks' wages. Amin's solution was simply to print more money. He often took private flights to Paris or London to go on luxury spending sprees with his closest friends.

At home in Uganda, Amin had a harem of wives and an estimated 25 to 35 children. He kept a collection of "trophies" from those he had killed in his home. When one of his wives, Kay, died in a bungled abortion attempt, he insisted that her legs and arms be removed and re-attached with the legs at the shoulders and the arms at the pelvis as a warning to his other wives. He kept the head of Jesse Gitta, the former husband of his wife Sarah in his freezer (which he referred to as his "botanical room"). Among many others was the head of Ruth Kobusinje, a one-time girlfriend whom he had suspected of infidelity. One nurse testified to decapitating six bodies and sending their shaved and preserved heads to Amin's home. He also confessed proudly to Henry Kyemba, the health minister, during a dinner party, that he had eaten the flesh of his human victims on many occasions.

Eventually, two events of international significance served to show the world the true extent of Idi Amin's madness. The first of these was his decision to expel all Asians from Uganda; the second was the Entebbe hostage crisis in 1976.

The expulsion of Uganda's Asian population was the final blow to the country's economy. Amin's justification was that the Asians had only come to the country to build the railways and, now that they had finished, they must all go home. In reality, Asians ran about 80 per cent of Uganda's small businesses. As they left the country, Asian families were usually stripped of all their possessions, including all jewelry and watches. Most of the Asian families expelled from Uganda sought asylum in the United Kingdom. All businesses which had been owned by Asians were handed over to Amin's army henchmen. The shops were first emptied, and then closed within a few weeks. By this time, the Ugandan people were close to starvation, but Amin, still lost in his fantasy world, did not, or would not, notice. He was still offering help to over 30 developing countries affected by drought, continuing to write cheques, seemingly with no idea of the terrible condition to which the Ugandan economy had been reduced.

When Palestinian militants hijacked an Air France flight from Tel Aviv to Paris via Athens, carrying around 300 passengers, they were given permission to land at Entebbe Airport in Uganda. From Entebbe, the hijackers publicized their demands; all passengers would be killed within 48 hours unless 53 Palestinian prisoners charged with acts of terrorism were released from jails in Israel and Europe. The deadline was extended following negotiations and non-Jewish passengers were released. The rest of the hostages were taken to the airport terminal where Amin, delighted by the attention, was filmed wandering, smiling, through the hostages. An elderly female hostage, Dora Bloch, with joint Israeli and British citizenship, choked on her food and had to be taken to hospital in Kampala. While she was receiving treatment, Israeli commandoes staged a spectacular rescue. Flying into Entebbe Airport, they took just under an hour and a half to rescue the hostages and destroy a flight of Mig fighter planes on the ground, to hamper pursuit. They killed 20 Ugandan army troops and all seven hijackers. One hostage died in the course of the rescue, along with the commandoes' leader.

When he heard about what had happened, Amin went wild with fury. Never one to allow anyone to humiliate him, he had Dora Bloch dragged from her bed in the hospital and killed. Her body was later found where it had been dumped on the outskirts of Kampala.

Amin subsequently attempted to invade Tanzania, but his army was forced to retreat. Amin suggested that the war be settled by a boxing match between himself and President Nyerere of Tanzania, but the proposal was ignored and Nyerere's troops simply continued their advance into Uganda.

In April 1979, Amin fled to Libya to seek refuge with Muammar Gaddafi. He lived there for the next few years, until Gaddafi threw him out, for reasons which remain unclear. Perhaps Gaddafi simply realized the extent of Amin's madness, but it is also rumored that Amin had raped, or attempted to rape, Gaddafi's 14-year-old daughter. The exiled Ugandan dictator ended up in Saudi Arabia, where he lived a life of luxury, on condition that he kept a low profile until his death, which came in August 2003. DL

Yasser Arafat

Bearing an Olive Branch and a Freedom Fighter's Gun

There is much debate as to whether Arafat should be deemed a hero or an asshole. Many argue that he was always only ever acting with the best intentions of attempting to gain an autonomous homeland for Palestinians, while others view him as a leader and supporter of terrorists.

Arafat was born Mohammed Abdel-Raouf Arafat As Qudwa al-Hussaeini, on 24 August 1929, in Cairo, Egypt. Supposedly, even before he turned 17, he was smuggling arms to Palestine for use against the British authorities and the Jewish settlers. While he was studying at the University of Faud I (later Cairo University) war broke out between the Jews and the Arab states. Wanting to fight, Arafat left university and fought against the Jews in Gaza. When the Arabs were defeated, resulting in the creation of the state of Israel, Arafat was in despair. Nevertheless, he held on to his dream of an independent Palestinian homeland, and, when he returned to university, he spent most of his time leading the Palestinian students.

In 1953, Arafat sent a famed letter to an Egyptian leader. His letter consisted of only three words, rumored to have been written with his own blood. The message was simple: "Don't forget Palestine."

The Palestine Liberation Organization (PLO) was established in 1964, and, in 1969, Arafat was appointed chairman. In Jordan, he developed the PLO into a state within a state, with its own military force. But King Hussein of Jordan expelled the PLO because of attacks on Israel, its powerful neighbor. Following the expulsion, Arafat attempted to establish a similar "state" in Lebanon, with greater success, owing to Lebanon's weak and embattled central government. During the 1970s, a number of leftist PLO groups emerged to take up the military struggle against Israel, attacking both military and civilian targets, inside and outside of Israel. From this point onwards, Arafat was seen by many as a terrorist.

In 1974, the Palestine National Council (PNC) approved a Ten Point

Program, drawn up by Arafat and his advisors, which proposed compromise with the Israelis. The program called for a Palestinian national authority to take power over every part of "liberated Palestinian territory," a reference to those areas captured by Arab forces in the 1948 Arab–Israeli War, meaning the present-day West Bank and Gaza Strip. This caused discontent among several of the PLO factions and, as a result, the Popular Front for the Liberation of Palestine (PFLP), the Democratic Front for the Liberation of Palestine (DFLP), and other groups formed a breakaway organization called the Rejectionist Front.

Israel and the United States have alleged that Arafat was involved in the 1973 assassination in Khartoum of five diplomats and five others. A 1973 US Department of State document, declassified in 2006, concludes, "The Khartoum operation was planned and carried out with the full knowledge and personal approval of Yasser Arafat." Arafat, however, denied any involvement with the operation, insisting that it had been carried out independently by the Black September group. Israel claimed that Arafat was in ultimate control of such Palestinian organizations, and had thus not abandoned terrorism. In the same year, the PLO was declared the "sole legitimate representative of the Palestinian people" and admitted to full membership by the Arab League at a summit in Rabat, the capital of Morocco. Arafat was the first representative of a non-governmental organization to address a plenary session of the United Nations General Assembly. In his UN address, Arafat condemned Zionism, but said, "Today I have come bearing an olive branch and a freedom fighter's gun. Do not let the olive branch fall from my hand." It was a speech which increased international sympathy for the Palestinian cause, even though it carried an implied threat.

The problem was that Arafat, while demanding peace and autonomy, made some foolish mistakes. During the Kuwait crisis of 1990, for example, he supported Saddam Hussein, thereby isolating himself, and the Palestinian cause, from most of the international community. Deciding he had no option but to negotiate with Israel for peace, Arafat, along with Shimon Peres and the Israeli Prime Minister Yitzhak Rabin, was jointly awarded the 1994 Nobel Peace Prize. The award was controversial because many accused Arafat of supporting and organizing terrorism, while in the Israeli military, it was Yitzhak Rabin that had ordered the expulsion of Arabs from areas captured by

Israel during the 1948 war. The winners all shook hands on the White House lawn in 1993, but there was no real resolution of these issues. When Arafat returned to Gaza the following year, such fundamental problems as the fate of Palestinian refugees had been left undecided, and the peace process was still fraught with difficulty. It was increasingly unclear why the Nobel Prize had been awarded to the three men in the first place. Nevertheless, Arafat continued to try to keep both the Palestinians and the Israelis committed to what he called "the peace of the brave."

From that time onward, Arafat's own life was far from peaceful. By 2000, all attempts at conciliation seemed to have failed, and a new, armed *intifada*, with Arafat as its figurehead, had been launched in the West Bank. Ariel Sharon accused Arafat of bringing terror to Israeli streets, and Israeli troops battered Arafat's Ramallah compound. Meanwhile, his Palestinian critics accused him of running a corrupt administration, and of having made too many concessions to, and placed undue trust in, the United States. Arafat seemed to have rendered himself ineffectual through his attempts to secure peace by keeping all sides happy. Perhaps it is unfair to castigate Arafat, as the Middle East problem has defeated all attempts at solution. But in reviewing Arafat's life, it seems that he was the one man who might have been able to bring the Palestinians to peace in his lifetime, but was simultaneously a man who was incapable of achieving that goal.

In October 2004, Arafat fell ill. Closely observed by the world's media, his condition deteriorated over following days. Eventually, Arafat was flown by French government jet to the Percy military hospital in Clamart, a suburb of Paris, where his doctors said that he was suffering from idiopathic thrombocytopenic purpura, a decrease in the number of circulating platelets to abnormally low levels. In November, as he lapsed into a gradually deepening coma, kept alive by life support machines, rumors ran riot, including speculation that he had been poisoned. Sheikh Taissir Tamimi, the head of the Islamic court of the Palestinian territories, who held a vigil at Arafat's bedside, declared that there was no question of disconnecting him from life support equipment since, according to the Sheikh, such an action was prohibited by Islam. Arafat was pronounced dead at 3.30 a.m. (Greenwich Mean Time) on 11 November 2004, at the age of 75. The exact cause of his illness remains unknown; what we do know is that the troubles between Israel and Palestine continue to this day. DL

Marion Barry

Bitch Set me Up

While he was Mayor of Washington DC, Marion Barry was busted for crack cocaine by the FBI. He later recovered from this major political setback to serve on the Washington DC City Council in 2005. "I've been knocked down," he told CNN. "Some people would say you fell down or knocked yourself down, but I got up!" Fair comment. But Barry has a long history of political banana skins.

In 1960, as a young man, he was involved in a lunch-counter sit-in in Nashville, Tennessee. According to the *Washington Post*, he helped register voters and conducted non-violence workshops while studying for a doctorate in chemistry at the University of Tennessee. Later he was involved in the burgeoning civil rights movement, moving to Washington DC where he became a leader on the Student Non-Violent Co-ordinating Committee. His opposition to racial discrimination gained him support in the district, and Barry moved on to a political career, winning an open School Board seat, and later a place on the city council. In 1978, he was elected mayor, an office which he held until 1990.

During his 12 years as mayor, Barry undoubtedly made some positive political moves. He helped to rejuvenate the city's downtown area, which in turn sparked off a construction boom, and his administration also succeeded in balancing the city's budget, a major issue which had dogged cities around the United States. One of his most distinctive initiatives was the District Youths Employment Act of 1979, which gave guaranteed summer jobs to any city youth who wanted one, regardless of their economic status.

However, on 18 January 1990, trouble arrived. Barry was arrested for crack cocaine use and possession while with his former girlfriend, Hazel "Rasheeda" Moore, at the Vista Hotel. He was caught out by a sting operation conducted by the FBI and DC Police. Footage of the incident was constantly shown on TV, with an enraged Barry railing at "Rasheeda" Moore, who had been acting as an FBI informant: "Goddamn setup . . . I'll be goddamn. Bitch set me up."

Barry was charged with three felony counts of perjury, ten counts of misdemeanor drug possession, and one misdemeanor count of conspiracy to possess cocaine. He was only actually convicted on only one charge, in October 1990: a single previous misdemeanor count of possessing cocaine, dating back to November 1989, for which he served six months in a federal prison. He was acquitted on one possession charge and a mistrial was declared on the 12 remaining charges. But the inevitable result of his arrest and trial was that Barry was forced to step down as mayor, in the middle of his campaign for a City Council seat.

Barry has many staunch supporters though, who saw him first and foremost as a champion of the poor, . In 1992, he was again elected to the Washington DC City Council, and, two years later, he was elected as mayor once again. It shows the regard in which he was held that he was so quickly forgiven by many. There's little doubt that he could have achieved much more had his reputation not been consistently tarnished by his various brushes with the law.

However, his fourth term as the city's leader was overshadowed by allegations of financial wrongdoing, and he decided not to run again in 1998. Barry seemed to crave attention though, and he did not stay in the shadows for long. In 2004, Barry ran for the City Council once again. He succeeded, having won more than 96 per cent of the vote in Ward 8, an extremely poor area with high unemployment levels. Barry insisted that his drug-taking was in the past, and that he was looking forward to the future. However, it was not long before it all went wrong yet again.

This time, he had apparently "forgotten" to pay his taxes and, in October 2005, he pleaded guilty to two misdemeanor charges for failing to file his income tax returns for 2000, following an IRS investigation, and a federal magistrate judge sentenced him to three years' probation. He had tested positive for cocaine and marijuana use the previous year, so the judge also ordered Barry to undergo drug treatment and counseling.

Even then, Barry couldn't keep out of trouble. On 10 September 2006, he was stopped by Secret Service Uniformed Division police officers and charged with driving under the influence, operating a vehicle while impaired, driving an unregistered vehicle, and the misuse of temporary tags. In June 2007, he was acquitted of the drunk-driving charges, but it nonetheless seems that every time Barry gets a chance to once again have a positive impact on the lives of disadvantaged people, he just can't stop himself from ending up in court and letting the opportunity slip away. DL

Osama bin Laden

Egotist, Terrorist, Rabbit

Osama bin Laden is perhaps the most infamous figure in the world today as the founder of al-Qaeda, a terrorist group with cells around the world, capable of causing mass destruction and death. Bin Laden is the world's most wanted man, and his hatred of the United States and all that it stands for is well documented. He has many supporters, but one can't help but wonder why this wealthy, middle-aged man should continue to incite young people to kill themselves, and others, for their beliefs. Does it make him a coward, or a hero? A great leader, or an asshole? From the Western media viewpoint, bin Laden is one of the biggest assholes of his generation, one among many waging war. His role is as a lynchpin in his own ideological battle, attracting thousands of disaffected youths to sign up for DIY warfare from the comfort of their Western bedrooms. His group manipulates others into killing themselves for his delusional, self-righteous cause. Many say that bin Laden abuses religious doctrine in pursuit of his message of hate.

It is claimed that bin Laden is the mastermind behind the 9/11 attacks in New York, and he seems happy to take the credit for this murderous attack. At the time, George W. Bush described the Saudi-born militant as an incarnation of evil and said he was wanted "dead or alive." In an interview on al-Jazeera TV station in 1998, bin Laden reportedly said, "Ever since I can recall, I despised and felt hatred towards Americans." Even before this, his activities were well known, and the bin Laden family disowned Osama officially in 1994, under pressure from the Saudi government.

Of course, some argue that the United States had a hand in building bin Laden up in the first place, since they once funded his operations, during the Soviet occupation of Afghanistan, between 1979 and 1989. It is reported that bin Laden fought alongside US units during the Soviet–Afghan war. When al-Qaeda set up their training camps in the Taliban's Afghanistan, they were using US weapons. This was, of course, during the Cold War with the Soviet Union, and it was in the United States's interest to support the Afghan fighters. During Osama's early years, his target was the Soviet Union. But after the collapse of the Soviet bloc, he seemed to turn on the United States.

Another perspective on this would be that the United States supported the Taliban in wresting power from the Soviets, and then turned against the Taliban when action had to be taken against the terrorist training camps after 9/11. There is little room for loyalty in the alliances of modern warfare. Al-Qaeda did more or less the same thing: they welcomed help from the United States in their fight against the Soviets, and then rechanneled their energy into bringing down their erstwhile allies. But none of this excuses bin Laden's personal war, and his cowardice in hiding away like a rabbit, while egging others on to give up their lives in his name.

Even though great efforts were supposedly made to discover bin Laden, no firm evidence of his whereabouts has been produced since the destruction of the World Trade Center, and he has never been found. Some sources argue that Osama bin Laden is dead. *Time* magazine (June 2002) reported that the news had been passed on from sources in Afghanistan and Pakistan six months previously. The story was that the fugitive bin Laden had died in December 2001, and was buried in the mountains of southeast Afghanistan. However, despite Pakistan President Pervez Musharraf repeating the information, US commentators refused to believe the growing rumors. True of false, the surviving members of bin Laden's gang have mostly stayed silent, either to keep his "ghost" alive, or because they have no safe means of communication. "The proof that he's alive is, we don't hear anything from Osama bin Laden," said Larry Johnson, a former State Department counter-terrorism official. "The proof that he's dead is, we don't hear anything from Osama bin Laden." (*Time* June 2002)

With his monstrous ego, it is hard to believe that he would have remained silent for so long if he were still alive. He has always liked to take credit, even for things he probably had nothing to do with. Would he really remain silent for years on end and not trumpet his own survival? His supporters point to the al-Jazeera Arab television broadcasts that show the world that he is still alive. However some observers have pointed out disparities in his appearance in these videos, and most of the broadcasts show only a picture rather than film footage. Nonetheless, these broadcasts all purport to bring messages and threats from the über-terrorist.

Another puzzling aspect of the bin Laden case is the fact that he has rarely been mentioned by President Bush or his senior advisors, who acknowledge that they do not know whether he was killed in an Afghan cave or is still alive and in hiding. Michael Sherry, an historian at Northwestern University in Chicago, is reported to have said, "They didn't find him, they don't know where he is and it's not in the administration's interest to keep reminding the American people of that . . . Every time bin Laden is mentioned, it's a reminder that they don't have a clue and it's a reminder of their failure to fulfil their own stated war aims and it's a reminder that the war on terrorism has become directionless and not very effective" (*Reuters*, 20 August, 2002). The brutal killings and pointless suicide bombings make it a tasteless comparison, but there is a touch of the Wizard of Oz about him, the threadbare figure behind the scenes sending out a fearsome apparition to the world. There's no doubt that if he's in hiding, he's just as cowardly.

Muslim clerics in Spain issued the world's first fatwa (an Islamic edict) against Osama bin Laden on 11 March 2005. The fatwa, issued on the first anniversary of the Madrid train bombings, called bin Laden an apostate and urged other Muslims to denounce the al-Qaeda leader. Even some of those who might be thought to be in the same camp as bin Laden don't like him. He is of course not the only man behind the current state of fear and anxiety, but he can be blamed not only for the many murders and crimes he takes credit for, but also for creating much misery and stress in the individual lives of Muslim and non-Muslim alike. DL

Tony Blair

Poodle of Mass Destruction

It all seemed to start so well . . . Tony Blair became Prime Minister of the United Kingdom in May 1997 with a landslide majority, bringing new hope to millions of Britons, who had become tired of the previous Conservative administration. Ten years later he left office, fated to be best remembered for taking his country into a deeply unpopular war. Although there were plenty of other reasons to regard his legacy as tainted.

In his years in office, he had increased the tax burden and implemented a series of pointless "target-led" policies for areas such as health, education, and welfare. He introduced market-based reforms in the education and health sectors (in other words reforms which allowed corporations to fleece the taxpayer); introduced student tuition fees, which remain controversial; and introduced "tough" but ineffective anti-terrorism and identity card legislation which, though very unpopular, the UK government remains committed to seeing implemented. Blair did introduce a minimum wage and some new employment rights have been enacted, but he also retained Margaret Thatcher's unpopular trade union legislation.

Blair's government took political spin – the tendency to manipulate and twist information to show it in the best possible light – to new heights. He was, after all, a lawyer, so perhaps bullshitting is in his blood. He is the first ever prime minister of the United Kingdom to have been formally questioned by police officers while in office, although he was not under caution when interviewed. Many also blame Tony Blair for eroding civil liberties and increasing social authoritarianism with new police powers – creating more arrestable offences, allowing DNA records to be taken and stored, and enabling the issuing of dispersal orders.

Apart from this sorry record, what will always remain as the inescapable foundation of Blair's legacy are the wars in Afghanistan and Iraq. Blair has been widely criticized for his dog-like allegiance to US president George W. Bush and for his Middle East policies including the war in Iraq, the failure to criticize Israel in the 2006

Lebanon conflict, and the seemingly unending Israeli–Palestinian conflict, which Blair continues with good intentions, but against the backdrop of the failed Iraq policy. Bush has lauded Blair and the United Kingdom as worthy allies. In his post-9/11 speech, for example, Bush stated that "America has no truer friend than Great Britain," though a majority of British people would probably prefer the relationship to be less one-sided – the alliance between Bush and Blair has seriously damaged Blair's standing in the eyes of many in the United Kingdom, to whom he became known as Bush's "poodle." Blair always argued that it is in Britain's interests to "protect and strengthen the bond" with the United States, regardless of who is in the White House, which is possibly true. But previous British leaders have also had the gumption to argue with flawed American policies. Harold Wilson had apparently resisted American pressure to send troops to Vietnam, whereas Blair seemed to feel it was his duty to commit wholeheartedly to even the most insane neocon adventures.

Although the invasion of Iraq, which was launched on 18 March 2003, was in theory complete by 1 May the same year, the war continues. The invasion was led by the United States, together with the United Kingdom and smaller contingents from Australia and Poland. Following the "fall" of Baghdad, Blair's government failed to oppose the disastrous US orders that criminals should be released from prison and the army and police force disbanded. While Baghdad was being looted by armed thugs, soldiers stood around doing nothing because their orders were simply to invade and remove Saddam. No effective plan appeared to be in place for the immediate aftermath. The result was a country in complete meltdown. Warring religious factions and street gangs took over, and continued to be a significant factor in the chaos over five years later.

The claimed objectives of the invasion were "to disarm Iraq of weapons of mass destruction, to end Saddam Hussein's support for terrorism, and to free the Iraqi people." Bush asserted that the actual trigger was Iraq's failure to take a "final opportunity" to disarm itself of nuclear, chemical, and biological weapons that US and coalition officials referred to as "an immediate and intolerable threat to world peace."

According to minutes leaked in UK newspaper the *Sunday Times* (1 May 2005), Tony Blair gathered senior ministers and advisors for a confidential, crucial meeting in the build-up to the Iraq War on 23 July 2002, eight months before the invasion. At this stage the official story was that war was not inevitable. Attending the meeting were the Prime Minister, the foreign secretary, Jack Straw, the defence minister, Geoff Hoon, the attorney-general, Lord Goldsmith, and military and intelligence chiefs. Also marked as present on the minutes are Alastair Campbell, Blair's director of strategy, Jonathan Powell, his chief of staff, and Sally Morgan, the director of government relations. The end result of this meeting would tarnish Tony Blair's long-term reputation. According to the article, the attorney-general warned of grave doubts about the legality of the proposed war. Jack Straw asserted that the case for war was "thin."

It seems that Blair and his inner circle set about finding a watertight way to justify an invasion of Iraq by finding the "right political context." (This was necessary because straightforward "regime change" would have been illegal under UK law). These attempts focused on Iraq's supposed collection and manufacture of weapons of mass destruction. The following day in parliament, Blair told the house: "We have not got to the stage of military action . . . we have not yet reached the point of decision." The report in the *Sunday Times* suggested this wasn't true: "It was typical lawyer's cleverness, if not dissembling: while no actual order had been given to invade, Blair already knew Saddam Hussein was going to be removed, sooner or later. Plans were in motion. The justification would come later."

A few years in to the seemingly never-ending Iraq War, the basis on which Blair took the UK into the invasion – the removal of Saddam Hussein and the location of his weapons of mass destruction (WMD) – came under serious challenge. It was reported by the BBC's *Today* program that the government had "sexed up" a weapons inspection report, in a way that gave the UK a reason to join the United States in invading Iraq and removing Saddam Hussein. Dr David Kelly, a former senior UN weapons inspector, was revealed as the man who had held an "unauthorized" meeting with BBC journalist Andrew Gilligan. Kelly was subsequently found dead, having committed suicide under stress according to the inquest, though there are of course conspiracy theorists who conjecture that he was murdered. The suicide of this decent man was an avoidable tragedy, as a decision had been made that allowed his leaked name to be confirmed – all part of a campaign to dismiss the news reports about the sexed-up dossier and protect the government's reputation.

When Blair finally left office in 2007, the unofficial figure for civilian deaths in Iraq stood at 655,000; at the time of writing there have also been over 4,000 US, and over 100 UK, military deaths. At least 77 journalists have died, and the death toll keeps rising. The questionable legality of the war hangs around Blair's neck like an albatross. No weapons of mass destruction were ever found. In January 2005, the Iraq Survey Group concluded that Iraq had ended its WMD programs in 1991, and had had none at the time of the invasion. DL

Michael Brown

A Heck of a Job

Political appointees are hardly rare in the heavily "networked" culture of Washington DC. Indeed, one of the biggest perks of any new administration is the ability to appoint people to a large number of offices, from cabinet level down, "at the pleasure of The President." And based simply on the number of positions requiring to be filled, it is reasonable to assume that a fair number of appointees are not neccessarily the best qualified candidates for their positions. However, no one in recent US history has appeared quite as dangerously out of his league and basically incompetent as former Federal Emergency Management Agency (FEMA) director, Michael Brown.

Brown's childhood and early adulthood are as blandly undistinguished as one would expect of a typical future bureaucrat. He received a Bachelor of Arts in Public Administration from the University of Central Oklahoma in 1978, and subsequently worked as an intern, assisting the City Manager of nearby Edmond, Oklahoma, mostly with labor and budget matters. He later earned a law degree from Oklahoma City University (OCU) in 1981, and on being appointed Finance Committee Staff Director, he oversaw state fiscal issues during 1982.

Brown then moved to Enid, Oklahoma, where he was involved in a few different ventures, with varying degrees of success. On the one

hand, the senior partner of the first law firm he worked for characterized him as "not serious and somewhat shallow," while, on the other,
he was apparently knowledgeable enough to teach at OCU's Law
School as an adjunct. Eventually, he became Chairman of the Board
for the Oklahoma Municipal Power Authority from late 1982 until
1988, in which role he was responsible for the building of several new
power plants, including, ironically enough, a hydroelectric dam,
bearing his name.

Attempting to cash in on these accomplishments, Brown ran for
Congress against the incumbent Democrat, Glenn English, who had
run unchallenged in the previous election. Brown was trounced by a
margin of three to one, but he vowed to run again in 1990, predicting,
"I have an excellent chance of prevailing. It's a Democratic state, but a
very Republican district." In fact, not only did Brown not run again in
1990, but he has never since run for elected office, and Glenn English
defeated his 1990 challenger by a margin of four to one.

For unknown reasons, Brown then moved away from all previous
areas of endeavor, and worked as Judges and Stewards Commissioner
for the International Arabian Horse Association (IAHA), from 1989
until 2001. It was, apparently, enough of a hardship-free post that Mr
Brown was able to remain in it for over ten years without significant
incident, until a March 2000 decision to pursue an investigation of
David Boggs, described as a "kingpin of the Arabian horse world."
Though the ethics board agreed with Brown's decision, and chose,
ultimately, to suspend Boggs from the association for five years, Boggs'
obstructionist countersuits against the IAHA and Brown took a toll,
both on the organization's finances, and its morale.

In an attempt to stem the damage being done to him, the embattled
commissioner started a legal defense fund for himself, soliciting
donations, both from the IAHA and the breeders it regulated, against the
likelihood of Boggs's ongoing lawsuit against him personally, becoming
more expensive. The board of the IAHA perceived this as a clear conflict
of interest, and demanded Brown resign from his position, which he did,
after the IAHA had agreed to pay all his personal legal expenses for all of
Boggs's cases, past and present, and the remainder of his $100,000 yearly
salary. This compromise arrangement on the part of the IAHA, while
probably legally savvy, was financially ruinous, and resulted in its merger
with a rival organization, the Arabian Horse Registry of America.

In January 2001, in a radical departure from his life up to that point,

Mr Brown went to Washington as part of an incoming wave of Bush Administration appointees. He had been brought in as General Counsel for the Federal Emergency Management Agency by long-time friend, and recently appointed FEMA Director, Joe Allbaugh, a campaign staffer from President Bush's 2000 election team. Following the 9/11 attacks, Allbaugh named Brown Deputy Director, as elements of FEMA and other affected agencies were reorganized under the auspices of the newly created Department of Homeland Security.

In August 2002, President Bush appointed Brown, to be "head" of the transition planning office, of the Emergency Planning and Response Division of the Department of Homeland Security. As acting FEMA Deputy Director as well, Brown was also in charge of the National Incident Management System, the National Disaster Medical System, and the Nuclear Incident Response Team. If Brown was overstretched by multiple positions of responsibility, he certainly never said so to anyone who mattered, and he remained a largely anonymous bureaucrat until the 2004 hurricane season.

At that time it came out that FEMA had disbursed $30 million in disaster relief to the residents of Miami, Florida, following Hurricane Frances, despite the fact that Miami had not been significantly affected by the storm. While Under Secretary Brown admitted to $12 million having been disbursed in error, blaming a computer glitch, an investigative exposé printed in the *South Florida Sun-Sentinel* presented credible evidence that Brown was responsible, and called for him to be fired. By January 2005, Democratic Florida Congressman Robert Wexler urged both President Bush and Homeland Security Secretary Michael Chertoff to fire Brown for the alleged improprieties, but due to the partisan demeanor of the Bush Administration and its loyalists, this outcry was dismissed with little to no comment in response.

While the 2004 hurricane season had seen more storms than usual, 2005 broke new records. By the end of summer that year, ten "named storms" had already occurred, two of them reaching hurricane status, and an eleventh, Hurricane Katrina, was about to make landfall somewhere on the Gulf Coast. At the time, the storm was deemed an "incident of national significance." Brown resumed "acting" Deputy Director status for an already overtaxed FEMA, and was put in charge of the agency's impending Rescue and Recovery response operations in the projected hurricane zone, despite having had only two days of valid training on the co-ordination of local, state, and federal disaster response elements. Brown's lack of experience, guidance, and ability to co-ordinate these multiple efforts soon became clear to all who witnessed the debacle that followed.

If Brown himself had misgivings, he chose to express them late in the process. On 29 August, five hours before the storm's projected landfall, Brown made his first request for additional Homeland Security rescue workers to be deployed to the area. He compounded his errors in deploying personnel by instructing fire and rescue workers in areas surrounding the projected disaster zone to refrain from spontaneously taking action, so as to avoid potential co-ordination problems, and his agency being seen as having overstepped its authority. These decisions, together with the poor handling of the evacuation of residents in the hurricane zone by local and state authorities, and breaching of the inadequate system of levees surrounding the city of New Orleans, combined to make Hurricane Katrina one of the worst natural disasters in US history.

In the absence of an effective co-ordinated response, those with the ability to act did so to the best of their ability. The US Coast Guard's Rescue and Recovery teams, along with the more loyal members of the New Orleans Police and Fire Departments, all attempted heroically to "step up" to the situation, and provide whatever aid they could, while a mystified public watched on TV the grim and often degrading struggle of survivors of the disaster, who were no less mystified. Whenever any attention was focused on Michael Brown, he frequently seemed confused by the situation, or worse still, made disastrous admissions, such as, for example, that he had been unaware until 1 September, of the evacuees in the Superdome, despite media coverage of their plight for a little over a day. He was also openly critical of those "who chose not to leave," which he saw as defiance of a mandatory evacuation order, rather than the far more likely inability to do so.

When President Bush arrived in the so-called Katrina Zone on 2 September, to survey the damage to the region and assess the recovery effort, he praised Deputy Director Brown with the phrase that would haunt the rest of his now curtailed career in public service, "Brownie, you're doing a heck of a job," which instantly became a catch-phrase for the remainder of that year, and slightly beyond, used whenever someone made a particularly poor or ill-advised attempt at anything. The immediate backlash against this praise, led to "Brownie" being relieved of all on-site relief duties a week later, pending further agency oversight and review.

By this time, of course, the public outcry had developed a momentum all of its own. As numerous Democratic Congressmen and Senators called for Brown's immediate firing, the news media found fresh, horrifying examples of how his incompetence had negatively impacted on thousands of Katrina survivors. On 12 September, Michael Brown officially resigned from FEMA, claiming that negative publicity surrounding him was distracting from relief efforts.

In response, Homeland Security Secretary Chertoff granted Brown two 30-day "extensions" on his contract, presumably so that the agency could figure out what had gone so terribly wrong with relief effort planning, and not "sacrifice the ability to get a full picture of Mike's experiences." Brown continued to draw his $148,000 annual salary in the interim, until resigning, more forcefully, on 2 November, when he left in the middle of his second contract extension, claiming that he was being made a scapegoat. Be that as it may, the controversy surrounding his management both of FEMA and of the response to Katrina continued to dog his footsteps.

A House committee investigating the botched response to the disaster released Brown's e-mails of the crisis period to the media, showing him often to be more worried about public perceptions of his efforts, than about co-ordinating critical elements of the response to the disaster. In addition, video footage from a teleconference before Katrina made landfall between an "on-site" Brown and his superiors in the form of Secretary Chertoff and President Bush also surfaced, and seemed to support Brown's assertion that those above him had met his predictions of impending disaster with blank non-comprehension. In the light of everything, however, the public could not help but come away with the opinion that this might serve as a worst-case scenario of what happens when unqualified political hacks get assigned to critical government agencies under crisis conditions, which, terrifyingly, is just about *nothing.* KD

George W. Bush

Dumb, Dumber, Dubya

Apparently, the "President Bush is an Asshole" group was deleted from MySpace.com in 2006. There were protests from its members, but was it really required? The whole internet is awash with short videos and blogs showing the president in various embarrassing moments, making his famous gaffes in speeches and gaffes in etiquette while meeting other world leaders. Go on, look him up! One doesn't know whether to laugh or despair that this is the man who won two terms of office as president of the United States.

It is rumored that Bush's advisors don't like him to make unscripted appearances. No surprise given the mess he makes of the scripted ones – one famed example is Bush's embarrassing campaign question, "Is our children learning?" instead of "are." Although he wasn't the first president to have problems with the meaning of the word "is", as Bill Clinton could confirm.

Where to start with Bush? Some argue his brain was affected by spending his early adult life as a drunk. His alcohol intake has indeed been used as an explanation for his less than impressive grades in college, although how he subsequently came to be in charge of one of the most powerful countries in the world remains a mystery. One public pronouncement revealed that he believes that the United States and Japan have been allies for a century and a half, instead of since the Second World War (don't confuse him by mentioning Hiroshima, then). Even some of those who have worked closely with him have been unable to avoid mentioning his incompetence. Richard Perle, his foreign policy advisor, apparently said, "The first time I met Bush . . . two things became clear. One, he didn't know very much. The other was that he had the confidence to ask questions that revealed he didn't know very much." David Frum, his former speechwriter, reportedly commented that "Bush had a poor memory for facts and figures . . . Fire a question at him about the specifics of his administration's policies, and he often appeared uncertain. Nobody would ever enrol him in a quiz show." So you don't want him on your quiz team, but you do want him as president?

Of course, George W. Bush is possibly the easiest president ever to make fun of. If it were only speech gaffes and comedy mishaps, it would not be so serious. It is his actions that are the real cause for concern.

Bush appointed Thomas White as Secretary of the Army because, as Bush saw it, White had great business experience. This was experience he'd mostly acquired at Enron. Bush apparently said that he wanted Thomas White to run the army like he would run a business. White's former employees at Enron unhelpfully spoke out to accuse him of being dishonest, and of helping to set up the fake partnerships which had led to Enron's bankruptcy. White's defence was that he had had no part in any illegal or fraudulent activities, because he wasn't really in charge of the operations. Is he a criminal, or merely grossly incompetent? Either you're in charge, or you're not, and if you're not then maybe the business experience wasn't such a good recommendation after all.

Bush ordered the US Army to war in Iraq to remove Saddam Hussein from power without a realistic plan for how the country's infrastructure would be replaced. The legality of this invasion remains a debatable point. Once the army reached Baghdad, US troops stood helplessly by as armed gangs looted and robbed the people of the city. This was because they hadn't been given the necessary orders to keep order in the city. The war planners had assumed that the Iraqis would be so overjoyed to see Saddam overthrown that everything else would just fall into place. The Bush Administration's attitude seemed to be that their job was done. If anything they seemed bewildered and angry at the Iraqis for behaving in such a savage fashion and ruining the script. Bush seems to have little knowledge or understanding of international politics, or of how the rest of the world perceives the United States. He doesn't even seem to have a passing acquaintance the history of modern warfare. To expect to be able to invade a country, remove its leader, in the hope that the population would automatically form themselves into the sort of country and form of government that Bush preferred is so naïve as to beggar belief.

Even with continued sectarian violence and the insurgency in Iraq ongoing (credible, if unconfirmed, reports suggest that 655,000 Iraqi civilians have been killed since 2003), Bush is at time of writing still insistent on achieving "victory" rather than seeking a solution. Around 4,000 US troops have been killed since the invasion of Iraq in 2003. The Bush Administration's initial response to the mounting death toll was to order that footage of coffins being flown home not be broadcast on national TV. This was presumably a vain attempt to avoid a Vietnam-style perception of a quagmire, but reflects badly on those who failed to challenge the decision. Here is a leader who waves soldiers off to war but then chooses to pretend they don't exist after they have died in battle.

Amnesty International has been among many who have criticized the Bush Administration's treatment of detainees at Guantanamo Bay, describing the facility as the gulag of our times (referring to the prisons in which political prisoners were held by the former Soviet Union). Bush and his cheerleaders responded quickly, dismissing the accusation as absurd. The Bush Administration specifically selected Guantanamo Bay with the intention of preventing the prisoners from having access to US courts. Bush has refused to call them prisoners of war, because this would mean they came under the legal protection of the Geneva Convention, despite the fact that the United States is fighting what he describes as a global "War on Terror." The conditions in which the inmates in Guantanamo Bay are held and the manner in which they have been treated have been well documented, but Bush's government has appeared to be turning a blind eye.

Since Bush became president, the economy has faltered, US foreign policy has disintegrated into a confused mess, constitutional freedoms have been undermined, and environmental protections have been weakened or swept aside, meaning that Bush's executive friends in the corporations and oil business can increase profits. Bush has governed, for the most part, in the manner of an airhead playing out a bad Hollywood script. He has taken for granted the international goodwill shown after 9/11, and allowed huge problems (including global warming; funding shortfalls for Medicare/Medicaid, Social Security, and veterans' benefits; and HIV/AIDS) to spread through a combination of vacuous incomprehension, and seeming indifference. Bush may be treated like a fool by many of those around him, but to the rest of the world, this is insufficient. He is in a position in which his stupidity has proved dangerous and damaging, and the results of this presidency will be with us for decades to come. DL

The Catholic Church

Infelicitous Solicitations

On Sunday, 17 August 2003, UK newspaper the *Observer* exposed a secret document written by the Vatican in 1962. The document instructed bishops around the world to cover up in cases of sexual abuse or else risk being excommunicated from the Church. According to the article, lawyers called this a "blueprint for deception and concealment." One UK lawyer acting for Church child abuse victims described it as "explosive." That children were being sexually abused by priests was known. The shocking implication of this report was that the Vatican had been aware of this child abuse for nearly 50 years, and, what is even worse, had decided to turn a blind eye to the suffering of abused children. One of the biggest, and most powerful, set of assholes in the world protecting their own power, one might say.

The 69-page Latin document bearing Pope John XXIII's seal reportedly sent to every bishop in the world. The instructions outlined the policy of "strictest" secrecy in dealing with allegations of sexual abuse. It also threatened anyone who spoke out with excommunication. They also called for victims to take an oath of secrecy at the time when they made a complaint to Church officials. These instructions were apparently to "be diligently stored in the secret archives of the Curia [Vatican] as strictly confidential. Nor is it to be published nor added to with any commentaries."

The document, confirmed as genuine by the Roman Catholic Church in England and Wales, is called *Crimine Solicitationies*, which is translated as "instruction on proceeding in cases of solicitation." It focuses on sexual abuse which came about as part of the confessional relationship between a priest and a member of his congregation. But the instructions also deal with what it calls the "worst crime," defined as an obscene act perpetrated by a cleric with "youths of either sex or with brute animals (bestiality)."

The document was proof that the Catholic Church had systematically covered up abuse and aimed to silence its victims. And, as the document dates back to 1962, it gives the lies to the Catholic Church's previous claim that the issue of sexual abuse was merely a modern, limited phenomenon. So many authenticated reports of victims having been intimidated to remain silent by Church authorities have now come out worldwide that to claim that such intimidation was the exception is no longer remotely sufficient.

Of course the vast majority of priests are thought never to have abused any children, but there are many confirmed reports of Roman Catholic priests who have been accused of being abusers. These men had easy access to children and were figures of authority, trusted in their communities.

One of the worst cases occurred in Ireland, where Father Brendan Smyth systematically raped and sexually abused hundreds of boys between 1945 and 1990. The Norbertine Order obstructed the investigation of the Smyth case. Such obstruction was also seen in other cases, including that of Father Jim Grennan, a parish priest, who abused children during their preparations for their first communion, and Father Sean Fortune, who committed suicide before he could be put on trial for the rape of children. The abuse by Grennan and others in the Diocese of Ferns in south-east Ireland led to the resignation of the local bishop, Brendan Comiskey. In 2005, the Irish government established the Ferns Inquiry into the allegations of clerical sexual abuse in Ferns. The inquiry reported back on its revulsion at the extent, degree, and duration of the sexual abuse perpetrated on children by priests there.

No one has successfully sued the Vatican for sexual abuse by priests, but individual dioceses, especially in the United States, have been forced into settling claims with significant payments. Mostly, however, the Catholic Church has continued to protect its priests. If the Church has lists of the accused, no such list has been made public. For decades, and possibly longer, child-abusing priests have got away with their horrifying activities because their church was more concerned with protecting its own reputation than it was with protecting children.

May their God have pity on their souls. DL

Ahmed Chalabi

Hero in Error

In January 1999, a *Foreign Affairs* article focused on the Iraqi National Congress (INC) after its head, Ahmed Chalabi told a US Senate hearing, "Give the Iraqi National Congress a base protected from Saddam's tanks, give us the temporary support we need to feed and house and care for the liberated population, and we will give you a free Iraq, an Iraq free of weapons of mass destruction, and a free-market Iraq. Best of all, the INC will do this all for free." The *Foreign Affairs* article stated, "The INC plan is so flawed and unrealistic that it would lead inexorably to a replay of the Bay of Pigs. US officials would ultimately face the choice of intervening directly or watching [the INC] get butchered."

Chalabi was advocating the removal of Saddam Hussein long before the 2003 invasion of Iraq. He wanted the war to overthrow Saddam. He claimed that the invading force would be met by jubilation and dancing in the streets and that the terror threat would end. Once Saddam and the Taliban were defeated, all other wannabe terrorists would get the message "You're next" and would cease their activities immediately. Of course, this was a lie, one which has cost hundreds of thousands of innocent lives. A price that Chalabi once insisted was "worth it."

In interviews after the fall of Saddam Hussein, Mr Chalabi discounted the possibility that he would seek a role in the future government. "Personally, I will not run for any office, and I am not seeking any positions. My job will end with the liberation of Iraq from Saddam's rule," he is quoted as having told the German weekly *Die Zeit*.

He had strong backing in the US Congress and the Pentagon, especially among the neocon elements, but little grassroots support in Iraq. Many of the opposition groups operating within Iraq sought to distance themselves from the INC.

Nevertheless, the United States installed Chalabi as the most powerful member of the Iraqi Governing Council (IGC), in which role he was widely regarded as a spy and US puppet. Businessmen operating in Iraq saw Chalabi as a bank embezzler and "aristocrat," and he treated US generals as though they were his minions. After all, Chalabi, unlike the US military top brass, had the ear of the most powerful men in the United States, including Cheney, Rumsfeld, and Wolfowitz. The United States had simply replaced one corrupt tyrant with another.

Chalabi was placed in charge of the "de-Ba'athification" program, where he dictated which Iraqi families could work, an issue of crucial importance in occupied Iraq. Many people warned that his rule would increase the level of violence in the country. Chalabi became the de facto political chieftain of the INC, which received more $3 million a year from the Defense Intelligence Agency (DIA) for the "Information Collection Program" that was the main source of intelligence on the Iraqi resistance for the Coalition Provisional Authority. In this capacity, Chalabi oversaw the debriefing of prisoners arrested by the occupation forces.

Investigations by the Senate, the Department of Defense (DOD), and the General Accounting Office (GAO) started to investigate INC fraud in fabricating the reports on weapons of mass destruction, misuse of US funds, and profiteering through lucrative contracts awarded by the neocons in the Pentagon. But instead of being removed from positions of trust, Chalabi was left in charge of intelligence collection operations in Iraq and was paid with US tax dollars to do so.

In response to the weapons of mass destruction (WMD) controversy, Chalabi told the UK's *Daily Telegraph* in February 2004, "We are heroes in error. As far as we're concerned, we've been entirely successful. That tyrant Saddam is gone and the Americans are in Baghdad. What was said before is not important. The Bush Administration is looking for a scapegoat." Yes, Chalabi was "entirely successful" in getting the United States to go to war in Iraq, overthrow Saddam Hussein, and cause hundreds of thousands of civilian deaths to get his own way. Nice man.

During the period from March 2000 to September 2003, the US State Department paid the Iraqi National Congress close to $33 million, according to a US General Accounting Office report. There were irregularities in the way these funds were used and further action was finally taken against Chalabi. He was still wanted for embezzling nearly $300 million through a bank he created in Jordan. In May 2004, Mr Chalabi's home and offices were raided. He denounced the raid, which he described as a political act, carried out by US agents and Iraqi police. There were even rumors in Washington that Chalabi had been playing the Americans for fools all along by spying for the Iranians.

In January 2004, Chalabi and his associates claimed that leaders around the world were illegally profiting from the Oil for Food program. Conveniently these charges were made around the same time that UN envoy Lakhdar Brahimi indicated that Chalabi might not be welcome in a future Iraqi government. Up until then, Chalabi had been mentioned several times in connection with possible future leadership positions. Chalabi was bitter at not gaining power and was hitting back. The US government was opposed to Chalabi's investigation into the Oil for Food program on the basis that it was undermining the credibility of its own investigation. Chalabi decided that he was being sidelined by Washington because his organization was one of the sources for faulty intelligence about Iraq's weapons of mass destruction. Perhaps even the neocons had finally realized what an embarrassment he had been to their cause.

The current charges against Ahmed Chalabi relate to alleged counterfeiting activities. He denies the charges, of course. DL

Dick Cheney

Deadeye Duck (Hunter)

When Dick Cheney, a Wyoming Congressman who had never served in the military was chosen in 1989 by former President George Bush as his Secretary of Defense, he had an immediate problem of credibility. Dick Cheney, also known as the "five-time draft dodger" has apparently admitted that he didn't know much about defense at all. Between 1963 and 1965, Cheney had relied on his student status (at Casper College and the University of Wyoming) when he received four 2-S draft deferments. As the war in Vietnam continued, Cheney continued to expand his deferments. In August 1964, as the prospect of a major expansion of the draft seemed imminent, he married his girlfriend

Lynne. This may have been for love, but it also had the advantage that even if his student deferment was lifted, his married status might influence the draft board. However, the list of those eligible for the draft continued to expand as the war deepened and Cheney was reclassified 1-A, which made him "available for military service." If Cheney had a child, he would be reclassified 3-A, removing him from the pool of those facing the probability of the draft. Precisely nine months and two days after the Selective Service eliminated special protections for childless married men, Cheney was blessed with his first child. He had dodged the draft yet again.

So it's no surprise Cheney knew "nothing about defense" – he'd managed to stay a few thousand miles away from the army when it really mattered. In the two decades since he served under Bush the elder, he has became one of the more hated world political figures.

There's plenty about him to find detestable. In spite of his own aversion to serving abroad he sent US troops into action in the Gulf War. At the conclusion of that was, Cheney was in favour of the US decision to leave Saddam in power. However, when the situation changed and the neocon gang of the George W. Bush Administration were beating the war drum, he was happy to promote the overthrow of Saddam. In the same way that leaked documents revealed that UK prime minister Tony Blair had been talking about invading Iraq long before the 2003 invasion, the Bush government were also secretly planning to remove Saddam long before this became public knowledge (CBS Journalist Bob Woodward, in *Plan of Attack*, 2004). Woodward describes Cheney as a "powerful, steamrolling force obsessed with Saddam and taking him out." He also notes, "Dick Cheney's view is that in a way, it doesn't matter how long the aftermath is . . . What matters is the ultimate outcome . . . whether there's stability and democracy." Cheney clearly had no coherent plan for the aftermath of the invasion and the removal of Saddam Hussein. And, in case we forget, it was Cheney who suggested that the whole invasion would be a "cake walk"? There speaks a man who never saw combat. This relaxed, over-confident attitude has influenced terrible decisions that fed straight into the hellish five-year (and ongoing) insurgency, and in all probability it helped to cause thousands of avoidable deaths.

Among his many pre-war statements, Cheney wrongly claimed that Iraq had been connected to 9/11, stating that it was "pretty well confirmed" that 9/11 hijacker Mohammed Atta had met with Iraqi intelligence officials. Cheney also claimed that Saddam was "in fact reconstituting his nuclear program" and that US forces would be "greeted as liberators" (*Meet the Press*, 16 March, 2003). In January 2005, the Iraq Survey Group concluded that Iraq had ended its weapons of mass destruction (WMD) programs in 1991, and had no WMD at the time of the invasion. The Iraqi government had not been involved with al-Qaeda, indeed the removal of that government allowed the terrorists to thrive in the wasteland created by a botched piece of nation-building.

Cheney has also been accused of manipulating the intelligence to strengthen the case for invasion. In November 2007, 21 Democrats officially called for the impeachment of Vice President Dick Cheney, citing deceit concerning Iraq and also covert operations in Iran. The impeachment attempt is unlikely to touch Cheney though. Bush's neo-conservatives behaved with an arrogance that comes from their need for control, and one effect of the "War On Terror" has been to greatly increase the power of the executive branch.

What is worrying at the time of writing is where they might strike next. Cheney continues to advocate pre-emptive military intervention in the Middle East while the rest of the world observes in fear and horror. He recently threatened Iran in a speech on board an aircraft carrier off Iran's coast (CBS *Face the Nation*, 19 March, 2006; *New York Times*, 11 May 2005).

Cheney's hardline stance against Iraq can also be regarded as hypocritical considering that during his tenure as Halliburton chief executive, Cheney pressed the UN Security Council to end their 11-year embargo on sales of civilian goods, including oil-related equipment, to Iraq. He apparently said that sanctions against countries like Iraq punish US companies unfairly – especially ones paying him, it would seem. Halliburton has also made huge profits in the attempts to rebuild Iraq.

Contrary to Cheney's assertions, Saddam was not a direct threat to the United States. His "weapons of mass destruction" have never been found, his terrorist connections remain unproven at best, and he almost certainly had nothing to do with the attack on the World Trade Center. Cheney's sudden concern for the poor Iraqis, who needed the United States to liberate them is pure hypocrisy. Saddam's treatment of the people of Iraq, terrible though it was, was no worse in 2001 than it had been in his most murderous period, when Iraq's heroic protectors, Dick

Cheney included, were still cheerfully trading oil and arms with Saddam (in Cheney's case, as recently as 1999).

There isn't a great deal that is funny about Dick Cheney. Even his most comical moment as VP is a bit grim – he shot his friend, Harry Whittington, in the face by accident while hunting and then tried to keep the incident quiet. Whittington said he and his family were "deeply sorry for all that Vice President Cheney and his family have had to go through this past week." Guess what? Cheney got off scot free on that one too. DL

Larry Craig

A Cloud over Idaho

Compared with almost any other negative character trait, hypocrisy is especially detestable. There is something particularly reprehensible about those who publicly encourage others to behave in one way, due to the supposedly virtuous nature of behaving in such a way, while privately doing the contrary when out of public view, sometimes even to an extreme. There may be no better, recent example – except, perhaps, for fellow former Congressman and Republican Mark Foley – than Idaho Senator Larry Craig.

As a Senator of the conservative western state, Craig seemed to be well aligned with the "traditional family values" of his constituents, and was a fairly successful politician. During both his ten years in the House of Representatives, and the 16 years he has so far served in the Senate, Craig distinguished himself in the eyes of those in his party as having a solid track record for voting in lock-step with other so-called Christian Conservatives on legislation to do with social issues. It is the deeply ironic nature of his secret personal life, however, that eventually turned this voting record into a badge of insincerity, hypocrisy, and obvious self-loathing.

The first inklings of the possibility of Craig having a double life came early in his career, but to no noticeable effect. Accused anonymously of using cocaine and having sex with teenaged, male congressional pages in 1982, the then unmarried Craig was able to brush all such allegations aside due to lack of evidence, his well-known conservative record on "gay issues," and the seeming credibility of his unwavering denial that he was in any way a homosexual. To further cement his claims in the minds of the media and the voting public alike, before the end of that year he had married a mother of three. Further, in 1989, as part of the House Ethics Committee, he lead an extended effort to ensure that Representative Barney Frank received the maximum penalty for his secret affair with a male prostitute.

His tenure in the Senate, starting in 1991, served as further evidence of the absurdity of the 1982 allegations. He became a member of a barbershop quartet with noted fellow conservatives Trent Lott, John Ashcroft, and James Jeffords in 1995, and stood firmly with them and other party members during the impeachment of Bill Clinton in 1999. When the Bush Administration was "voted in" a year later, however, Craig finally got his chance to prove publicly how deep his commitment to the conservative social agenda really was.

As acting Senate Republican Policy Committee Chairman at the time, a post he had held for the previous three years, Craig was free to pursue whichever aspect of his party's larger agenda he thought deserved more attention. When the GOP (the Grand Old Party, the Republican Party) took control of Congress during the interim election of 2002, Craig and fellow Republicans wasted little time before flexing their newfound political muscle, gained through this consolidation of their power. The first clue was Craig's vote, along with most of the rest of his party, against a proposed amendment to Federal Hate Crime laws, which would have extended them to include sexual orientation. Following their success in defeating the proposed amendment, they tried, in 2004 and 2006, to pass the Federal Defense of Marriage Act, which would have defined marriage under federal law as an institution between a man and a woman *only*. They did not succeed, except, perhaps, in proving to their narrow-minded constituents that their "concerns" were being acted on.

Other strong evidence of Craig's party loyalty came from the GOP faithful, in the form of the American Conservative Union, which, in 2005, awarded him a score of 96 out of a possible 100 for voting for their agenda. Conversely, the liberal Human Rights Campaign gave the Senator a score of 0 out of 100, for numerous reasons, though mainly for his active efforts to curtail gay rights. It is these public judgments that make the events in Larry Craig's life on 11 June 2007, so especially damning and ironic.

According to the arresting officer, on that date Larry Craig attempted to solicit an anonymous sexual encounter with him, in a Minneapolis–Saint Paul International Airport men's room notorious for such behavior. The incident was part of a larger effort by area police to reduce or eliminate complaints of lewd behavior by "cruising" gays in the public facility, by utilizing standard "sting" tactics. After Craig allegedly signaled his interest in such a public sexual encounter to the undercover officer, he was immediately taken into police custody for booking.

At the airport's police station, Craig was "Mirandized" (informed of his right to remain silent to avoid incriminating himself) and inter- viewed about what had happened in the men's room. According to the interviewing officer's report, Craig then identified himself as a US Senator by producing his business card, and inquired if the police could hold his flight, which was imminent. When the police had no luck contacting the airline, they proceeded with the interview.

Craig claimed to have tapped the arresting officer's foot, the initial signal in a two-part secret code, known to those active in this particular gay sub-culture, due to having a "wide stance" and thus needing to spread his feet far apart to conduct his "business" on the toilet. When asked about his use of the follow-up signal, which involves hand gestures visible from the adjacent stall, Craig claimed he was attempting to pick up a piece of paper, which was immediately refuted by the arresting officer. It was noted in the arrest report that the Senator frequently disagreed with the police version of events, but also seemed to have difficulty recalling the events himself, at least in terms of the order in which they had occurred. He was cited, issued with a plea petition, and released.

Oddly enough, following the incident, the Senator returned to the airport police station on 22 June to complain about how he was treated, and supposedly to obtain information for his lawyer. That lawyer, if consulted at all, must have been dubious of Craig's chances of beating the case, as he returned a guilty plea petition to the District Court of Hennepin County, along with $575 which had been levied as a fine, on 1 August,   for the misdemeanor charge of disorderly conduct.

Interestingly, the plea petition contained the clearly spelled out provision that the court could not accept it from anyone who claimed to be innocent of the charges, and that by signing the petition, the defendant was clearly admitting guilt of the charge. The document was duly entered into the court record on 8 August and became one of several critically important documents in the ensuing scandal.

Less than three weeks later, on 27 August, the Congressional newspaper, *Roll Call*, broke the story of Craig's arrest and subsequent guilty plea, making the matter public among Craig's peers and associates. After this conviction came to light, the *Idaho Statesman* published a story the following day about three past allegations of Craig's homosexual conduct which they had previously not published due to a lack of verifiable evidence. One had come from a man who had been attempting to pledge Craig's fraternity at the University of Idaho in 1967, who claimed Craig had used their group affiliation as an opening to sexually proposition him. Another incident involved a self-defined gay man, who claimed that in 1994, Craig had followed him around a Boise area REI store for over half an hour, allegedly attempting to "cruise" him. The last "incident report" had come from a closeted Republican, who claimed that he and Craig had engaged in oral sex in Washington DC's Union Station in 2004. When the reporter compiling the story in the spring of 2007 called the Senator's office for comment, Craig himself issued a vehement, on-record denial of ever having engaged in any homosexual behaviour of any kind, causing the reporter to put the story on hold pending solid proof.

When the article was eventually published, Craig held a press conference the same day and stated for the public record: "I am not gay. I never have been gay . . . In June I overreacted and made a poor decision. I chose to plead guilty to a lesser charge in hopes of making it go away . . . Please let me apologize to my family, friends, and staff and fellow Idahoans for the cloud placed over Idaho. I did nothing wrong at the Minneapolis airport. I did nothing wrong, and regret the decision to plead guilty and the sadness that decision has brought on my wife, on my family, friends, staff, and fellow Idahoans." He further claimed that his lack of good judgment in entering the guilty plea had come about due to the stress of being constantly harassed by the *Idaho Statesman*, which was orchestrating a witch-hunt, he claimed, in their investigation of claims that the Senator was a homosexual.

The *Idaho Statesman* responded two days later with an editorial demanding Larry Craig's resignation. Further, The Minneapolis–Saint Paul Airport police released their unedited interview tapes to the national news media, to clarify their assertions about the Senator's actions both during, and following, the 11 June incident. This led to Craig's loss of a position in Mitt Romney's presidential campaign, and to the political watchdog group Citizens for Responsibility and Ethics in Washington filing a complaint against him with the Senate Ethics Committee, demanding an immediate investigation into Craig's conduct. Further, numerous fellow Senate Republicans were publicly calling for his resignation "for the good of the party," and the Senate GOP leadership were asking him to step down from all his committee seats, at least temporarily, until the scandal had been resolved, which, to his credit, Craig did.

On 1 September, Larry Craig announced his plans to resign at the end of the month. Three days later, though, a spokesman for Craig's office indicated that the embattled Senator had reconsidered, and was instead looking into the possibility of overturning his conviction, and thus regaining his committee assignments in the Senate, along with the confidence of the people of Idaho, hopefully. His attorneys filed a motion requesting a hearing to withdraw Craig's by now infamous plea.

The hearing was held before Judge Charles Porter Jr, on 26 September. Craig's attorneys argued that the charge of disorderly conduct was unwarranted as the Senator had barely made any movements at all, and had not touched, or even spoken out loud to the arresting officer. They also argued that the mail-in plea agreement used by the Senator was "defective" because it lacked a judge's signature. Following the hearing, Craig released a statement saying that he would remain in office until the presiding District Judge had ruled on his motion.

On 4 October, Judge Porter denied Craig's motion, ruling that the Senator's plea had been accurate and voluntary at the time, and was supported by police evidence. After the ruling, Craig announced that he would still not resign as he was now determined to serve out the rest of his term so that he could continue his fight to clear his name before the Senate Ethics Committee, which he could not do if he were no longer a Senator. Upon further reflection, he announced that he was also attempting to overturn the lower court's verdict with an appeal.

As of December 2007, eight gay men have come forward to the *Idaho*

Statesman alleging sexual encounters with, or claiming to have been "cruised" by, Craig. Four of the men in question have gone so far as to give graphic, recorded details to the paper, which have been posted on the newspaper's website. One of the four is Mike Jones, the male escort who is alleged, in 2006, to have had an ongoing sexual relationship with, and provided methamphetamine to, Evangelical Church leader Ted Haggard, another noted Christian Conservative.

Craig has denied all these allegations, especially those made by Jones, claiming that the former prostitute Jones's only motivation is to boost sales of his upcoming "tell all" book. It is a strange state of affairs indeed when a meth-addicted male escort is seen as having more credibility than a Congressman with close to thirty years of "public service" under his belt. But while Mr Jones may well have sold sex to other men to support a self-destructive addiction, he never publicly denounced those who did, especially not in exchange for power and privilege, and that important distinction makes him, and others like him, a far better man than Larry Craig. Hypocrisy can prove to be an ugly, and costly, luxury. KD

David Duke

Knight of the Ku Klux Klan

Following the seeming defeat of numerous racist, pro-segregation legal policies, along with many of the politicians who had supported them, with the passing of Federal Civil and Voting Rights laws during the 1960s, overt white supremacist organizations such as the Ku Klux Klan were under increasing pressure to modify their tactics to make them more "subtle," and less violent, or continue to suffer defeat in the form of continued federal prosecution. During the 1970s, this largely Southern subculture saw a shift away from the use of naked aggression and overt intimidation, to a more "media-friendly" approach, under the new racist concept of white separatism. One of its chief proponents,

David Duke, proved how dangerous this newfound "subtlety" was, with his repeated, but as yet unsuccessful, attempts to gain public office, as a candidate of both major US political parties, with his deeper ideology serving as the true platform of his campaigns.

Duke started life as the son of an engineer working for Shell Oil, which led to the family living in many different locations around the world, before finally settling in Louisiana. David became interested in racial politics at an early age, joining the pro-segregationist National Alliance, and later the Ku Klux Klan, in the late 1960s. When he later attended Louisiana State University in 1970, Duke gained notoriety for forming a student group known as the White Youth Alliance, which was notable for such "pro-white" activities as wearing Nazi uniforms in public, picketing for the right to have Hitler's birthday recognized as a "holiday," and protesting a public appearance by liberal author James Kuntsler at nearby Tulane University. Ironically, even though Duke was an award-winning member of his campus's Reserve Officers' Training Corps chapter, he was rejected for military service in the Vietnam War for his overtly controversial beliefs.

On graduating from LSU in 1974, Duke formed a Klan "splinter group," the Knights of the Ku Klux Klan, a self-described "white nationalist" political lobby, presided over by a "National Director" rather than a more traditional and grandiose-sounding Grand Wizard, in line with its stated goal of replacing traditional white, hooded robes with business suits. To support these efforts, he tried to raise funds, initially by publishing a supposed "self-help" book for women, under the pseudonym Dorothy Vanderbilt, which counseled women to be sexually subservient to men in order to achieve romantic success. When this effort failed completely, Duke concentrated his efforts on an unsuccessful run for the Louisiana Senate as a Democrat in the model of segregationist George Wallace.

Following his defeat, Duke disappeared from public life to engage in high-risk financial investing, and even professional gambling. By 1980, he had resurfaced as the founder of the "white nationalist" group, the National Association for the Advancement of White People, having decided the Klan's history of violence was counterproductive in advancing the larger goal of "white separatism." To this end, Duke revamped his appearance with plastic surgery and shaved off his mustache, before a highly unsuccessful run for president, first as a

"Wallace Democrat," and then as a nominee of the fringe Populist Party, in 1988.

These defeats served as lessons rather than deterrents to Duke's later political career, firstly by encouraging a switch in his party affiliation from Democrat to Republican, and, secondly, by revising the scope of his goals, motivating a run for the far more attainable office of Representative to the Louisiana State House in 1989. Surprisingly, he achieved a narrow victory in the primary election, despite significant support for his opponent from the then President, George H. W. Bush, and former President Reagan, before suffering a resounding, and antic- ipated, defeat in the state's general election later that year. Still undaunted, he ran for the US Senate in 1990, again as a Republican candidate, when the only challenger in his party, State Senator Bernard Bagert Jr dropped out of the race two days before the election. Concerned that Duke's extreme views would lead to the damaging perception that they were accepted by the larger Republican political community, numerous Republican politicians endorsed his Democratic challenger, Bennett Johnston, rather than the overtly racist candidate of their own party.

Undeterred by these events, Duke continued his attempts to gain public office in Louisiana with a 1991 run for governor. He successfully defeated the incumbent Republican governor in the primary election of that year, drawing national attention to his general election contest against Edwin Edwards, a Democratic former governor, whose record had been marred by allegations of corruption. Despite strong financial support for his campaign from various white supremacist and far-right organizations, Duke was again defeated during the later contest by a margin of nearly two to one, even with Edwards's supporters seemingly touting their candidate's corrupt public image, with bumper stickers exhorting the public to "Vote for the Crook. It's Important."

The remainder of the 1990s saw Duke remain a perennial candidate for any major elected office in Louisiana, with an unsuccessful run for the Senate in 1996, against Mary Landrieu, and an equally unsuc- cessful campaign in the run-off election in 1999, created by the scandal- driven resignation of House Representative Bob Livingston. In between such efforts, he took time to publish his autobiography, *My Awakening: A Path to Racial Understanding*, in 1998. Though denounced by groups such as the Anti-Defamation League as racist, sexist, antise- mitic, and homophobic, it was still a noteworthy accomplishment, as, in some ways, it was a symbolic shift of Duke's activities from the realm of elected politics, to the realm of supposedly academic discourse.

This emphasis on public discourse, and the exchange of ideas between racial separatist and anti-Zionist groups took many unusual twists and turns during the early twenty-first century, especially in the light of the US "War on Terror," as well as with regard to widespread "ethnic tensions" in former Soviet Bloc and communist countries. Duke utilized both to great advantage, as components of a developing world view, espoused through his website, www.davidduke.com. The website became mildly notorious in 2002 for espousing the theory that the 9/11 terrorist attacks were actually a secret plot executed by Israel's secret service, Mossad, despite considerable evidence to the contrary.

In 2003, Duke published *Jewish Supremacism: My Awakening on the Jewish Question*, a supposedly scholarly take on the growing menace of the "Global Zionist Conspiracy," "researched" by Duke while he was also preparing a dissertation for a PhD in History from a Ukrainian institution, the Interregional Academy of Personnel Management. It is claimed that the first 5,000 copies of the widely available book sold out in just a few weeks, even being sold in a gift shop in the Duma, the lower house of the Russian parliament, the popularity of the book underscoring reports of ethnic division throughout the former "Second World." By 2004, the book had finally been published in the United States, and, by 2006, its author claimed that the book had been translated into eight languages, and had sold an estimated 500,000 copies worldwide.

The past few years have seen Duke try to consolidate his newfound international notoriety as an anti-Zionist advocate in a variety of contexts and venues. First, in May 2004, he helped to organize the New Orleans Protocol, an agreement between US-based far-right racists to avoid both public violence and private infighting in pursuit of their goal of protecting white "racial supremacy" in the United States. On 3 June 2005, following his receipt of a PhD from the Interregional Academy of Personnel Management, Duke co-chaired a conference held at the Ukrainian institution, called "Zionism as the Biggest Threat to Modern Civilization." A year later, in June 2006, he spoke at the "White World's Future" conference in Moscow, and, about six months later, he appeared at the International Conference to Review the Global Vision of the Holocaust, held in Tehran and sponsored by Iranian President Mahmoud Ahmadinejad. Though held in "ethnically" very different locations, all the conferences were unanimous in their inherent distrust and hatred of the world's Jews.

In 2007, Duke published an updated version of *Jewish Supremacism*, noteworthy, according to its author, for "better paper stock" and a full-color dust jacket, rather than for any revision or refinement of its highly questionable assertions and "theories." It is not possible to know what new publications, public appearances, or outrageous sound-bites the world may be subjected to at any moment by the self-styled "racial defender." What *is* certain is that these will be directed at combating any perceived enemies of "Aryan Peoples," through the use of deception, propaganda, and political "will," rather than by means of a more overt method, such as "ethnic cleansing," for example. One can only hope that such divisive and delusional theories and rhetoric will remain in semi-obscurity, part of the dull roar of the US and global "lunatic fringe." KD

Jerry Falwell

Hammer of the Teletubbies

Until his sudden death in May 2007, there was no higher "earthly authority" within the ranks of the US "religious right" than Jerry Falwell. As the founder of both Liberty University and the so-called Moral Majority, he was instrumental in defining the values and guiding the policies of what became the Social Conservative movement within the Republican Party. Initially he did this through his relationship based on public and political policy with President Ronald Reagan, and later through similar relationships with both George H. W. Bush and George W. Bush. A vocal critic of anything he perceived to be anti-Christian, anti-family, or anti-American, the pastor of the prototypical Thomas Road Baptist "megachurch" was noteworthy throughout his career as a religious figure for numerous provocative, inflammatory, and/or insensitive remarks based on his narrow views, supposedly based on Christian scriptures and traditional American patriotism.

Falwell was born in Lynchburg, Virginia, in August 1933, along with twin brother Gene, into a family which was not particularly religious. His father was a one-time bootlegger, who later became a small-time entrepreneur, though without much success. After a seemingly unremarkable childhood, Jerry first attended the local secular Lynchburg College, before transferring to Baptist Bible College, in Springfield, Missouri, during his sophomore year, to pursue a degree in Divinity. Having "answered God's call" with vigor, zeal, and enthusiasm, Falwell graduated from the institution in 1956, and wasted no time in founding the Thomas Road Baptist Church that same year.

Typical of its time in the pre-integration South, the church's exclusively white congregation later became a haven for pro-segregationist views. One of Falwell's most notable sermons of the period was a 1965 speech in which he criticized fellow minister and Civil Rights leader Martin Luther King Jr, renaming his cause the "Civil Wrongs Movement," and openly denouncing its values and goals as un-American. Falwell's radio program, *The Old Time Gospel Hour*, which began broadcasting around the same time, was equally notorious for airing live the views of pro-segregation guests such as Lester Maddox and George Wallace.

Not content with merely providing such "spiritual guidance," Falwell founded Liberty University, a fundamentalist Christian college in Lynchburg, in 1971. The institution's early survival was jeopardized almost immediately when the Securities and Exchange Commission (SEC) investigated Falwell's organization on charges of bond fraud, allegedly uncovering $6.5 million in unsecured church bonds in the course of the investigation. In the end, however, Falwell and his church were exonerated of all charges in federal court, in 1973, and used the incident to re-finance the university's outstanding $2.5 million debt, through the Reber–Thomas Christian Heritage Foundation, after its coffers had been refilled with $3.5 million in donations from Christian "cult leader," the Reverend Sun Myung Moon.

While this scandalous state of affairs failed to gain much attention nationally – in all likelihood due to the Watergate scandal and the ensuing investigations into the Nixon White House – the Reverend Falwell was one of many conservative, religious voices whio later backed anti-gay activist Anita Bryant's Save Our Children movement, which sought to limit the civil rights of homosexuals, based on their inherently "sinful" and "un-Christian" lifestyle. "Gay folks would just as soon kill you as look at you," he is noted for having said during one rally on behalf of this cause. Two years later, in 1979, he founded the socially conservative and "fundamentalist" Christian advocacy group, the Moral Majority, to combat directly any perceived "anti-Christian" activities in the United States in an organized way on a national level.

The organization was founded by Falwell on basic tenets which were zealously adhered to by leader and followers alike, aimed at creating a US society which was pro-family, pro-life, pro-defense, and pro-Israel. The group was openly praised by then presidential candidate Ronald Reagan, for its anti-gay, anti-abortion, and pro-Cold War outlook, and the true era of the "social conservative movement" had begun. Having seemingly been granted licence, if not authority, to influence national social views, and thereby political policy, the group wasted little time in espousing its point of view to anyone prepared to listen.

Falwell and company's rhetoric throughout the 1980s left little doubt as to the narrowness and zealousness of their views and convictions. He was criticized in the early 1980s for openly suggesting that "AIDS is not just God's punishment for homosexuals, it is punishment for the society that tolerates homosexuals," and for depicting gays as "brute beasts" allegedly requiring utter annihilation by the Almighty to return the world to His graces. Falwell was also notable for his support for the repeal of federal abortion rights laws, his negative criticism of all sanctions and divestment by the United States in apartheid South Africa, and for suggesting that "labor unions should study and read the Bible instead of asking for more money. When people get right with God, they are better workers."

The most notorious public incident involving Falwell during this era resulted from a crude parody of the good reverend in the November, 1983, issue of the pornographic magazine *Hustler*, published by fervent civil libertarian, Larry Flynt. The "joke" in question was a fake ad for Campari, suggesting that Falwell had gotten drunk on the product for the first time in an outhouse, before losing his virginity to his mother. The $45-million lawsuit that followed alleged that the crude jest had invaded Falwell's privacy, was libelous, and had intentionally inflicted mental distress. When Falwell was not successful in the original civil trial, he repeatedly appealed to higher and higher courts, until he was finally ruled against by the Supreme Court in 1988, who decided in favor of the defendant, stating that public figures cannot circumvent First Amendment protections of the right to free speech by alleging distress caused by parodies and other obvious jokes.

Falwell fared no better as the defendant in a 1984 lawsuit brought by gay activist Jerry Sloan. In July that year, Falwell denied ever having made his notorious comments about gays being "brute beasts" in need of "annihilation" and when Sloan countered that he had a tape of the reverend saying as much, Falwell promised he would pay him $5,000 dollars if he could produce it. When Sloan did just that, and Falwell reneged on his public offer, Sloan successfully sued, making it known that he intended to donate the proceeds from the suit to help build the Sacramento, California, Lambda Community Center, to serve the local gay, lesbian, bisexual, and transgendered community in the area. When Falwell later tried to appeal, the court ruled against him again, and he was ordered to pay an additional $2,875 in sanctions and court costs, ending the matter once and for all.

When the last vestiges of the "Reagan Revolution" were removed from the White House with the defeat of the former Vice President George H. W. Bush in 1992, Falwell wasted little time in changing his national role, from unwavering supporter of the US presidency, to unwavering partisan critic and "watchdog." In 1994, he funded the production and sale of the straight-to-video documentary, *The Clinton Chronicles*, a slickly produced collection of disproven conspiracy theories concerning the supposed wrongdoing of the Clintons during Bill Clinton's time as governor of Arkansas. Falwell himself appeared in the 80-minute "infomercials" for the tape, at one point even interviewing one of the supposed journalists behind it, who appeared only in silhouette, allegedly due to the fear of reprisals including abduction and murder, which had supposedly befallen others who had delved too deeply into the Clintons' affairs. Although it was learned years later that the supposed journalist was actually the tape's producer, Patrick Matriasciana, of the conservative group Citizens for Honest Government, Falwell's endorsement of the product was a powerful element in a well-orchestrated Republican effort to limit the effectiveness of the Clinton presidency by any means possible.

As just one voice in a chorus of conservative criticism of the Clinton White House, Falwell spent much of the 1990s in the background, limiting his activities and interests to tightly focused sermons to the already converted, in an effort to galvanize Christian conservatives against all things "liberal" or "secular." However, in the February edition of his *National Liberty Journal* he chose to "out" children's TV character Tinky Winky from the popular *Teletubbies*. Tinky Winky was obviously gay, supposedly, because of his "pro-gay" purple color, the triangular shape of his antenna – a triangle being a gay pride symbol – and his magic bag, which the article insisted was a "purse." Falwell lent further weight to these preposterous accusations by claiming that "role modeling the gay lifestyle is damaging to the moral lives of children." He also used a tongue-in-cheek article in the *Washington Post* in which Michael Colton had named Tinky Winky as an "in" gay icon, to substantiate his claim. *Teletubbies* creator, Steve Rice, dismissed the remarks about his creation as "absurd and kind of offensive."

When Clinton left office, having been replaced by fellow conservative Christian Republican, George W. Bush in 2001, Falwell seemed almost to come out of hiding, and he attempted to bolster Bush's public profile with vocal and unconditional support. But he took this too far, perhaps, when, following the terrorist attacks of 9/11, during an appearance on the religious right talk show *The 700 Club*, he said, "I really believe that the pagans, and the abortionists, and the feminists, and the gays, and the lesbians who are actively trying to make that an alternative lifestyle, the ACLU, People for the American Way, all of them who have tried to secularize America. I point the finger in their face and say, 'You helped them.'" After immediate and strong public objections to the remarks, in the light of the grave nature of the national tragedy, Falwell apologized and relented slightly, but added, "If we decide to change all the rules on which this Judeo-Christian nation was built, we cannot expect the Lord to put his shield of protection around us, as he has in the past."

Also noteworthy at the time was Falwell's obvious support of the Bush Administration's so-called "faith-based iniatives," which sought to limit federal spending on social programs by funding private, and frequently religious or church-based charities instead, to solve social problems and community crises. While the reverend supported such a plan on a broad and theoretical level, he had specific reservations about the program concerning where the funding might go and what restrictions might be put on churches in the use of these public funds. "My problem is where it might go under his successors," explained Falwell. "I don't want to put any of the Jerry Falwell Ministries in a position where we might be subservient to a future Bill Clinton, God forbid . . .

It concerns me that once the pork barrel is filled, suddenly the Church of Scientology, the Jehovah's Witnesses, the various and many denominations and religious groups – and I don't say those words in a pejorative way – begin applying for money – and I don't see how any can be turned down because of their radical and unpopular views. I don't know where that would take us."

Still, with such unwavering advocates for Christian conservatism as the Bush White House and its GOP allies, Falwell remained largely free of scandal and controversy for the rest of his adult life. He was in the news in 2005, when he was hospitalized for two weeks with a viral infection, before being taken back into hospital just days later as a result of respiratory arrest. President George W. Bush personally contacted the reverend during this health scare to wish him well. Falwell made one final appearance in the national media, on 31 July 2006, on an episode of CNN's *Paula Zahn Now*, on the topic of the Apocalypse, in which he stated, "I believe in the premillenial, pre-tribulational coming of Christ for all of his Church, and to summarize that, your first poll, 'Do you believe Jesus coming the second time will be in the future?' I would vote yes with the 59 per cent, and with Billy Graham, and most evangelicals."

If the Second Coming really was imminent, Falwell did not live to see it, as he was found unconscious and without a pulse in his office at 10:45 a.m. on 15 May 2007. Although he was resuscitated and rushed to Lynchburg General Hospital, efforts to stabilize his condition were unsuccessful and he was declared legally dead at 12:40 p.m. Eastern Standard Time (EST), with all the members of his immediate family at his bedside as he died. Falwell was buried a week later, having lain "in state" both at this church and at Liberty University before a small, private memorial service, closed to members of the public and press. On his arrival in the afterlife, one can only imagine his conversations with Jesus and "the Almighty," especially in the light of the good reverend's impassioned defense of both throughout a controversial career, allegedly devoted to "religious" service. KD

Mark Foley

Revolting and Unforgivable

One of the most frightening "tactical preferences" of many sex offenders, especially child molesters, is their use of stealth and deception to achieve their "goals." Someone who seemed to understand this better than most was Florida Congressman Mark Foley, who was perceived, by those in the general public familiar with his work, to be a staunch and tireless "child advocate," both willing and able to combine a deep understanding of the criminal threat to children with strong legislation, in an attempt to stem the tide of a disturbing, and growing, threat to public safety. In the scandal that broke in the fall of 2006, Foley's public identity proved to be a longstanding facade, of the type maintained by the kinds of criminals the good Congressman had been attempting so publicly to thwart. The scandal shocked members of his own party, as well as members of the media, law enforcement agencies, and child advocacy organizations, many of whom, ironically, were already well aware of the specifics and peculiarities of this kind of criminal activity.

Mark Foley's initial political career certainly gave no clue as to his hidden nature. Initially elected to the House of Representatives on behalf of Florida's Sixteenth Congressional District in 1994, Foley's first term was largely unremarkable, apart from his appointment to the powerful Ways and Means Committee. The moderate Republican was re-elected in 1996 by an even greater margin, despite rumors in the gay and lesbian press that he was "secretly gay," alleged to be "backlash," some said, for the Congressman's socially moderate voting record.

Examples of such moderation were to be found in Foley's membership of the Republican Majority for Choice, and in his staunch support for Hate Crimes legislation, which was balanced by his loyal support of the Patriot Act, and the Federal Death Penalty. In addition, he was always a strong and vocal supporter of any and all legislation aimed at apprehending and punishing child molesters to the fullest extent of the law. Foley became increasingly involved in "victim's rights" causes, which probably fostered his eventual partnership with the National

Center for Missing and Exploited Children, and the television show *America's Most Wanted.*

Still, rumors persisted about Foley's alleged homosexuality, and these are thought to have been part of the reason he aborted his attempt to gain the Senate seat left open by the retiring Bob Graham in 2003. In the earliest days of that campaign, stories which had begun, once again, as mere whispers in the gay and lesbian press, turned into much bigger stories in publications such as the *New York Times.* While Foley called such questions "revolting and unforgivable," his critics claimed this proved their allegations, as he said nothing directly to refute the charges.

Despite this setback, Foley's political career in the House progressed fairly smoothly. He regained his seat easily, with his usual majority of more than 60 per cent. On top of successful reforms, relating to background checks on anyone working with children, and the imposition of stricter limits on the role of underage models on the internet, along with tougher sentencing guidelines for repeat offenders, Foley was viewed as a sincere public servant, vigorous and dedicated to his cause. This reputation made him a frequent media spokesman for any impending House legislation of this kind, and a "must have" guest for programs like NBC Dateline's *Internet Predator* "sting" shows.

His entire public record, however, was put into stark and ironic contrast on 28 September 2006, when a former Congressional page, in an ABC News interview, claimed that Foley had sent him e-mail messages which made him feel "weird," and had requested a picture of the teenager as well. The official response from Foley's office dismissed the young man's reaction by saying that such a request was standard for anyone seeking a professional recommendation from the Congressman, as the former page had, in fact, done. In the light of Foley's reputation, many saw the allegation as a harmless misunderstanding, blown out of proportion by a sensation-seeking, "liberally biased" media.

That is, until the next day, when ABC News broke the story of new allegations, again by a former congressional page, concerning inappropriate attention paid to him by Foley, and most damningly, with verifiable proof in the form of saved instant messages from the Congressman. Though censored in media coverage, these messages made clear references to sex acts and organs. The young page also alleged that he had been warned by fellow pages, on beginning work, to avoid contact with

Foley, as he seemed to be "weird" around teenage boys. The story added to a disturbing picture, which was in stark contrast to the public image of the celebrated children's and victims' advocate.

On the same day, Foley's former chief of staff, Kirk Fordham, was also contacted by ABC News before the airing of the controversial interview, seeking any additional comment or insight he might be willing to give, about the accusations made by yet another page. After Fordham issued a terse "no comment," he informed both his current employer, New York Congressman Tom Reynolds, and Speaker of the House, Dennis Hastert, of the impending interview, and its sensational, but plausible accusations. Fordham was tasked with collecting Foley's resignation – as Hastert and Reynolds made it clear that Foley would be expelled from the House if he did not resign – which he dutifully delivered to Speaker's office later that day. Foley's letter of resignation, addressed to both Hastert and Florida Governor Jeb Bush, consisted of a single sentence: "I am deeply sorry and I apologize for letting down my family and the people of Florida I have had the privilege to represent."

On 2 October, in an attempt to deflect fallout from the scandal away from both his office and the Republican Party in general, Hastert made public the ultimatum he had given Foley with regard to his recent resignation. Meanwhile, Foley himself was also in the news, having checked himself in to a rehab facility for an alleged alcohol abuse problem. In a statement issued through his lawyer, the disgraced Congressman revealed that he had been molested by a priest as a teenager, and despite his recent "bad judgment calls," he did not consider himself a pedophile, but rather a gay man suffering from the effects of his alleged abuse at the hands of the priest. These claims did little to silence his detractors though, especially after the media was flooded with numerous additional allegations by other former pages, in some cases around a decade old, as well as from former Congressional staffers, both of which pointed to Foley's inappropriate interests and behavior, and allegations that Hastert's office had been aware of the problem and had chosen to do nothing about it.

This information stirred up even more negative sentiment, both because of Foley's conduct and his lack of honesty about it, and because Hastert was aware of what was going on, yet did nothing to put a stop to it. The conservative *Washington Times* even went so far as to call for the Speaker's resignation, as having been aware of the "Foley problem" and doing nothing about it was seen as a grave dereliction of duty, especially given the "tough on crime" stance of the GOP. While Hastert simply kept his mouth shut, and weathered the storm, this and other scandals caused him to resign the office of House Minority leader, after numerous scandals cost the Republicans their majority status in both Congress and the Senate in the mid-term elections in 2006. Hastert's retention of his own seat is testament to the loyalty of his constituency; to the rest of the country he appeared a controversial buffoon.

The most interesting opinion on the scandal came in an interview with a retired Catholic priest, Anthony Mercieca, on 19 October. He told the *Sarasota Herald-Tribune* of his two-year relationship with the then teenaged Mark Foley. The former priest, living in Malta, acknowledged that the two had taken nude saunas together, and engaged in some incidents of "light touching," but he denied that there had been any overtly sexual contact. Such a denial, in the light of how Foley had turned out as a result of such "spiritual guidance," was more than a little hollow, and of little consequence, other than perhaps giving an insight into the type of priest the "good father" really was. It also spoke volumes about how Mark Foley had become the man he had: internally divided, self-loathing, and false.

Probably one of the more sickening footnotes to the case has been how, over a year later, Foley had still not been more vigorously investigated and/or punished for any of his criminal misdeeds. It is not known whether his treatment for alcohol addiction has been successful, or whether he has undergone treatment of any kind to deal with his attraction to underage boys. All that is known for sure is that, for the time being at least, he has slipped through the fingers of the very legal system he sought to empower, seemingly guilty of the kinds of things which he supposedly wanted to stop. That final irony, together with other aspects of the case, is a very bitter one indeed. KD

George Galloway

Big Cat

The younger generation in the United Kingdom know George Galloway not as a Member of Parliament (he was once in the Labour Party, but ended up founding his own Respect Party), but as the man who pretended to be a cat in the UK version of *Celebrity Big Brother*. The Big Brother figure controlling the show asked the participants to try some animal role play exercises to warm up for their upcoming tasks. Galloway acted out his "animal role play" with actress Rula Lenska. He went down on all fours and pretended to lick milk from her cupped hands. Meanwhile she rubbed the "cream" from his "whiskers" stroking his head and behind his ears while he purred and mewed. The performance began to seem like the start of a bad porn movie as Rula said, "Oooh yes, has it been a trying day with all those people coming into the house, has it? You just like being alone with your mummy, don't you?"

When Galloway is playing politics rather than playing the fool, he can be an intriguing figure. Strident in his anti-Iraq War stance, he was widely criticized for his decision to desert politics for reality television for up to three weeks spent in the Big Brother house. Many felt he should instead have been looking after his constituents in the East End of London. He claimed that he did this to raise young people's awareness of the war in Iraq, because the Blair government had made it hard for him to publicize his anti-war message through normal political channels. A large part of his constituency was Muslims, who had been drawn to support him because of his anti-war message. Instead of giving them a voice, he ended up with a transvestite and a topless glamor model on TV.

It was no wonder that his Muslim constituents responded with bemusement. Galloway insisted that he had talked about politics often in the Big Brother house, but that the producers had edited it out, a claim that was denied by BB producer Peter Bazalgette. Those working for the MP are said to have stated that he had been prepared to suffer indignities such as the animal role-playing in the belief that his political message was getting across to the mass audience. But, they claimed, when he discovered that his political message had been silenced, he would be furious.

Long before this particular debacle, Galloway was widely viewed with suspicion. A fervent socialist, he nonetheless seems to revel in a degree of wealth; he has a holiday home in the Algarve; he smokes Cuban cigars; and he makes odd political mis-steps, like calling for Staffordshire Bull Terriers (a relatively harmless breed) to be made illegal. There just seems to be something odd about the man. He is, however, an extremely effective public speaker and his tirades against the Iraq War are mostly valid. He has been accused of being an apologist for the Saddam regime, but one can perhaps view his actions as attempts to keep channels of communication open.

It just always seems as if Galloway's activities veer too far into pure attention seeking. At an anti-Israel rally in London on 22 July 2006, he showed support for Hezbollah terrorists, making a speech in which he stated, "What I'm about to say is illegal in this country . . . Hezbollah has never been a terrorist organization. I am here to glorify the Lebanese resistance, Hezbollah, and to glorify the resistance leader, Sheikh Hassan Nasrallah . . . I'll see you in court, Mr Blair." As with his meeting with Saddam, he seemed far too willing to overlook the faults of Hezbollah, even as he tried to make a point about censorship.

Galloway is known as a maverick, something of a rebel. He'd probably like to be known as a dissident. Either way he is a powerful campaigner for his favored issues: Palestine, Iraq, Scottish home rule, whatever. But that's the key point here: the "whatever." It sometimes seems as if he will latch onto the causes of others and then hijack them simply to promote himself. It is frequently hard to establish whether he is bringing new light to an issue or whether he just wants people to turn up and cheer him.

Then there are the reports about his conduct with regard to finances. In 1987, he faced inquiries over his financial stewardship of the charity War on Want, for whom he had been general secretary for several years. He was exonerated after he volunteered to repay some of the contested expenses. Indeed his repayment went beyond the repayment required by the auditors, as he subsequently stressed.

In January 1994, TV pictures showed him apparently praising Saddam Hussein for his courage, strength, and indefatigability. When he opposed the invasion of Iraq, this skeleton in his closet was once again aired in the UK media, even though some of the prominent members of the Bush Administration had also met with Saddam for their own reasons. He has since insisted that he was lauding the people of Iraq, not their leader. Watching the footage though, it is unclear how one is expected to make this distinction. In 1998, he brought a young girl, Mariam Hamza, from Iraq to Glasgow for much-needed treatment for leukemia. This was an act of charity, inspired by the fact that medical sanctions prevented Mariam from receiving treatment in Iraq. Again, his detractors called it a PR stunt. As so often with Galloway, we are presented with the problem of trying to disentangle the elements of self-promotion from the sincere politics.

Galloway has had some memorable moments. The United States became aware of him during a hearing on Capitol Hill in Washington DC, in May 2005, which was referred to as "the confrontation of his career" by the *Guardian* (18 May 2005). In response to claims that he had profited illegally from Iraqi oil sales, he faced down the US Senate. He called the Oil-for-Food scandal as the "mother of all smokescreens." In his speech he hurled a series of accusations at the Senate. "I'm here today, but last week you already found me guilty. You traduced my name around the world without ever having asked me a single question." He went on to say, "I met Saddam Hussein exactly the same number of times as Donald Rumsfeld met him. The difference is that Donald Rumsfeld met him to sell him guns, and to give him maps the better to target those guns," (*Guardian*, 18 May 2005). Many cheered him on at this moment, but later in the year he perhaps wasted the goodwill with some questionable remarks about sectarian violence in Iraq.

Some insist that Galloway is pilloried purely because he is such an effective critic of the war. He has certainly been one of the loudest opposition voices, and the only one to gain a seat as an MP because of his opposition to the war. It's just there are always those times, as with the 2006 anti-Israel rally, when he goes too far. He has been accused of implicitly inciting British troops to disobey lawful orders. The UK press was outraged when he referred to terrorist insurgents in Iraq as martyrs just four weeks after the 7/7 bombings in London, in 2005. Almost anybody else would have realised that there is a time and a place for such comments, and that in context they would be seen as inflammatory and stupid.

Galloway is rumored once to have said that only an idiot has no regrets. He makes a point of never apologizing. Will he ever look back on his career and feel that he took too many wrong turns, made too many bad moves? Only he can answer that question. DL

Kim Jong-il

Dear Leader

According to official biographers, Kim Jong-il's birth, on 16 February 1941, was foretold by a swallow and marked by a new star in the heavens and the appearance of a double rainbow over Baekdu Mountain. As the leader of North Korea – more properly known as the Democratic People's Republic of Korea – he is officially referred to by North Koreans as "Dear Leader." In 1991, Kim was appointed Supreme Commander of the Korean People's Army, the fourth largest standing army in the world, the final step in the long process of grooming him for leadership, managed by his father, Kim Il-sung.

Although Kim is the General Secretary of the Workers' Party of Korea, the ruling party, by all accounts he leads a life of truly decadent luxury. When, following North Korea's 2006 nuclear test, the United Nations imposed restrictions on the import of luxury items, Reuters noted, "No one enjoys luxury goods more than paramount leader Kim Jong-il, who boasts the country's finest wine cellar with space for 10,000 bottles. Kim has a penchant for fine food such as lobster, caviar, and the most expensive cuts of sushi that he has flown in to him from Japan." While Kim is reported to spend $700,000 a year on Hennessy cognac, the average North Korean must get by on the equivalent of roughly $900 a year. And just in case Comrade Kim feels like going for a drive, it is a requirement that North Korean roads keep a lane free for him.

Not only does Kim have a taste for the finer things in life, he has also often been condemned by other countries and international non-governmental organizations for human rights abuses. In North Korea's largest concentration camp, Camp 22, up to 50,000 men, women, and children accused of political "crimes" are held. There have been many reports of gross human rights violations by guards, such as the murder of babies born to inmates.

Kim has also been accused of ordering at least two bombings carried out by North Korean agents, although there is no incontrovertible evidence for this – in fact, his father, Kim Il-sung, is reported to have been in charge of North Korea's international activities at the time. Whoever was ultimately responsible, in 1983, in Rangoon, Burma (Yangon, Myanmar), 17 visiting South Korean officials, including four Cabinet members, were killed; another bomb, in 1987, killed all 115 people on board a South Korean airliner.

North Korea has also long been suspected of having a nuclear capability, but Kim's attempts to elevate his dictatorship into the ranks of the nuclear superpowers, have proved as ineffectual as his efforts to develop long-range missiles. On 3 October 2006, North Korea announced that it was going to conduct a test of a four-megaton nuclear device, an historically low yield for such an inaugural test. Nevertheless, the announcement sparked panic in the international community, causing diplomats to threaten North Korea with grave consequences. But when North Korea conducted the test, six days later, very little happened. "Is that it?" was the almost disappointed response from the international community. According to seismic analysis, the force of the explosion was less than one kiloton, or, according to some observers, only half of that. By way of contrast, the first ever test of technology for a nuclear weapon, the Trinity test carried out in the United States in 1945, generated a force of 20 kilotons. In fact, the North Korean test generated less force than many tactical nuclear weapons, and could even have been simulated using conventional explosives. A small amount of trace radiation in the atmosphere around the site was the only proof that there had, in fact, been a nuclear explosion of some kind.

Needless to say, no one was particularly impressed by Kim Jong-il's feeble new plaything. The international community condemned the test, but did not seriously consider military action. Kim is supposed to have apologized to the Chinese ambassador for having conducted the test, and, that same month, he meekly agreed to re-enter the six-nation negotiations regarding North Korea's "nuclear arms program."

Unsurprisingly, Kim Jong-il is a constant target for parody and satire, especially in the United States. A Kim-like character often features in the "Celebrity Jeopardy!" sketch on comedian Jay Leno's *The Tonight Show*, in which "Kim" feuds with a George W. Bush character, and comedian David Letterman refers disparagingly to the North Korean dictator as "Li'l Kim." But while Kim Jong-il may be a figure of fun, he is nevertheless a potentially dangerous one. DL

David Koresh

Vernon the Messiah

Never trust anyone who changes his or her name. Born in 1959, David Koresh was originally Vernon Wayne Howell. At the age of 20 he joined the Seventh-Day Adventist Church, but he developed different ideas from the church leaders, and was asked to leave the church, apparently for shouting and screaming at the congregation. In 1981, he joined the Branch Davidians, who had themselves been expelled from the Seventh-Day Adventist Church in the 1930s. The Branch Davidians had established their headquarters at a ranch about nine miles outside of Waco, Texas in 1955. They called it the Mount Carmel Center, after the Biblical Mount Carmel.

Koresh, then still Vernon Howell, an asshole with a persecution complex and a belief in his own righteousness, felt right at home. Branch Davidians believe they are God's chosen people for the Last Days. Because of this they believe that God will always send a prophet to guide them. The Branch Davidians have had five prophets: Ellen White, Victor Houteff, Ben Roden, Lois Roden, and David Koresh. Conveniently for wannabe messiahs like Koresh, Branch Davidians believe that the Bible teaches that no one can be perfect – but those who believe "Present Truth," the latest teachings from God, are the most righteous. It is only by constantly following the new teachings from God that believers will be saved. The group still exists and continues to believe that they are being sent divine messages.

In 1983, Koresh began to claim that he had acquired the gift of prophecy. He was in a sexual relationship with Lois Roden, who was the prophetess and leader of the sect. She was in her late sixties at the time. She claimed that God had chosen him to father a child with her, who would be the "Chosen One." Koresh began to teach his own message which caused some controversy in the group as Lois Roden's existing son, George Roden, had intended to be the group's next leader. Clearly deeply religious, George Roden eventually forced Koresh and his group off the Mount Carmel Center property at gunpoint.

Koresh and around 25 followers then set up their own camp at

Palestine, 90 miles from Waco, where they proceeded to recruit new followers from California, the United Kingdom, Israel, and Australia. In 1985, Koresh traveled to Israel where he claimed to have conversed with God and it was here that Koresh changed his name from Vernon Wayne Howell to David Koresh. The switch came about because he believed that he was now the head of the House of David, from which, according to biblical tradition, the Messiah will come. The name Koresh was derived from the Hebrew name of Cyrus, the Persian king who allowed the Jews who had been dispersed through Babylonia to return to their ancestral homeland. King David and Cyrus are each referred to as Messiah in the Old Testament. Koresh, who was full of new ideas about his godliness, now set up the Davidic Kingdom in Jerusalem. However by 1991, he was convinced that his martyrdom should be in the United States, so he returned to Waco, in the belief that the Mount Carmel Center would be the center of his kingdom.

At the camp in Palestine, Texas, Koresh began to realize his messianic dream. He arranged things so that he was the central figure in every relationship. As his teachings became more self-delusional, he taught his followers that all previous bonds and attachments, family or otherwise, meant nothing, a standard tactic with cult leaders. This is something that increases the vulnerability of cult members. By this time, he was already proclaiming that he was "the Son of God."

In 1986, after Lois Roden died, Koresh announced that polygamy was allowed, although only for him, and amazingly all his followers fell for it. In March 1986, Koresh slept with Karen Doyle, aged 14, and claimed her as his second wife. Not long afterwards, in August 1986, Koresh secretly began sleeping with 12-year-old Michele Jones, his wife's younger sister. Seemingly delighted that he was getting away with this behavior, Koresh began to preach that he was entitled to 140 wives – 60 women as "queens" and 80 more as concubines. Koresh then developed an entirely new theology based around his marriage to Doyle.

He called his theology the New Light, with a doctrine of polygamy for himself and his women. Analysts have said that Koresh's doctrine of polygamy almost certainly arose out of his deep desire to have sex with young girls. He convinced himself that this was God's will, and then he was able to have guilt-free sex with as many young girls as he wanted.

Some former members of the cult have also alleged that Koresh felt he could claim any of the females in the compound. Evidently he fathered at least a dozen children by his harem. The other adults in the compound were told by Koresh not to talk to anyone else about this because they wouldn't understand. Former cult members have also claimed that Koresh would annul all marriages of couples who joined his cult. This served a joint purpose of severing all previous emotional ties and allowing him to have exclusive sexual rights to the women.

By late 1987, support for rival George Roden's organization at Waco had declined. He challenged Koresh to a messianic contest, centering on raising the dead. The contest even involved digging up one corpse to practice on it. Koresh returned to Mount Carmel in camouflage, with seven armed followers. All but one – who managed to escape – were arrested by the local police after the sound of gunfire was heard. Deputy sheriffs arrived and ended the shoot-out. They found Koresh and six followers firing their rifles at Roden, who had already suffered a minor gunshot wound and was trapped behind a tree. As a result, Koresh and his followers were charged with attempted murder. Koresh testified at the trial that he went to Mount Carmel to find evidence of corpse abuse by George Roden. Koresh's followers were acquitted, and his trial was declared a mistrial.

In 1988, Roden murdered Dale Adair with an axe after Adair stated his belief that Koresh was indeed the Messiah. Roden was convicted of murder and, as he owed thousands of dollars in unpaid taxes, Mount Carmel was put up for sale. Koresh and his followers managed to raise the money and bought the property, which he subsequently renamed "Ranch Apocalypse." Koresh was now free to play God without a significant challenger.

On 28 February, 1993, the Bureau of Alcohol, Tobacco and Firearms (BATF) attempted to execute a search warrant at the Branch Davidian ranch at Mount Carmel. An exchange of gunfire resulted in the deaths of ten people, four agents and six Branch Davidians. The ensuing 51-day siege by the Federal Bureau of Investigation (FBI) only ended on 19 April when fire destroyed the complex. Seventy-six people, including 21 children and two pregnant women, along with David Koresh died in the incident. FBI officials had planned a final assault in which the Branch Davidians would to be expelled from their building by force. However in the course of the assault, the church building caught fire, leading to the tragedy.

Twenty-one children, aged from five months to 12 years, were released from Mount Carmel after negotiations at the beginning of the siege. These children were put into the custody of the Child Protective Services and housed together. Over the next two months, these children were cared for by a multidisciplinary treatment team. Child-care and mental health professionals from various institutions and organizations carried out extensive evaluation and assessment. They reported that the children had been raised in an abusive setting. The children said that at various times they had been instructed by Koresh to refer to their natural parents as dogs and to call him their father. The children's testimony helped to piece together a fuller picture of Koresh's truly evil behavior.

Children who were not biologically related to Koresh, or that he had not adopted, were referred to as bastards. Like most dictatorial leaders, Koresh undermined all relationships within the community that didn't involve him, including sibling relationships, marriages, and even friendships. If Koresh judged a relationship to be more important to an individual than dependence on him or God, then it was not tolerated. The Branch Davidian children had been taught to view Koresh as God.

David Koresh was an absolute asshole, exploitative and manipulative of children and young women, exposing them to a variety of inappropriate sexual content, including graphic descriptions of sexual intercourse and sexual technique in his sermons, which lasted for hours at a time, and at which children were present. Furthermore, the young girls were brought up to believe that sex with Koresh was normal, and desirable as part of God's plan for them. All the young girls were being groomed to be his wives, and to view such a state of affairs as healthy and desirable. There have been many cult leaders who have exploited their followers but few have been so completely beyond the pale as Koresh. DL

Oliver North

Neat

For those who don't know it, the motto of the United States Marine Corps (USMC) is *Semper Fidelis*, Latin for "ever faithful." Long associated with the history, traditions, and culture of that branch of service, the expression is sometimes used as a greeting in its shortened form, "Semper Fi," by the Corps "faithful," and is also often printed on commemorative and souvenir items for those who claim to have a strong bond with that particular military community. And like all employees of the US federal government, members of this branch of the armed forces swear an oath to defend and protect the United States and its constitution from all enemies, both foreign and domestic. It is these two elements of Marine Corps culture that make the "service" record of USMC Colonel Oliver North both ironic, and disturbing.

Following an uneventful childhood in upstate New York, North attended State University of New York, Brockport, but after taking a Marine Platoon Leader's course in Quantico, Virginia, as part of his Reserve Officers' Training Corps roster, North decided to make a career in the Marine Corps, and transferred to the United States Naval Academy in the fall of 1963. Aside from a year missed due to injuries sustained in a motor accident, his time at Annapolis was unremarkable, and he graduated as a Second Lieutenant in the spring of 1968.

North remained a lieutenant throughout his initial tour of duty in Vietnam, following which he returned to Quantico as an instructor at the Marine Corps Officer Basic School. In 1970, North returned briefly to Vietnam as a witness in the court marshall of Corporal Randy Herrod, who had been charged with the mass killing of Vietnamese civilians. Having negotiated that challenging "assignment," North was promoted to Captain shortly afterwards, assuming the post of Commanding Officer of the Marine Corps Northern Training Area in Okinawa, Japan, in 1971.

When North returned to the United States, he was assigned to Marine Headquarters in Arlington, Virginia, and promoted to Major. This was followed by two years spent as operations officer for the 2nd Marine Division at Camp Lejeune, North Carolina. In 1981, shortly after graduating from the Naval War College, North began his service with the National Security Council (NSC), where he earned his final promotion to Lieutenant Colonel, and spent the remainder of his military career. It was at the National Security Council that North became enmeshed in activities that lead to one of the biggest scandals of the Reagan Administration.

The first of North's questionable activities involved the Reagan Administration's attempt to influence Hezbollah guerillas, who had taken a number of hostages from many different nations in the multilateral Lebanese civil war of the early 1980s. In an attempt to curry favor with Shi'ite Muslim extremist groups, the NSC agreed to sell conventional anti-tank rockets to the Shi'ite "holy land," Iran. Given the relatively recent return of US hostages from Iran just two years previously, and the bombing of the Marine Corps barracks in Beirut by Hezbollah-friendly group Islamic Jihad in the fall of 1983, the sale of the weapons was arranged as covertly as possible to avoid a US public outcry, especially from those who had voted for President Reagan as the embodiment of a forceful US foreign policy.

The proceeds from the sale of the weapons were used as a covert source of funding for the Contras (forces opposed to Sandinista's Communist government in Nicaragua) even though this violated the Boland Amendment, which, when passed in December 1983, had substantially limited the Reagan White House's attempts at "regime change" in the region. North channeled funds through a shell organization, the National Endowment for the Preservation of Liberty, from Washington DC bank accounts to the Nicaraguan "freedom fighters," beginning with an initial instalment of $2.8 million. The Endowment also funded "training operations" in El Salvador, Honduras, and Guatemala, among other anti-Communist activities in the region, which often utilized abduction, torture, and assassination to achieve their aims.

In 1986, North even "befriended" Panamanian dictator Manuel Noriega, a notorious regional "strongman," alleged to be involved in bribery, corruption, drug smuggling, and money laundering. In an NSC e-mail, in August that year, North informed his superior, Admiral John Poindexter, that Noriega would be willing covertly to "take care" of the Sandinista leadership, if the United States would be willing to help him "clean up" his image, by lifting the US ban on the sale of weapons to Panama's defense forces. In the same e-mail, North suggested to his superior that such aid would be valuable, and further suggested that paying Noriega $1 million dollars out of their "Project Democracy" funds would be money well spent.

The entire operation began to come to light on 3 November, when a Lebanese magazine, *Ash-Shiraa*, broke the story of the United States selling weapons to Iran. Another recent, well-publicized story told of a supposed missionary aid plane which had been downed over Nicaragua and found to be carrying a load of weapons. The pilot, when questioned by the Nicaraguan authorities, claimed to be working for the US Central Intelligence Agency (CIA). Increasingly, the NSC began to find itself in hot water for its supposedly clandestine activities. President Reagan himself informed the US public about the nature and scope of these operations in a press conference, which attempted to pass the mess off as a well-intentioned, but ultimately misguided, attempt to foster better relations with Iran. Reagan also claimed to have had no knowledge of the illegal, covert funding of the Contras, and promised to take action to get to the bottom of what had been going on.

Meanwhile, according to the later sworn testimony of North's then secretary, Fawn Hall, by late November, the good Colonel was busy destroying or removing potentially incriminating documents from his NSC archives. Fired shortly afterwards, he became a key witness in the hearings of the Tower Commission, which began an official investigation into any potential wrongdoing by the NSC on 25 November 1986. The commission's report, in February 1987, was scathingly critical of North and Poindexter's activities, but cleared President Reagan of having had any direct knowledge of their activities.

Not content with simply presenting such findings, Congress held its own televised hearings to determine the extent of these wrongdoings, presided over by a special joint committee. The Iran–Contra Hearings, as they were to become known, dominated that summer's news, and featured public testimony from all parties concerned, including Colonel North who was finally called to the witness stand. The photographs of North being sworn in became iconic of the increasingly notorious scandal. Seemingly a "good Marine" to some of the viewing public, he admitted to all the illegal activities alleged in the Tower Commission's report, as well as to lying to Congress at the time, and justified his actions by saying he believed in the Contra's goals as "freedom fighters," and that the covert operation funded by arms sales was a "neat idea."

By March 1988, however, that "neat idea" had earned Colonel North 16 felony indictments, on a variety of federal charges, of varying degrees of severity. Those who had been impressed by his seemingly forthright demeanor and willingness to accept blame at earlier hearings now became convinced that North was a loyal American, guilty only of following orders, who had been made a scapegoat by those he had served faithfully. As a result of this belief, many championed his cause, making donations to various legal relief funds on his behalf. These funds were established, unsurprisingly, by groups with conservative, Republican ideologies and agendas.

In the end, the Colonel was convicted of only three charges: accepting an illegal gratuity; aiding and abetting in the obstruction of a Congressional inquiry; and the destruction of documents. He was sentenced to a three-year suspended prison term, two years probation, $150,000 in fines, and 1,200 hours of community service. Appealing against even these seemingly minor convictions, with the help of the American Civil Liberties Union (ACLU), North had them all quashed, after arguing successfully that his trial had been unduly affected by media coverage of his Congressional (and "immunized") testimony. As a result, as of 20 July 1990, Oliver North was a free man.

Following the scandal, North attempted to run for Congress in 1994, looking to become the Junior Senator for the commonwealth of Virginia. However, he was shunned by senior Virginia Senator John Warner, who endorsed instead his independent challenger, Marshall Coleman, and by former First Lady Nancy Reagan, whose claims on the eve of the election that the colonel had lied to her husband when discussing Iran–Contra matters, were viewed by many as being decisive in his defeat at the hands of incumbent Democrat Charles Robb. Nevertheless, North's failed campaign gained some notoriety a couple of years later, as the subject of the 1996 documentary, *A Perfect Candidate*.

Since then, North has kept busy writing a series of bestselling "patriotic" action novels, presenting a series on Fox News, *Oliver North's War Stories*, and making a number of cameo appearances in the military legal drama series *JAG*. He also founded the Freedom Alliance, a non-profit organization dedicated to "advancing the American heritage of freedom, by honoring and encouraging military service, defending the sovereignty of the United States, and promoting a strong national defense." In the light of such stated goals, it would be very interesting indeed to hear Colonel North explain how selling weapons to known enemies of his nation, and then channeling the proceeds into an illegal covert war, waged by death squads and drug dealers, fits in with such otherwise noble and patriotic aims. The answer would probably not be "neat." KD

General Augusto José Ramón Pinochet Ugarte

I Feel like an Angel

Of the bloody coup d'état in Chile, in 1973, in which he played a commanding role, General Pinochet has said, "We only set about the task of transforming Chile into a democratic society of free men and women." What followed were the deaths of over 3,197 people, mainly on his orders. Some political scientists have ascribed the relative violence of the coup to the stability of the existing democratic system, which required extreme action to overturn.

Pinochet was born in Valparaíso on 25 November 1915, the son of Augusto Pinochet Vera, who worked as a customs official, and Avelina Ugarte Martínez. He went to primary and secondary school at the San Rafael Seminary of Valparaíso, the Rafael Ariztía Institute (Marist Brothers) in Quillota, and the French Fathers' School of Valparaíso. He entered Military School in 1933, graduating after four years of study in 1937 with the rank of *alférez* (Second Lieutenant) in the infantry.

Pinochet rose quickly through the military ranks, eventually reaching the rank of Major. In 1963, he was appointed Sub-Director of the War Academy, following which his military career continued to progress successfully. In 1968, he was named Chief of Staff of the Second Army Division, based in Santiago, and, at the end of that year, he was promoted to Brigadier General and Commander in Chief of the VI Division, garrisoned in Iquique. In his new post, he was also appointed Intendant of the Tarapacá Province.

In a surprise move, Pinochet was then appointed Army Commander by the president, shortly before parliament voted for a resolution calling for President Allende's removal, by force if necessary.

The Chilean Coup of 1973 began on 22 August, when the Chamber of Deputies of Chile passed, by a vote of 81 to 47, a resolution calling for Allende's removal. The military intervened in the mounting social crisis, staging a violent coup d'état under the direction of Pinochet.

Ground forces surrounded and attacked the Presidential palace, while the air force bombed it. President Allende died before being captured. The exact circumstances of his death are still disputed, although an autopsy in 1990 found that Allende's wounds were consistent with the most widely accepted explanation, that Pinochet had committed suicide.

In his memoirs, Pinochet confirmed that he had been the leading plotter of the coup, and had used his position as Commander in Chief of the Army to co-ordinate a comprehensive plan with the other two branches of the military and the national police.

After the military's seizure of power, Pinochet engaged in brutal political repression, aiming to destroy all remaining support for the defeated Popular Unity (PU) government. In October 1973, General Pinochet despatched General Aurellano Starck on the notorious operation that became known as the Caravan of Death. General Starck flew out of Santiago by helicopter on 30 September, heading first south, then turning towards the copper-rich north of the country. Everywhere Starck's helicopter landed, prisoners were taken out and murdered. Four in Cauquenes, 12 in Valdivia, 15 in La Serena – until the final stop in Calama, on 19 October, where 26 political prisoners were killed. The Caravan of Death had lasted 19 days and, in total, 72 prisoners had been killed. This was by no means the highest death toll during the course of one operation under Pinochet, but it is one of the few which can be linked directly to orders given by him.

Almost immediately upon taking power, the junta banned all the leftist parties that had constituted Allende's UP coalition. Much of the Pinochet regime's violence was directed toward those it viewed as socialist or Marxist sympathisers, though any dissidents who spoke out against the government were persecuted. In the first few months after the coup, thousands were murdered, becoming what came to be called, "the disappeared." Thousands more were jailed, torture was commonplace, and up to one million fled into self-imposed exile. A state of siege was declared and martial law imposed. Parliament was temporarily closed; the media was censored; the universities purged; books burned; Marxist political parties outlawed; and union activities banned. At least five new prison camps had to be established for the increasing numbers of political prisoners.

Some accounts state that up to 250,000 people were detained in those first months. Stadia, military bases, and naval vessels were initially used as short-term prisons. The newly formed secret police, the National Intelligence Directorate (NDA) created a reign of terror at home and organized the assassination of opponents in exile overseas. Civilian courts were supplanted by military tribunals.

It is not known exactly how many people were killed by government or military forces during the 17 years that Pinochet was in power – the exact numbers of "the disappeared" are not known. The Rettig Commission listed 2,095 deaths and 1,102 "disappearances," with the vast majority of victims coming from those opposed to Pinochet at the hands of the state security apparatus. In 2004, the National Commission on Political Prisoners and Torture produced the Valech Report after interviewing an estimated 35,000 people who claimed to have been abused by the regime. About 28,000 of these testimonies were regarded as legitimate. According to the Commission, more than half of the arrests occurred in the months immediately following the coup – approximately 18,000 of those testifying claimed they were detained between September and December of 1973.

A military junta was established immediately following the coup, made up of General Pinochet, representing the Army, Admiral José Toribio Merino, representing the Navy, General Gustavo Leigh, representing the Air Force, and General César Mendoza, representing the *Carabineros* (uniformed police). The new junta embarked on a campaign to remove the influence of the UP from all social institutions.

Once the junta was firmly in power, Pinochet consolidated his control. First, he retained sole chairmanship of the junta. Pinochet, an admirer of Spanish dictator Francisco Franco, was appointed President on 27 June, 1974. He began immediately to rule as an iron-fisted autocrat.

In 1977, making it clear that he had started as he meant to go on, Pinochet announced that there would be no early return to democracy. The junta alone would determine when civilian government could be reinstated. As head of state and commander in chief of the military, he exerted absolute control over the country and ensured that his cronies controlled all key posts.

Pinochet allowed a referendum on the legitimacy of his regime in 1978, following which he claimed that more than 75 per cent of the population endorsed his rule. Pinochet's position had by now become unassailable. He passed an amnesty law to protect military officers accused of human rights abuses committed since the 1973 coup, decree law 2191, published on 19 April 1978, which was personally drafted by the justice minister, Monica Madariaga, a relative of Pinochet. Anyone who had committed crimes, had been an accomplice to crimes, or had covered up crimes between the day of the coup and 10 March 1978, was exculpated from criminal responsibility. Technically, the law is still in force today.

In 1981, Pinochet promoted himself to the supreme army rank of Captain General, a title previously granted only to colonial governors and Bernardo O'Higgins, a hero of Chile's war of independence. The rank was reserved exclusively for those who were head of both the government and the army. He introduced a new constitution, which allowed him to remain as president until 1989. The new constitution also entrenched the military's domination of the government and allowed Pinochet to restrict freedom of association and speech, and to arrest or exile any citizen, with no right of appeal except to Pinochet himself.

The political activities of unions and community organizations were restricted and politicians were barred from advocacy roles for such groups. Local governments were abolished and Pinochet gave himself the power to dissolve the House of Representatives. This meant that the constitution could not be amended without Pinochet's approval.

Pinochet lost the 1988 referendum, in which 55 per cent of the votes cast rejected an extension of the Presidential term. Open Presidential elections were held the following year, during the same period that congressional elections would have taken place. Pinochet left the presidency on 11 March 1990, transferring power to Patricio Aylwin, the new democratically elected president.

Due to the transitional provisions of the constitution, Pinochet remained as Commander in Chief of the Army, until March 1998. That same year, Pinochet, who still had much influence in Chile, traveled to the United Kingdom for medical treatment. While there, he was arrested under an international arrest warrant issued by a Spanish judge, Baltasar Garzón, and was placed under house arrest, initially, in the clinic where he had recently undergone back surgery, and later in a rented house. The charges included 94 counts of torture of Spanish citizens, and one count of conspiracy to commit torture. The government of Chile opposed his arrest, his extradition to Spain, and his trial.

He was arrested and then released by the UK government and, finally, arrested and prosecuted by the Chilean government itself. In

April 1999, along with Margaret Thatcher, Pope John Paul II, and George H. W. Bush, the Dalai Lama called upon the UK government to release Pinochet. They all urged that Pinochet be allowed to return to his homeland rather than be forced to go to Spain. There were questions about Pinochet's allegedly fragile health. After medical tests, the UK Home Secretary, Jack Straw, ruled, despite the protests of legal and medical experts from several countries, that he should not be extradited to Spain and, on 2 March 2000, Pinochet returned to Chile.

Shortly after this verdict, Pinochet resigned from the Senate and kept a low profile. He rarely made public appearances and was notably absent from the events marking the 30th anniversary of the coup, on 11 September 2003.

In a rare interview, broadcast by the Miami-based, Spanish-language television station WDLP-22 on 24 November 2002, Pinochet said he had no regrets about his time in power and refused to apologize for the abuses of his regime.

"I never aspired to be a dictator because . . . I considered that to be a dictator would end badly . . . I always acted in a democratic way . . . Who shall I ask to be pardoned by? They say I should ask for forgiveness, what shall I ask to be forgiven for? . . . I feel like an angel. I have no resentment . . . I am a man who does not carry any hate in his heart . . . I don't want future generations to think badly of me. I want them to know what really happened."

Many see him as a brutal dictator who ended democracy and led a regime characterized by torture and favoritism towards the rich. As well as trials for human rights abuses, Pinochet stands accused of tax evasion and fraud. Others believe that he saved the country from Communism, safeguarded Chilean democracy, and led the transformation of the Chilean economy into Latin America's most stable and fastest growing. He has many supporters in the international community, including, famously, ex-UK Prime Minister Margaret Thatcher, who thanked the General for "bringing democracy to Chile." Apparently they often enjoyed tea together and, indeed, Thatcher's free-market policies, which decimated the UK in the late 1980s and 1990s, were not so different from those of Pinochet.

Pinochet died on 10 December 2006. DL

Karl Rove

Turd Blossom

If you have ever wondered how George W. Bush got elected to *any* political office, let alone two terms as a partisan, politically divisive Republican president, the explanation is most likely Karl Christian Rove. The veteran political campaign strategist and advisor has been called "Bush's Brain" by parts of the media, and is alleged to be known as "turd blossom" by those in the Bush White House's inner circle, a metaphor for the wily operative's ability to create things of supposed beauty out of a stinking mess. Though he resigned from his role as Deputy Chief of Staff to George W. Bush on 31 August 2007, one can be fairly sure that this was only the end of a particularly successful episode in a political lifetime of covert action and dirty tricks on behalf of the Grand Old Party.

Born, ironically (to detractors, anyway), on Christmas Day, 1950, Karl was raised by his mother, Reba Wood, and his stepfather, Louis Rove Jr. Reba's first two children, Karl and his older brother Eric, were the children of an unknown man with whom she had been romantically involved, but who had left without having married her before Karl was born. To Louis Rove's credit, he raised the boys as if they were his own, and never even hinted that they were not his biological children, which, while noble, was the first of many secrets to be kept by Karl throughout his life.

As a precocious, but socially awkward, child, Karl made his first political allegiance, at the age of nine, to Richard Nixon during the 1960 election, getting into a physical fight with an equally young girl who supported John F. Kennedy. Rove lost. When the family moved from Denver to Salt Lake City in 1965, Rove took the opportunity to reinvent himself, by being elected student council president during his junior and senior years at Olympus High School, despite being, by his own admission, a "complete nerd." In 1968, Karl got his first taste of real political campaigning, supporting the successful re-election run of Wallace F. Bennett to the US Senate, and in the process befriending the senator's son Bob Bennett, a future Utah Senator.

In the fall of 1969, Karl started college at the University of Utah, joining the Pi Kappa Alpha fraternity, and majoring in Political Science. By the end of his first semester, the only man Rove had ever known to be his father, divorced his mother for reasons unknown at the time (though it was later reported that it was because he was allegedly homosexual). As if this event wasn't shocking enough for Karl, he also learned from his aunt and uncle that the senior Rove was not his biological father, which, conversely, only strengthened Karl's love for a man he later described as a loving and selfless father.

The other major source of stress in Karl's life at the time was the recently enacted Selective Service Draft "lottery," which was held at around the same time. With a draft number of 84, putting him squarely in the middle of the field of potential draftees, he made a point of maintaining a 2-S ineligibility status by attempting to maintain the necessary grade point average and full-time student status, despite being only marginally interested in his studies. For while the young Rove was a reasonably talented scholar, following his involvement in his first political campaign the previous year, he was far more interested in the "real world" practice of political science, than its classroom "theory."

His first taste of real-world politics came in 1970, through his involvement with the University of Utah's Hinckley Institute of Politics, which had secured him an internship with the Utah Republican Party, and later landed him a position on the unsuccessful re-election campaign of Illinois Senator Ralph Smith. During this seasonal tenure in Illinois politics, Rove is alleged to have broken into the offices of Illinois Democratic State Treasurer candidate Alan J. Dixon, and stolen 1,000 of his campaign's official letterhead stationery, which he used to print fliers, making the bogus claim that there would be free beer, food, and girls available at an upcoming Dixon rally. Though Dixon won despite the attempt at sabotage, and Rove dismissed the incident as a "youthful prank" in later interviews, the incident gave a strong indication of the kind of campaign strategies and tactics that were to become his stock in trade.

By June 1971, Rove had left Utah for good, to take a paid position as the Executive Director of the College Republican National Committee (RNC), under the guidance of then National Chairman, Joe Abate. His primary role at the time was as an instructor at weekend seminars for campus conservatives, to show them how to organize their relatively few members in taking aggressive stances against "leftist" and "counter-cultural" values and related policies which were far more popular with college students of that era. By 1972, he was a seasoned junior political operative of Richard Nixon's re-election campaign for president of the United States, under the guidance of no less than future convicted Watergate co-conspirator Donald Segretti, a man well acquainted with media smear tactics.

Following the successful re-election of Nixon in 1972, Rove campaigned for the post of National Chairman of the College Republican National Committee which he had so far served so well. With Lee Atwater as his campaign manager, Rove spent much of the spring of that year drumming up support from campus conservatives all over the country, before trying to win the election by having his opponent forfeit it due to an obscure loophole in the group's charter. When the story was leaked to the *Washington Post*, by that same rival, that he and other members of the College Republicans had allegedly been schooled by Rove, in 1972, in how to carry out various dirty tricks against the McGovern Presidential campaign, Karl only escaped prosecution due to his status as an underling, leaving many to speculate as to how this would affect the decision of the then Republican National Committee Chairman, George H. W. Bush, with regard to the contested election in the party's collegiate ranks.

Ultimately, the elder Bush appointed Rove to the position of Chairman despite the public controversy, which resulted in the forging of a strong alliance between the two which would serve them both well politically in the years to come. Rove is credited with introducing Lee Atwater to the Bush family patriarch, undoubtedly helping his chances of an eventual RNC Chairmanship of his own, as well as a position as a campaign advisor to Bush's run for president of the United States in 1988. Rove's role as a special assistant to George H. W. Bush also created an alliance between Rove and George W. Bush, when Rove was sent on an "errand" to take a spare set of car keys to the George W., who was down in Texas, in the fall of 1973. The rest of his tenure in Washington DC was occupied by acting as a special assistant to RNC co-chair Richard Obenshain, and continuing his still incomplete studies at nearby George Mason University.

After a short tenure as finance director for the Republican Party of Virginia, notable for its use of direct mail as a fundraising device, in 1976, Rove moved to Texas a year later, presumably to complete his degree at the University of Texas at Austin, but almost equally assuredly to cash in on his recently cultivated connections in the state through the RNC and George H. W. Bush. His initial job on completing his studies was as a legislative aide to Fred Agnich, a Texas state representative. Rove was later appointed Executive Director of the Fund for Limited Government, a Houston political action committee, headed by James Baker, a local attorney who later served in both the Reagan and Bush Administrations. The political action committee later served as the core membership of the 1980 Bush primary election campaign.

Karl's first foray into Texan electoral politics came in 1978, when he helped Bill Clements Jr become the first Republican Governor of Texas in 100 years. This initial success was dampened somewhat by his inability to produce similar success for George W. Bush in his first run for Congress that same year. He fared slightly better two years later, as a campaign advisor to the elder Bush's 1980 campaign for president, staying on board even after his boss accepted a vice-presidential position under leading candidate Ronald Reagan, only to be fired halfway through the national election campaign for making unauthorized leaks to the press.

With his freshman attempt at advising a national political campaign so abruptly ended, Rove refocused on Texan politics, forming direct mail consulting firm Karl Rove & Company to that end, in Austin, in 1981. His firm's first campaign, William Clements Jr's re-election bid, was defeated by Clements's Democratic challenger in the 1982 gubernatorial election, but their second, on behalf of conservative Democrat Phil Gramm, was sufficiently successful to ensure not just a win for that campaign, but also for Gramm's senatorial campaign in 1984. Karl Rove & Company also handled the direct mail for the 1984 Presidential re-election campaign of Ronald Reagan and Bush Sr, following which Rove played an advisory role during the rest of the 1980s to a variety of Texan Republican candidates.

After helping to have William Clements Jr re-elected as Governor in 1986, and assisting Tom Phillips to become the first Republican to be elected to the Texas Supreme Court in 1988, Rove took a rare wrong turn in 1990 when he backed an attempt to have George W. Bush elected as governor, before Bush dropped out for unspecified reasons, and the Republican candidate was soundly defeated. Rove was more successful in backing Rick Perry to become Agricultural Commissioner and Kay Bailey Hutchison in her campaign to become State Treasurer of the Lone Star state that same year. Partisan appeals to party loyalty were a common characteristic of all these campaigns, as was a reliance on smear tactics, leaks, and dirty tricks, though none was ever traced directly back to Rove or any of his known associates.

The remainder of the 1990s saw Karl's focus shift to national GOP politics, but with mixed success. While unsuccessful in his advisory role to Dick Thornburgh during his 1991 senatorial campaign in Pennsylvania, and to President George H. W. Bush's presidential re-election campaign in 1992, Rove saw victories on behalf of the Kay Bailey Hutchison campaign for Senator of Texas in 1993, the 1994 Alabama Supreme Court campaign of Perry Hooper, George W. Bush's run for Governor of Texas, and John Ashcroft's run for Senate that same year. Karl finished the decade with a 1996 win for Harold See's campaign for Alabama Associate Supreme Court Justice, and the re-election campaign of George W. Bush in 1998. All these campaigns were notable for the increasingly higher fees earned by Rove, in exchange, one imagines, for increasingly underhand tactics. In 1999, Rove sold Karl Rove & Company to two of his senior, trusted subordinates, Ted Delisi and Todd Olsen, as a prelude to his first hands-on role as a primary political advisor in a presidential election, for Republican candidate George W. Bush.

Rove's two known contributions to the successful campaign are his well orchestrated smear campaign against Republican primary election challenger, John McCain, whom Rove and company intimated was too "shell-shocked" to be president, and whom they falsely implied may have fathered a "bi-racial" child out of wedlock, and by directing an "emergency response" of Republican politicians and activists to Florida at the end of the election, when close returns in that state threatened to result in a recount, and victory for Democratic challenger Al Gore on a technicality. His reward for this success was his appointment as Senior Advisor to the president in January 2001, a position notable for its considerable access to and influence on White House policies and agendas, with relatively little oversight by other branches of government, or accountability to any elected officials other than the president himself. It is a role Rove reveled in, giving an increasingly public impression of being the Bush Administration's ultimate "black knight" to the people of the United States, whenever his frequent covert activities were revealed in the national media.

The nature of Rove's new job became clear in 2002, when he chaired meetings of the White House Iraq Group, which was charged with making the case for war against Iraqi dictator Saddam Hussein as part of the recently initiated "War on Terror." Comprising Bush loyalists such as Vice President Dick Cheney, National Security Advisor Condoleezza Rice, Cheney's Chief of Staff Lewis "Scooter" Libby, Rice's Deputy Stephen Hadley, and communications strategists Mary Matalin, Karen Hughes, and James R. Wilkinson, the secret group was charged with the task of educating the US public about the danger to US national security allegedly posed by Iraq and its dictator. When undercover CIA operative Valerie Plame later attempted to present evidence contrary to the group's claims that Saddam Hussein was seeking to purchase black market uranium in order to produce "weapons of mass destruction," in early 2003, someone within the group blew her cover to *Washington Post* columnist Robert Novak, a noted conservative and Bush White House ally, kicking off the so-called Plamegate investigations that began in August that year and continued until the summer of 2006.

A far more overt accomplishment came in the 2004 re-election campaign of George W. Bush against Democratic challenger John Kerry. While it has been alleged that Rove was behind such tactics as raising the national "terror alert level" every time Kerry pulled ahead of the president in public opinion polls, as well as the partisan attack ads of the Swift Boat Veterans for Truth, a group of conservative Vietnam veterans who were publicly critical of Kerry's naval service record and subsequent anti-war activities, no proof of this has ever been found. Some have even gone so far as to allege that Rove was behind the Killian Documents, which, when leaked to CBS News, forced the resignation of veteran anchorman Dan Rather, because they had been inadequately authenticated before being aired. While the Killian Documents bear all the hallmarks of a typical Rove tactic, he has never been credibly linked to the controversy.

Whatever celebrations there might have been after such a hard-won victory petered out quickly as the charges and allegations of Plamegate forced outgoing Attorney General John Ashcroft to assign a special investigator, Patrick Fitzgerald, to the matter in order to determine conclusively, who, if anyone, had leaked her identity as a CIA operative to members of the national press. As a result, much of 2005 went by with incremental, and at times contradictory, accounts of how various members of the White House Iraq Group claimed to have spoken to the press about the run-up to the Iraq War, their case for the conflict – now known to be flawed – and who they may have spoken to, and when, about Valerie Plame and her evidence which contradicted the central plank of their argument. It took until 2006 for Fitzgerald to reach the conclusion that Rove had done nothing legally wrong and for Richard Armitage to claim responsibility for the leak, which was convenient, given that his 2005 resignation from the State Department had made him immune to disciplinary actions, and for Fitzgerald to file perjury and obstruction of justice charges against Lewis "Scooter" Libby as the sole defendant uncovered in the lengthy investigation.

Aside from some over-confident predictions concerning the upcoming mid-term congressional election results, Rove spent the remainder of 2006 keeping a low profile. In the light of more recent lobbying scandals in the House and Senate involving GOP lawmakers, as well as sex scandals concerning Congressman Mark Foley and Senator Larry Craig, and the trial of Lewis Libby, it seemed as though even the considerable powers of the party's most capable covert partisan were not sufficient to "spin" such events, or stem the inevitable tide of Democratic victory. Six months later, by March 2007, Rove's concern with continued Republican political success had been replaced by the more immediate goal of saving his career.

When the recently elected congress with a Democratic majority was sworn in during January 2007, its members were greeted by a large number of requests from the Justice Department of Attorney General Alberto Gonzalez, under the auspices of the Patriot Act, to make permanent the appointments of US attorneys who had been temporarily appointed. When close examination by the Senate Judicial Committee revealed that many of the temporary US attorneys had replaced longer standing employees for no apparently good reason, a series of well-publicized hearings were convened to determine the extent of the problem, and who in the Bush Administration had authorized the firings. When it was revealed, in February, that one of the temporary US attorneys was a former member of Karl Rove's staff, with considerably less legal experience than the man he had replaced, congressional operatives wasted no time in demanding an in-depth investigation into the questionable firings and appointments.

By March, it had been determined that Rove was behind the firing of all 93 attorneys in January 2005, proven in numerous e-mails, which were first subpoenaed by congress, before being released to the press. By July, as the hearings wore on, and evidence of Rove's culpability grew increasingly more obvious, Senator Patrick Leahy, chairman of the Judiciary Committee announced that he was issuing a subpoena for Karl Rove to appear before the committee, based on an increasing lack of confidence in the accuracy of the testimony of Alberto Gonzalez. Despite his obvious involvement in the firing of the US Attorneys, Rove refused to comment on the matter publicly, and the White House claimed Executive Privilege as a reason for Rove not needing to appear before the committee, unless it was off the record and in a private session not open to the press, based on an alleged need for national security.

The two arms of government tussled with each other, with the Judicial Committee having already proved Rove's involvement in the firings with evidence from his own e-mails, and the White House standing firmly by its decision to shield Rove from the Judiciary Committee's subpoena. To further complicate matters, Rove candidly informed the *Wall Street Journal* in a 13 August interview that he would resign from the Bush Administration at the end of that month, expressing a desire to spend more time with his family. With no other recourse, the Judiciary Committee focused its full attention on Alberto Gonzalez, all but interrogating the hapless Attorney General, who couldn't seem to recall anything related to the matter from the time he had assumed the office of Attorney General, despite the evidence of numerous documents and the sworn testimony of other witnesses to the contrary. As a result, Gonzalez announced his own resignation on 27 August, effective from 17 September, and Rove left his role as Senior Advisor to the Bush White House four days later.

It was not known, as Karl Rove left the White House, what he would do next. Many speculated that he would return to his adopted state of Texas, and perhaps make further forays into state political elections. Rove himself said at the time of his resignation that he intended to write a book about his career in politics. Whatever he gets up to, Rove's post-White House life is sure to be lived for the greater good of the Republican Party, as an exemplary "turd blossom." KD

Donald Rumsfeld

Secretary of Torture

Donald Rumsfeld resigned as Secretary of Defense in November 2006. His departure was widely seen as a potentially crucial shift in the direction of US foreign and defense policy. Rumsfeld had been fiercely criticized on a number of fronts, including misleading statements about the Iraqi regime during the run-up to war, his failure to plan adequately for post-invasion problems, and his handling of Abu Ghraib detainee abuse scandal.

Following the 11 September 2001 attacks, Rumsfeld was in charge of the military planning and execution of the US invasion of Afghanistan and the Iraq invasion in 2003. Approximately five hours after the attack on the World Trade Center, Rumsfeld reportedly told aides he wanted certain information fast. He asked them to make a judgment as to whether the information was good enough to hit not only Osama bin Laden but also Saddam Hussein. Right from the start, the focus was Saddam, regardless of the likelihood he had nothing to do with the attack. Rumsfeld subsequently made public statements regarding Iraq's alleged weapons of mass destruction. Arrogant to the end, he is the asshole who is largely credited with creating the mess that is now Iraq.

Shortly after 11 September 2001, Rumsfeld was in a meeting about the review of the Department of Defense's (Contingency) Plan in the event of a war with Iraq (US Central Command OPLAN 1003–98). The plan, as it was conceived at that stage, was for troop levels of up to 500,000. Rumsfeld's opinion was that this was far too many. He also vetoed the use of certain military equipment including the drone Predator bomber because it would be too expensive and require too many troops. This thrift-store approach to war has almost certainly been responsible for a significant number of deaths. By 2007, it had become widely acknowledged by the US Army leadership that the war in Iraq had been initiated with an inadequate number of troops.

After the invasion of Iraq, things began to go very badly wrong very rapidly. While US troops looked helplessly on, many government buildings, major museums, electrical generation infrastructure, and even items of importance to the oil industry were looted and vandalized during the time between the fall of Saddam Hussein's regime and the establishment of the Coalition Provisional Authority. A violent insurgency started shortly after the occupation started, encouraged by the US administration's failure to allow for the need to police an invaded country. The insurgency has continued for over five years.

Rumsfeld was characterized by an unwavering, arrogant insistence that war in Iraq was the right path for the United States and that his way of fighting that war was the only way. His adamant refusal to admit to mistakes in the prosecution of that war was equaled only by President Bush's steadfast loyalty to Rumsfeld. Previously, during Rumsfeld's tenure as Pentagon chief, he reportedly offered Bush his resignation twice as a result of the scandal of Abu Ghraib, but on both occasions Bush refused to accept it.

One of Rumsfeld's better known statements was that a US pullout from Iraq would result in "a haven for terrorists . . . It would be an enormous victory for the violent extremists" (*NewsHour with Jim Lehrer*, 8 December 2005). He also came under heavy criticism for using a signing machine instead of personally signing over 1,000 letters of condolence to the families of soldiers killed in action in Iraq and Afghanistan. An asshole with neither a brain nor a heart.

Rumsfeld also stubbornly refused to recognize the gradual transformation of the conflict in Iraq into a bloody counter-insurgency against surprsingly effective Sunni militias. In April 2003, shortly after the invasion of Baghdad, as the situation on the streets deteriorated in violence, Rumsfeld argued that "free people are free to make mistakes and commit crimes and do bad things" (*New Yorker*, 20 November 2006). Even when many, on the ground in Iraq and even within Rumsfeld's inner group in Washington, could acknowledge the ominous signs of a growing insurgency, Rumsfeld insistently declined to call it that.

In December 2004, Rumsfeld was again slammed by the media after a "town hall" meeting with US troops. Rumsfeld responded to a soldier's comments about inferior military equipment by saying, "You go to war with the army you have, not the army you want." Yet, as we've already seen, he had from the start refused requests for more sophisticated equipment or more troops.

In November 2006, the former US Army Brigadier General Janis Karpinski, who had been in charge of Abu Ghraib until early 2004, told Spain's *El Pais* newspaper that she had seen a letter that Rumsfeld had signed, allowing civilian contractors to use techniques during interrogation such as sleep deprivation. "The methods consisted of making prisoners stand for long periods, sleep deprivation . . . playing music at full volume, having to sit in uncomfortable positions . . . Rumsfeld authorized these specific techniques." She pointed out that this was contrary to the Geneva Convention, which states that: "Prisoners of war who refuse to answer may not be threatened, insulted, or exposed to any unpleasant or disadvantageous treatment of any kind."

According to Karpinski, the handwritten signature was over Rumsfeld's printed name and the same handwriting in the margin there was a comment: "Make sure this is accomplished." There has been little or no response from either the Pentagon or US Army in Iraq on Karpinski's accusations.

This asshole also went on to vigorously defend the Bush Administration's decision to detain alleged illegal enemy combatants without protection under the Geneva Convention. Many still feel that Rumsfeld should be held personally responsible for the Abu Ghraib torture and prisoner abuse scandal. Rumsfeld himself said, "These events occurred on my watch as Secretary of Defense. I am accountable for them." However, military investigations into the scandals did not find him responsible for any wrongdoing that had taken place.

As criticism of Rumsfeld grew to a clamor, Bush finally announced after the elections, on 8 November 2006, that Rumsfeld would resign as Secretary of Defense. Many Republicans were unhappy with the delay, believing they could have done better in the elections if voters had known that Rumsfeld would be going. Even his own party had become frustrated by his arrogance and blamed him for the loss of Senate seats.

Before his resignation, Rumsfeld had been the subject of a number of lawsuits. In March 2005, the American Civil Liberties Union and Human Rights First filed suit against Rumsfeld in an Illinois federal court on behalf of eight detainees who they alleged were subjected to torture and abuse by US forces. In December 2006 Donald Vance, a US citizen, filed suit against Rumsfeld and the US government alleging that he had been the subject of illegal incarceration and torture in Iraq. Vance's lawsuit against Rumsfeld and the US government alleges that he was tortured and had his rights of *habeas corpus* violated. Earlier in 2004 Wolfgang Kaleck, Michael Ratner, and Peter Weiss of the US-based Center for Constitutional Rights (CCR) pressed for criminal charges for war crimes in German courts. In November 2006, 11 former prisoners of Abu Ghraib and Guantanamo were backed by over 30 human rights organizations who supported the charges by Wolfgang Kaleck and the CCR lodged at the German Federal Attorney General (*Generalbundesanwalt*) against Rumsfeld. A complaint has been filed in a French court that accuses Rumsfeld of authorizing and ordering torture, in contravention of the United Nations Convention Against Torture, ratified by both the United States and France. This states that signatory countries must prosecute a torturer or someone who knowingly oversees torturers, irrespective of where the torture occurred. Criminal charges against Rumsfeld were also brought in Argentina in 2005 and in Sweden in 2007.

Whether the Iraq War was an endeavor doomed from the start is a question that will be debated for decades to come. The question now is whether the asshole Rumsfeld will ever be held to account for his arrogance, ineptitude, and mismanagement. As Michael Ratner says, "We will not rest until those US officials involved in torture are brought to justice. Rumsfeld must understand that he has no place to hide." DL

Saddam Hussein

"Victor"

In 1957, at the age of 20, Saddam joined the revolutionary pan-Arab Ba'ath Party, of which his uncle was a supporter. He already had a considerable reputation as a thug and an assassin after frequently walking to school carrying an iron bar as a weapon. Two years later, Saddam Hussein was one of an eight-man hit squad chosen for a US-backed plot to assassinate Prime Minister Qassim. The plot failed miserably as the would-be assassins were clearly idiots, and the plot had not been thoroughly thought through.

Army officers with ties to the Ba'ath Party eventually overthrew Qassim in a bloody coup in 1963. Saddam became a gun-toting

bodyguard on the right of the party. He won favour through his willingness to dispose of opponents by the most direct methods. He even
offered to blow away the leader of the party's left faction. His offer was
politely refused by Hassan-al-Bakr, his boss, who didn't want to set a
precedent which would put his own life at risk. Saddam was apparently
never without a machine-gun and at least one revolver, and he flourished in such a lawless environment. It was thought that his limited
"skills" – idiocy and aggression – were particularly appropriate to the
Ba'ath preference for violence over diplomacy, and Saddam was
promoted to the position of Secretary and eventually, Leader, a
position he shared with Abdel al-Shaikhili. Saddam's appointment was
unprecedented. He had no credentials and no experience, and he was
not accepted by the rest of the party. As a result, he was compelled to
resort to his customary method of achieving power – he had his co-
appointee, Abdel al Shaikhili, murdered, thereby putting himself in sole
charge.

Saddam actively fostered the modernization of the Iraqi economy at
the same time as he created a strong security apparatus to prevent
coups within the power structure, and insurrections outside of it. At the
centre of this strategy was Iraq's oil. On 1 June 1972, Saddam oversaw
the seizure of international oil interests, which, at the time, had a
monopoly on the country's oil. A year later, world oil prices rose
dramatically as a result of the 1973 world oil shock, and skyrocketing
revenues from oil enabled Saddam to expand his agenda.

In 1976, soon after becoming Deputy President, Saddam demanded
and received the rank of four-star General despite his lack of military
training. At the time, he was considered an enemy of Communism and
radical Islam, and regarded as being integral to US policy in the region,
which sought to weaken the influence of Iran and the Soviet Union.

In 1979, Iran's hereditary ruler, Shah Mohammad Reza Pahlavi,
was overthrown by the Islamic Revolution, and Ayatollah Khomeini
established an Islamic republic. The influence of revolutionary Shi'ite
Islam grew rapidly in the region, particularly in countries with large
Shi'ite populations, especially Iraq. Saddam feared that radical Islamic
ideas – hostile to his secular regime – were spreading rapidly among
Iraq's majority Shi'ite population.

Iraq quickly found itself bogged down in one of the longest and most
destructive wars of attrition of the twentieth century. During the war,
Iraq used chemical weapons against Iranian forces and Kurdish

separatists. On 16 March 1988, the Kurdish town of Halabja was attacked with a mixture of mustard gas and nerve agents, killing 5,000 civilians, and maiming, disfiguring, or seriously debilitating 10,000 more. Saddam's intention was to depopulate Kurdistan, a traditional bastion of resistance, while attention was still on fighting at the front. By mid-1989, he had destroyed 4,000 Kurdish settlements. A UK documentary film-maker managed to smuggle out conclusive evidence of the atrocities: bodies piled high in desolate villages, a film over their eyes and a horrible slime pouring out of their noses and mouths, their skin peeling and bubbling. A US Senator tried to get a Prevention of Genocide Act passed, but Reagan's government quashed it, still thinking its interests lay in keeping Saddam sweet. The attack occurred in conjunction with the 1988 al-Anfal campaign designed to reassert central control over the majority Kurdish areas of northern Iraq and to defeat the Kurdish Peshmerga rebel forces. The United States maintains that Saddam ordered the attack to terrorize the Kurdish population in northern Iraq, but Saddam's regime claimed that Iran was responsible for the attack. To the end, Saddam never acknowledged responsibility for any of his actions or orders.

The bloody eight-year Iran–Iraq war ended in a stalemate. There were hundreds of thousands of casualties; perhaps upward of 1.7 million died on both sides. Both economies, previously healthy and expanding, were left shattered. This didn't stop Saddam declaring himself the victor, and raising monuments and awarding himself an endless string of titles to back up his claims.

Under Saddam, torture became a customary experience, used not to extract information, but to re-model the very thoughts of the population. Extracting confessions to non-existent crimes was a means of compelling victims to surrender their individuality, to accept without question the truth as represented by the state. In order to heighten the impression of the Ba'athist organization as omniscient and divine and to have the people accept its leader, the security services attempted to cultivate a sense of guilt in people by acting anonymously and selecting victims at random. No explanations were ever offered for these arrests, which were efficiently calculated to suggest unimaginable horrors. As Samir al-Khali, an Iraqi dissident and author, wrote: "The pattern [was] for agents to pick someone up from work, or at night from his house . . . what one assume[d] to be the corpse [was] brought back weeks or maybe months later and delivered to the family in a sealed box. A death certificate [was] produced for signature to the effect that the person [had] died of fire, swimming, or other such accidents. Someone [was] allowed to accompany the police and box for a ceremony, but at no time [were] they allowed to see the corpse. The cost of proceedings [was] demanded from the family in advance . . ."

Acid baths were commonly used to make thousands of corpses disappear. Amnesty International has detailed 30 methods of torture used in Iraq, from beatings to mutilation, from rape to electrocution, including the gouging out of eyes, the cutting off of noses, breasts, penises, and limbs. Heavy metal poisoning was a favored means of killing "undesirables"; lead and thallium were administered to prisoners in soft drinks during uneventful, but deliberately prolonged, interrogations. Children were routinely tortured to extract confessions from their parents. In 1985, 300 children were held at Fusailyya Prison, where they were whipped, sexually abused, and given electric shocks. In order to assist their work, the security forces became master players of the rumor machine. They used it to create an enemy within and then to spread rumors of the horrendous punishments that traitors received. A constant stream of videos showing confessions, trials, and executions were released to the public. Ba'ath officials were required to take part in executions and were filmed doing so, thus binding themselves together in responsibility with "blood cement."

On 2 August 1990, Saddam invaded and annexed the neighboring oil-rich emirate of Kuwait. For the first several days following the invasion, US President George H. W. Bush responded cautiously. On the one hand, Kuwait, prior to the Iraqi invasion, had been a virulent enemy of Israel, and on friendly terms with the Soviet Union. On the other hand, Iraq controlled ten per cent of the world's crude oil reserves and, by invading Iraq, it had increased its control to 20 per cent. The United States was heavily invested in the region, and the invasion triggered fears that the price of oil, and therefore the stability of the world economy, was at stake. The United Kingdom, which had had a close historical relationship with Kuwait dating back to the days of the British Empire, was also concerned. The United Kingdom also benefited from billions of dollars of Kuwaiti investment. UK Prime Minister Margaret Thatcher underscored the risk the invasion posed to Western interests to President Bush in a one-on-one meeting on the day following the invasion, famously telling him, "Don't go wobbly on me, George."

Co-operation between the United States and the Soviet Union made possible the passage of resolutions in the United Nations Security Council, giving Iraq a deadline to leave Kuwait, and approving the use of force if Saddam refused to comply.

Saddam ignored the Security Council deadline. With unanimous backing from the Security Council, a US-led coalition launched round-the-clock missile and aerial attacks on Iraq, beginning on 16 January 1991. Israel, though subjected to attack by Iraqi missiles, refrained from retaliating in order not to provoke Arab states into leaving the coalition. A ground force, comprising largely US and UK armored and infantry divisions, ejected Saddam's army from Kuwait in February 1991, and occupied southern Iraq as far as the Euphrates. Before Iraqi troops left Kuwait, Saddam ordered its oil wells to be torched.

As part of the ceasefire agreement, Iraq agreed to abandon all chemical and biological weapons and to allow UN observers to inspect the sites where these had been produced and stored. UN trade sanctions would remain in effect until Iraq complied with all terms.

The Iraqis were barred from selling crude oil – their only export commodity – in the hope that Saddam would be left too impoverished to reconstitute his shattered army. The result, predictably, was that he took money from wherever he could to re-arm, leaving his people desperately hungry and devoid of proper amenities, including even basic medicines. Some US politicians openly admitted that they hoped the misery inflicted on Iraq would provoke "regime change" in the form of a successful revolution. It did not. For over a decade Saddam remained defiant, sometimes deliberately breaching the UN sanctions, while the United States continued to send cruise missiles into Iraq in retaliation. Meanwhile, Saddam routinely cited his survival as "proof" that Iraq had, in fact, won the war against the United States. This posturing earned Saddam a great deal of popularity in many parts of the Arab world.

Increasingly, Saddam portrayed himself as a devout Muslim in an effort to co-opt the conservative, religious elements of Iraqi society. Some elements of Sharia law were reintroduced, such as the 2001 edict imposing the death penalty for homosexuality, rape, and prostitution; "honor killings" were legalized; and the ritual phrase "*Allahu Akbar*" ("God is the greatest"), in Saddam's handwriting, was added to the national flag.

After al-Qaeda attacked the United States on 11 September 2001,

Iraq was suspected of supporting terrorists, and of preparing weapons of mass destruction for terrorism. In addition, there were rumors of terrorist training camps, which sowed the seeds of "Operation Iraqi Freedom," the US plan to invade Iraq.

On 4 April 2003, satellite channels worldwide broadcast footage of the besieged Iraqi leader touring the streets of his bombed capital, as smoke rose from oil fires in the background. As US-led ground troops advanced towards the Iraqi capital, a smiling Saddam Hussein, clearly so arrogant as to believe that nothing could touch him, greeted cheering, chanting crowds in the streets of Baghdad.

The Iraqi government and military collapsed within three weeks of the beginning of the US-led 2003 invasion of Iraq, on 20 March, and Saddam went into hiding. He was eventually captured, on 14 December 2000. It was reported that he had been found in an underground "spider hole" bunker at a farmhouse in ad-Dawr near his home town, Tikrit, in what was called Operation Red Dawn. Saddam was photographed in custody with a full beard and hair longer and curlier than his familiar appearance, which a barber later restored for him. His identity was later reportedly confirmed by DNA testing, and he was legally handed over to the interim Iraqi government, with the intention that he stand trial for war crimes, crimes against humanity, and genocide. Particular attention would be paid to his responsibility for violent campaigns against the Kurds in the north, during the Iran–Iraq War, and against the Shi'ites in the south, in 1991 and 1999, during the suppression of rebellions.

Saddam Hussein was found guilty, and was hanged on 30 December 2006. The situation in Iraq remains an ongoing humanitarian disaster.
DL

Kenneth Starr

Bong Hits for Jesus

One of the most significant characteristics of the 1990s in the United States was that the most powerful figure in US politics was neither of the presidents elected during that decade. Even more surprisingly, it was not even a member of Congress, or any of the Supreme Court Justices appointed during that era. Instead, Kenneth Starr of the Office of Independent Counsel was probably the most powerful political figure in the country at that time, with almost limitless power to investigate any alleged malfeasance of President Clinton and his administration, no matter how small the infraction, or how baseless or petty the claim might turn out to be. As a result, the practically anonymous partisan bureaucrat would be responsible for the impeachment of a president, for possibly the most mundane charge in the history of such proceedings.

Starr's early life was largely unremarkable, growing up as the son of a minister and part-time barber, in the rural Texas town of Lockett. Initially, he attended Harding University in Arkansas, before transferring to the more prestigious George Mason University in the Washington DC area, where he graduated with a BA in 1968. He quickly followed this achievement with a Master's degree from Brown University, and later a law degree from Duke University, in 1973.

That same year, following his graduation from Duke, Starr became a clerk for fifth Federal Circuit Court Judge David Dwyer, and then for Chief Justice of the Supreme Court, Warren Burger, in 1974. He took a short break from public service in 1977 to work for LA-based law firm Gibson, Dunn, and Crutcher, working out of their DC-area office, but returned following an appointment as Counselor to US Attorney General William French Smith in 1981. The Reagan Administration later boosted Starr's career considerably by appointing him to a Federal Judge position on the DC Circuit Court of Appeals from 1983 to 1989, increasing the likelihood of an eventual Supreme Court nomination if the fledgling jurist's rulings stayed in line with the conservative political agenda of the recently elected administration of George H. W. Bush.

In 1989, Starr was appointed US Solicitor General, a post he held until the election of Democratic President Bill Clinton in 1992. He was noted during his tenure for his neutral, thorough, and non-partisan investigation of a scandal involving Republican Senator Bob Packwood. However, this conduct had a negative effect on a 1990 Supreme Court Nomination to replace out-going Justice William Brennan, with Starr's superiors in the Department of Justice expressing concerns to President George H. W. Bush that the Solicitor General might not be sufficiently conservative to promote consistently Republican policies and agendas within the court. With the shift of political power that occurred two years later, Starr found himself momentarily directionless in the spring of 1993, but his predicament did not last for long.

In the summer of 1994, considerable partisan political pressure had been mounting from the recently elected Republican majority in Congress to investigate President Bill Clinton's business dealings with the Whitewater Development Company, a firm the Clintons had invested in – and lost money on – during Bill's tenure as Governor of Arkansas. By July of that year, a three-judge panel had been convened, which recommended the appointment of Independent Counsel to investigate the validity, if any, of those claims. By August, Starr had been appointed to the position, which conferred broad powers to investigate and subpoena nearly anyone with information relevant to the case, which rapidly spun off into separate investigations of the Clintons involving recent firings in the White House Travel Office; alleged political abuse of FBI files; the Clintons involvement with Madison Guaranty and the Rose law firm while Bill Clinton was Governor of Arkansas; their potential involvement in the suicide of White House Counsel Vince Foster; the ongoing sexual harassment lawsuit brought by Paula Jones; and, eventually, the president's adulterous affair with White House intern, Monica Lewinsky.

What is noteworthy about these investigations, besides their exhaustive attention to potential sources of political scandal, is how little they eventually revealed for all the time, money, and effort expended. Nevertheless, such tireless pursuit of even the most trivial allegations was used by conservative political commentators and their supporters as evidence that the Clinton Administration had something to hide, otherwise, it was publicly pondered, why would there be so many investigations into their conduct? While, in the end, Starr only uncovered that Bill Clinton had engaged in an adulterous affair with Monica Lewinsky, and then perjured himself in an attempt to cover the matter up, this was enough "evidence" for Clinton detractors of the president's "lack of moral fiber" and served as grounds for impeachment proceedings, and an almost automatic settlement of Paula Jones's civil claim against him, which had thus far proved fruitless. It also earned both men the title of Man of the Year for *Time* magazine's 1998 year-end issue, and is remembered as an enduring stain on Bill Clinton's reputation, especially by his detractors.

Ken Starr's life following his resignation from the Office of Independent Counsel has been far less public and embarrassing by comparison. He worked as a visiting law professor at New York University and at George Mason University School of Law, as well as continuing his work as a partner for the Kirkland & Ellis law firm as a litigator. In the latter capacity, Starr acted as counsel for a class action lawsuit filed a by a bi-partisan coalition of conservative and liberal groups (including the American Civil Liberties Union and the National Rifle Association) opposed to the provisions of the recently passed Bipartisan Campaign Reform Act of 2002, known informally in the media as the McCain–Feingold Act.

Starr remains a low-key, but actively partisan political and academic figure, holding the office of Dean of Pepperdine University's School of Law, as well as that of a litigator supportive of conservative causes and agendas. Most notably, he has represented the Juneau, Alaska, School Board in its 2006 Supreme Court case against student Joseph Frederick, successfully arguing that the School Board had the right to suspend the student for displaying a sign that read, "Bong hits for Jesus" during a public ceremony in which runners carried the Olympic Torch through the city. He has also agreed to represent Blackwater Worldwide, in that private military company's countersuit against relatives of dead Blackwater contractors, arguing that they have no right to learn the details of their dead loved ones' demise, due to "non-disclosure" stipulations in their employment contracts with the firm. He has also announced plans to challenge portions of the Sarbanes–Oxley Act, seeking to limit the oversight of publicly traded companies by the Federal Government, despite numerous scandals in the financial community that seem to warrant greater legal regulation of affected markets and firms.

When asked if he had any regrets about the Clinton/Whitewater years, which Starr is known to refer to openly as "the unpleasantness," the former Independent Counsel has been surprisingly candid. In his personal opinion, he is said to believe that the biggest mistake of the government's handling of the investigation of the Clintons, was Justice Department oversight of the Lewinsky investigation, and their appointment of him to conduct their inquiry into the matter. In his own opinion, the most fundamental thing that should have been done differently was that someone other than him should have been found to investigate the matter, and present his or her findings free from any perceptions of partisan bias. Small comfort, one supposes, for the subjects of his relentless investigations, and the majority of US citizens who had voted for Bill Clinton, and bitterly ironic when compared with the nature of the political scandals involving Clinton's successor, which have taken place without a similar level of scrutiny in the years that followed. KD

Clarence Thomas

The Silent Justice

In 1991, long-serving Supreme Court Justice Thurgood Marshall announced his plans to retire from the highest court in the United States. When asked the reason for his retirement, the 83-year-old jurist, who had been a member of the Supreme Court since his 1967 appointment by Lyndon Johnson, responded simply, "Because I'm *old*." His retirement presented an opportunity to Republican opponents to replace the outspoken and independent-minded Justice with one who was ideologically more in line with their policy agendas and goals. The difficulty lay in replacing one of the greatest judicial champions of civil rights with someone holding openly contrary views, which would be a potential source of controversy if the nominee were Caucasian, and therefore perceived as inherently racist. The Republicans' solution was to appoint obscure Federal Appeals Court Judge, Clarence Thomas, making him the second African-American appointment to the federal bench.

Thomas was born in 1948, in Pinpoint, Georgia, a rural community outside Savannah. His father abandoned the family when Clarence was two, and he was raised by his struggling single mother. By the time Clarence turned seven, the challenge had proved too much, and he was sent to live with his maternal grandfather, Myers, in Savannah, working even at that young age, helping his grandfather to deliver goods such as fuel oil and ice. Myers taught Clarence to maintain a self-reliant and competitive work ethic, which directed him towards texts like *Race and Economics*, which argued that individual effort was a more effective tool in combating the evils of organized racism than either federal reform laws, or even black nationalism. Thomas later embraced the writings of conservative philosopher Ayn Rand, and required every member of his staff to view the film adaptation of her novel, *The Fountainhead*, if they were not already well acquainted with her work.

Initially, however, he followed his grandfather's wishes closely, and attempted to become a Catholic priest, entering the Conception Seminary College in Missouri in the late 1960s. Though his grandfather had threatened to disown him if he did not follow this specific and demanding career path, Thomas nevertheless dropped out in the spring of 1968, after overhearing white seminary students expressing their approval for the recent shooting of civil rights leader Martin Luther King, especially after hearing them add that they hoped the "son of a bitch" would die. Instead, Thomas attended the College of the Holy Cross in Worcester, Massachusetts, where he graduated *cum laude* with a Bachelor's degree in English, in 1971. While he followed this up with the impressive achievement of a Juris Doctor's degree from Yale Law School in 1974, Thomas remained bitter about his achievement, believing that it had been perceived by fellow white students at the time as being solely the result of affirmative action, rather than personal merit, which ran directly contrary to his emerging "objectivist" philosophy.

Regardless, Thomas shrugged off these more academic considerations on starting work as an Assistant Attorney General in Missouri, under then State Attorney General John Danforth, in which role he continued to work until 1977. When Danforth was elected as the Senator for Missouri, Thomas took a short tenure in a Corporate Counsel position with local pharmaceutical firm Monsanto, until returning to work for Danforth as a Legislative Assistant, in 1979. By 1981, with Danforth's guidance and support, Thomas had his previous loyalty rewarded in the form of a posting as Assistant Secretary of Education for the Office of Civil Rights. In 1982, Thomas was appointed Chairman of the US Equal Employment Opportunity Commission, even as such "liberal" social programs were facing drastic cuts to their funding as a result of the recently elected Reagan Administration.

In 1990, Thomas was appointed by President George H. W. Bush to the US Court of Appeals for the District of Columbia Circuit. Towards the end of that year, Supreme Court Justice Thurgood Marshall, who was elderly and whose health was known to be failing, announced that he would be vacating his seat on the federal bench just as soon as the White House was ready to appoint a suitable replacement. It was a great surprise when Clarence Thomas was named as Marshall's replacement, given that he had only a year's experience as a judge of any kind, federal or otherwise, and the fact that only half of the American Bar Association rated him as qualified for such a post. Even more surprising were allegations concerning the personal conduct of Thomas that cast an even bigger pall over the prospective Justice.

Thomas was already perceived as a provocative choice for confirmation by groups such as the National Association for the Advancement of Colored Peoples, the Urban League, and the National Organization of Women as a result of his critical views of Civil Rights laws, and his conservative opinions of the *Roe v. Wade* case and the abortion rights laws supported by that precedent. Further negative opinion was generated when National Public Radio reporter and commentator Nina Totenberg broke the story that a former colleague and one-time assistant of Thomas at the Equal Employment Opportunity Commission (EEOC) and the Department of Energy, law professor Anita Hill, had accused the nominee of sexually harassing her during their time as co-workers. Her testimony as to the nature of Thomas's inappropriate speech and behavior was some of the most graphic and obscene ever to be presented in the history of similar government proceedings.

Hill alleged that Thomas had made numerous, crude sexual advances towards her, including inquiring if there was a pubic hair of hers on a can of Coke she'd just brought to him, and frequently discussed inappropriate topics, such as the pornographic exploits of adult entertainer "Long Dong Silver," making her time at work both unpleasant and difficult. Before Thomas was allowed to offer any counter-testimony on the matter, former EEOC co-worker Angela Wright came forward claiming that Thomas had repeatedly made unwanted comments about her appearance and inappropriately requested dates, though she was later discredited before the Nominating Committee when it was revealed that she had been fired by Thomas for using the word "faggot." Still, her claims were bolstered when yet another of Thomas's assistants, Sukari Hardnett, stated for the record, "If you were young, black, female, reasonably attractive, and worked directly for Clarence Thomas, you knew full well you were being inspected and auditioned as a female." In his defense against so many troubling charges for a potential Supreme Court Justice, Thomas made numerous impassioned remarks, which he ended as follows: "This is not an opportunity to talk about difficult matters privately or in a closed environment. This is a circus. It's a national disgrace. And from my standpoint, as a black American, it is a high-tech lynching for uppity blacks who in any way deign to think for themselves, to do for themselves, or to have different ideas, and it is a message that unless you kowtow to an old order, this is what will happen to you. You will be lynched, destroyed, caricatured by a committee of the US Senate rather than be hung from a tree."

In the end, after extensive debate, the committee sent the nomination to the full Senate for a confirmation vote without a recommendation of any kind. The vote saw Thomas approved by a 52–48 vote, largely along party lines and, on 23 October 1991, Clarence Thomas was sworn in as the 106th Associate Justice of the Supreme Court.

Since his nomination, Thomas has done little to distinguish himself, either positively or negatively, in the court's many proceedings, no matter how controversial the case in terms of establishing an ultimate legal ruling on contested case law. Like strict "federalist" judge Antonin Scalia, he is a staunch proponent of "states' rights" over federal regulation, except in matters relating to the medical use of marijuana and abortion rights, voting in step with the senior jurist 91 per cent of the time. He is also a staunch advocate of capital punishment, as well as of so-called expansions of power by the executive branch of government, and in fourth amendment matters pertaining to the legality of search and seizure, he favors law enforcement agents over defendants in the majority of his decisions. Despite all this, he is statistically the Justice second most likely to support the first amendment right to free speech, except in extreme cases such as "cross burnings" and anything resembling "child pornography."

What is perhaps most fascinating about Thomas' by now well-known judicial habits is that he has asked the fewest questions of any kind of all the sitting Justices during the oral argument section of all cases brought before the Supreme Court during his tenure. Thomas has said that this is more a matter of personal habit, having learned to be a good listener as child, while his detractors have claimed it seems more like an indifference to, or disdain for, the rapid back-and-forth arguments by attorneys during this part of the court's proceedings. At the very least, such behavior seems to be in line with other obvious, "low-key" tendencies in Thomas' character, pointing to a man more comfortable with anonymously doing and thinking what he's told to by others with the same political agenda, rather than doing anything that might discourage or betray that support, to which he obviously remains beholden for having been granted power in the first place. While this would be an understandable strategy for a politician, who is only temporarily elected as a representative of the public will, it is a baffling course of action for someone appointed for life to a post with far-reaching and long-standing legal implications for an entire nation. Given his relative youth, it remains to be seen how long Thomas' silence will continue, or how long the good Justice can continue to attempt to live as an "invisible man." KD

Linda Tripp

Patriotic Duty

Contrary to what the American public might believe, the Washington DC area is far less politically partisan than most of the rest of country. Indeed, "across the aisle" friendships are almost a tradition, such as those between Ronald Reagan and Tip O'Neill, Hunter S. Thompson and Pat Buchanan, or G. Gordon Liddy and many of the 1960s' radicals he arrested or prosecuted. Admittedly, this tradition has been in decline in recent years, as the political macro-climate has become increasingly divisive and mean-spirited, and many factors may be to blame – the strange "friendship" between Linda Tripp and Monica Lewinsky could certainly have been a significant factor.

While the two women had different political outlooks, came from opposite sides of the country, and differed in age by 24 years, they had both worked at the White House (Lewinsky as an intern and Tripp as an employee), and had both come to work at the Pentagon's Public Affairs Office in the mid-1990s. In 1997, when the two women had known each other for about a year and a half, Monica made the shocking revelation to Linda Tripp that as a White House intern she had had an affair with none other than President Bill Clinton himself. The events that followed proved how little Linda Tripp understood both friendship and the confidentiality it usually entails.

Tripp was also friendly with Lucianne Goldberg, a literary agent and partisan Republican, who was working on a book about the mysterious death of President Clinton's Deputy White House Counsel Vince Foster. Like many Republicans at the time, Ms Goldberg seemed convinced that every incongruity in the story and any improper action on the part of the president was proof of a more sinister design, which should be exposed and attacked by any means necessary, allegedly for the good of the nation. With this in mind, she recommended that Tripp attempt to find out more about the affair, and even go so far as to tape telephone conversations with Lewinsky, without Lewinsky's knowledge or consent.

As it turned out, 1997 was a critical year for Clinton detractors. In January, the Supreme Court had heard arguments appealing against a lower court's decision not to allow Paula Jones' ongoing lawsuit for sexual harassment, based on Clinton's status as a sitting president. In May, the court agreed with the plaintiff that the office of the presidency was not above US civil law. In August, Tripp alleged to *Newsweek* magazine that she had witnessed a disheveled Kathleen Willey exiting the Oval Office. These events set the stage for the ensuing scandal.

In January 1998, Tripp disclosed to Independent Counsel Kenneth Starr, that she was aware of the relationship between Monica Lewinsky and Bill Clinton, that Monica had executed a false affidavit to federal court officials overseeing the *Clinton v. Jones* lawsuit, and had attempted to suborn Tripp's perjury regarding the relationship, as well as her knowledge of the Kathleen Willey incident. To back her claims, Tripp presented Starr with all her covert recordings of her conversations with Monica, and also informed him of the existence of a certain, and later infamous, blue dress in Monica's possession. The dress was alleged to have been marked with the president's semen, and Tripp herself claimed to have convinced Monica not to have the garment dry cleaned. In exchange for the illegally recorded tapes and the other information, Starr granted Linda immunity from federal prosecution.

Based on the Tripp tapes, Starr was able to secure an expanded investigation into the Clinton–Lewinsky relationship, on the basis of looking for incidents of perjury in the *Clinton v. Jones* lawsuit. Ultimately, enough evidence was uncovered to warrant the appearance of both Clinton and Lewinsky before a grand jury in Washington DC to answer the perjury charges, which were largely substantiated by Tripp's recordings and the blue dress. When offered the opportunity to make final remarks with regard to the case, Monica responded as anyone who had been so completely betrayed and embarrassed by a supposed friend might. "I really hate Linda Tripp," she said.

The US public seemed to agree with this sentiment, and Tripp was repeatedly parodied by comic actor John Goodman in drag, on the sketch comedy program *Saturday Night Live*. Even among Republicans, only the most partisan condoned Tripp's decision to betray the confidences of a supposed friend in the name of "patriotic duty." For her part, Ms Tripp took most of the criticism in her stride, but said that some of the Goodman material had "hurt her feelings." Under the circumstances, her protestations received little sympathy.

And if the broader US public were not terribly sympathetic, the Democratic Party-controlled Maryland State Legislature was even less so. Forty-nine members of that body signed a letter to the State Prosecutor, demanding that Tripp, who was resident in Columbia, Maryland, be tried for violating the state's wiretapping laws. However, prior to any trial, the state court ruled that due to Linda's immunity agreements with the Independent Counsel's Office, substantial amounts of the state's evidence were inadmissible. While a pre-trial hearing was attempted, calling Monica as a witness to establish testimony untainted by the immunity agreement, the state court again ruled in favor of Linda, claiming Ms Lewinsky's testimony could not be seen as credible, given her record of perjuring herself. In the end, all charges were dismissed on 26 May 2000, due to lack of sufficient evidence.

Tripp herself filed a lawsuit in 2003, claiming that information leaked to the press during the 1998 scandal by her superiors at the Department of Defense, concerning her lying about her past on a security clearance form, was improper and had violated her privacy. In this case, a settlement was reached which required Tripp to be paid $595,000, reflecting a retroactive promotion for the years 1998–2000, and the retention of her pension. Tripp appeared on *Larry King Live* in December that year, having obviously had extensive plastic surgery, to make hair-splitting distinctions about how her invasion of privacy case was somehow different from her invasion of Monica Lewinsky's privacy. Her decision to record her friend's confessions, she claimed, was all to protect her against possible retaliation by the Clinton Administration for refusing to protect the president during *Clinton v. Jones*.

Ms Tripp is currently living in Northern Virginia, and has married her long-time sweetheart, German architect Dieter Rausch. As it was very unlikely that she would ever again be employed by the Federal Government, she has opened a year-round Christmas shop, called the Christmas Sleigh, in Middleburg, Virginia. In light of her deplorable behaviour though, I doubt even jolly old St Nick would be inclined to include her on anything but his Naughty List. KD

Media Assholes

Martin Amis

Godlike

"I have a godlike relationship with the world I've created. It is exactly analogous. There is creation and resolution, and it's all up to me." (*Guardian Unlimited*, 2007)

Born on 25 August 1949, Martin Amis, is an English novelist, essayist, and short-story writer. As a novelist, he is widely read, and also much criticized. The people who read his books and those who critically dismiss them come, for the most part, from completely different sectors of society, and it is his asshole of a self-aggrandizing "god-like" persona that seems to most irk his critics.

After Oxford, he worked at the *Times Literary Supplement*, following which, he became literary editor of the *New Statesman* at the age of 27, then a feature writer for the *Observer*. His father, Kingsley Amis, is reported to have had no interest in his son's work, allegedly saying that it broke the rules, mucked about with the reader, and drew attention to the author. Amis' characteristic traits were evident from his early novels, which demonstrated a dark sense of humor, fascination with the zeitgeist, clever literary tricks such as authorial presence in the plots, and a casualness that bordered on ennui. His characters often suffered humiliating misfortunes which made one feel that they were the playthings of a cruel god (or author) rather than fully rounded characters. The most obvious common theme was Amis himself, who was inescapably present in every page of every novel. Even his best-known novels, and the most critically respected – *Money, London Fields,*

Time's Arrow, and *The Information* – are marked by this sense of solipsistic egotism.

Amis frequently responds to interview questions using quotations from his books to back up his point, as if his fiction is somehow more worthwhile than real-life opinion. Worse still, on several occasions, he has written journalistic pieces in newspapers, giving his views on topical issues, as if all the world were characters in his misanthropic fiction. On the eve of the fifth anniversary of 9/11, he wrote an essay, "The Age of Horrorism," in UK newspaper the *Observer* (Sunday 10 September 2006) in which he analyzed his reactions to the rise of extremist Islam, offering a critique of Islamic fundamentalists, and questioning the West's faltering response. According to the essay, in the West, religion is only followed by the ignorant and Islamic extremists are the ignorant, waging war on all facets of modern civilization. "The most extreme Islamists want to kill everyone on earth," he writes, "except the most extreme Islamists; but every jihadi sees the need for eliminating all non-Muslims, either by conversion or by execution." Amis goes on to write that wherever Islam gets an army the result is a massacre, fratricide, or genocide. Once again his theory is espoused through a fictional character, Ayed, and Islamists spend their time coming up with break-through ideas for committing mass murder, while the West fatuously goes shopping.

In an interview with Ginny Dougary (*Times*, 9 September 2006), Amis played with the idea that, "The Muslim community will have to suffer until it gets its house in order. What sort of suffering? Not let them travel. Deportation – further down the road. Curtailing of freedoms. Strip-searching people who look like they're from the Middle East or from Pakistan. Discriminatory stuff, until it hurts the whole community and they start getting tough with their children . . ." Unsurprisingly, these pronouncements caused a huge outcry and debate raged over whether or not Amis was a racist. Given his misogyny, and apparent distaste for the characters he creates, it would not be a big jump to brand him as such.

A row broke out between Amis and the Marxist intellectual Terry Eagleton, who accused him of being Islamophobic because he has abandoned traditional Western values of liberalism following the 9/11 attack on the World Trade Center. In an introduction to the 2007 edition of Eagleton's classic book, *Ideology: An Introduction*, Professor Eagleton attacked the views of "Amis and his ilk" for taking an adversarial stance against Islam in general instead of propounding tolerance and understanding. He branded Amis' alleged argument as a means of "hounding and humiliating [Muslims] as a whole [so] they would return home and teach their children to be obedient to the White Man's law."

The attack also extended to Amis' novelist father, the late Kingsley Amis. Professor Eagleton called Amis senior "a racist, anti-Semitic boor, a drink-sodden, self-hating reviler of women, gays, and liberals," adding "Amis has clearly learnt more from him than how to turn a shapely phrase." Eagleton may have a point.

Pompous as ever, Amis continues to defend his position, rather than accept that his original statements were at best too simplistic, and at worst hateful. He spoke during a debate at Manchester University, in which he told a packed auditorium that only a machine would not have experienced "retaliatory urges" upon learning in August the previous year of the alleged plot to bomb transatlantic aircraft, in which, Amis said, 3,000 people could have died. Furthermore, in a letter published in UK newspaper the *Independent* (11 October 2007), Amis wrote, "Islamism, in most of its manifestations, not only wants to kill me – it wants to kill you." The fact that he has now spent over a year defending his position and speaking or writing of this rage is proof of how reluctant he is to simply disown his original comments, or to fully dispel the misinterpretations he believes they have suffered from.

Let's finish with another quotation: "After a week of thunderous rumblings as academic titans laid about one another, yesterday began with a plea from one side [Amis]: 'Can I ask him, in a collegial spirit, to shut up about it?'

Fat chance." (Maev Kennedy, *Guardian*, Saturday, 13 October 2007)

It would seem Amis prefers the sound of his own voice above all others. DL

John Wayne Bobbit

Frankenpenis

When John Wayne Bobbitt's story entered the national media in June 1993, he seemed the victim of a particularly disturbing crime, deserving sympathy. As he had lain sleeping, his wife Lorena was alleged to have cut off half his penis, got into her car, driven for "a while," and then thrown the severed appendage into a nearby field, before eventually stopping again to dial 911. It was the kind of shocking and bizarre crime that generates a media feeding frenzy, and on the basis of these facts alone, made just about every man who heard of the case cross his legs and wince in sympathy.

What could possibly have provoked such a vicious and degrading attack, the public wondered. How crazy was this woman? Would the poor man ever recover, and if so, to what degree? By the time the facts were known, of course, Lorena had become a sort of twisted feminist icon to some, and John had become a comical and cautionary example of machismo gone very, very wrong.

Immediately following the incident, after police had recovered the missing portion of his penis, John was given emergency surgery. After nine-and-a-half hours, Dr James Sehn and Dr David Berman had reattached the penis, estimating that John could be fully recovered after about a year's "rehab."

Lorena, meanwhile, had been taken into police custody and charged with malicious wounding. She is alleged to have told police that, "[John] always have orgasm and he doesn't wait for me to have orgasm." Such a comment, taken as her only motivation for the attack, seemed only to underscore that this was a deranged and dangerous woman. It would take her trial to change these perceptions. Meanwhile, the late-night comics and radio shock jocks had a field day, emphasizing the sensational nature of the case, and attempting to satisfy the public's curiosity as to Lorena's sanity, or otherwise.

It was probably the 1994 trial that turned the tide of public opinion. Lorena testified that on the night of the attack, John had come home drunk, demanding sex, and when she declined, raped her before falling asleep. Further, she alleged that their relationship had been physically, sexually, and emotionally abusive, that John had had numerous affairs which he had flaunted, and that he'd forced her to have an abortion almost exactly three years prior to the night of her attack. Lorena's attorneys alleged that this constant abuse, combined with her relative social isolation as a "mail-order bride," caused her to snap, and so she was not guilty by reason of insanity.

While John did ultimately confess to some of the allegations of abuse, he downplayed the severity of his actions, and under cross-examination, his statements often conflicted with known facts and the testimony of credible defense witnesses. This severely weakened the prosecution's case, and when all was said and done, the jury sided with the defense after a mere seven hours of deliberation. Under state law, Lorena was ordered to undergo a 45-day evaluation period in a state mental hospital, to be followed by her release, pending psychiatric approval.

Under normal circumstances, this would have been the end of the story, but like his name, and the case that made him famous, there was little that was normal about John Wayne Bobbitt. In 1994, he attempted to cash in on his notoriety by making the pornographic film *John Wayne Bobbitt Uncut*, which sold about 80,000 copies worldwide, despite John's complete lack of acting talent, shaky sexual performance and the grotesque appearance of his famous member. This was followed in 1996 by the adult film *Frankenpenis*, which sold considerably fewer copies, despite being promoted by John himself on the *Howard Stern Show* and elsewhere. Apparently it never occurred to him that freak shows rarely do a lot of repeat business.

Far more consistent than John's post-trial "career" in "show business" were his run-ins with law enforcement agencies. In 1994, he was convicted of misdemeanor domestic battery by his former fiancée, Kristina Elliot, which resulted in a 15-day jail sentence. In September 1999, he was sentenced to five years probation for his role in the theft of $140,000 in clothing from a store in Fallon, Nevada, as well as the payment of $5,000 restitution and 100 hours of community service. In 2004, he was tried for two separate incidents of domestic abuse against his third wife, Joanna Ferrell, resulting in a conviction and an acquittal. While still awaiting sentencing for this conviction, he was arrested in September 2005, on the same charge. This case also resulted in a not guilty verdict by the presiding municipal judge, due to insufficient evidence. It seems clear in Bobbitt's case that some people do indeed never learn from their mistakes.

More than anything else, one can't help but wonder at the motivation for such repeated bad behavior. John Wayne Bobbitt's name alone suggests his parents had a narrowly focused notion of what constitutes masculinity. Bobbitt's stint as a US Marine is highly unlikely to have undone these notions derived from his parents; if anything, it probably further embedded them in his psyche. The fact that Bobbitt had gone to the considerable effort of securing a "mail-order bride" strongly suggests a need for a submissive, servile woman devoted solely to his needs. When Lorena turned out to be anything but submissive and servile, it is perhaps not surprising that he continued to seek out relationships with women over whom he could assert his dominance.

Whatever his reasoning, it is clear that he was, and in all likelihood remains, unrepentant of his desire to assert his will over whichever women became, or might yet become, involved in his life. In a better world, one could hope that his contemptible conduct towards women might eventually result in a solid conviction on a substantive charge. Of course, it's possible that the real problem is that Lorena cut off the wrong portion of his anatomy, simply, though understandably, misunderstanding the true source of John Wayne Bobbitt's problem with women. KD

Ann Coulter

Is she for Real?

Following the controversial election of George W. Bush and the terrorist attacks of 9/11, Republican and right-wing media commentators assumed an increasingly partisan and rabidly patriotic stance, which would continue to build through the run-up to the eventual war with Iraq, the divisive presidential election of 2004, and beyond. More mainstream, and, as such, more middle-of-the-road pro-GOP commentators adopted a classic and fairly predictable "America: love it or leave it" position, while more extreme voices from so-called

Christian Right outlets openly blamed all left-wing values, political policies, and philosophies for the war with "Muslim extremists," while being equally zealous in their defense of all US military actions in the world, even openly advocating torture and assassination in defense of the supposedly superior "American" and "Christian" way of life. A hybrid of the two views developed during that time, and soon gained media prominence, in the person of one Ann Coulter, a figure who would find ways of espousing some of conservative America's most extreme and partisan views in some of the most mainstream and high-profile US media outlets.

Born in New York City in the early 1960s, Ann spent the rest of her childhood in suburban Connecticut, the product of a self-defined "upper middle class" background. She graduated *cum laude* from Cornell University in 1984, and obtained a law degree from the University of Michigan, where she gained recognition as the editor of the *Michigan Law Review*, a respected publication of that prestigious institution. Following her graduation, she served as a law clerk for Pasco Bowman II of the United States Court of Appeals for the Eighth Circuit, worked as a staff member of the Senate Judiciary Committee following the Republican "take-over" of Congress in 1994, and later became a litigator for the Center for Individual Rights.

She entered the realm of media commentary in 1996 when she was hired by cable news channel MSNBC as a legal correspondent. Though photogenic and quick-witted, Coulter was fired twice during her tenure, first for insulting comments made about a recently deceased US ambassador during coverage of her funeral service, and later for off-topic and insulting remarks made in an exchange with a disabled Vietnam veteran who was a spokesman for the International Campaign to Ban Landmines. Coulter took the dismissal in her stride, however, and moved on to publish her first book, *High Crimes and Misdemeanors: The Case against Bill Clinton* in 1998, cashing in on the popularity of the "movement" to impeach the scandal-embroiled president, among the GOP audience which she was clearly courting.

Having established herself with such partisan credentials, Coulter continued to raise her public profile in the late 1990s with regular columns in *George* magazine, and as a columnist for Universal Press Syndicate, providing her with enhanced distribution for her narrowly defined but humorously expressed views. Nonetheless, she was the subject of controversy once again in 2001 when she was hired by the

National Review Online, and then fired, for a piece written after the terrorist attacks of 9/11, which was viewed as too controversial and which she was unwilling to revise. She attempted to make her case on the national TV show *Politically Incorrect*, claiming she had been censored for her views, but she was publicly contradicted by the NRO's editor-at-large, who claimed that she had been fired for her lack of professionalism and loyalty to the online venue.

By 2002, Coulter seemed to have hit her stride with the publication of her second book, *Slander: Liberal Lies about the American Right*, which eventually gained and held the number one spot on the *New York Times* Bestseller List for seven weeks. A book of partisan observations, it was openly critical of the supposedly unfair media coverage that had been given to President Bush up to that time, from its "distortions" about his contested 2000 election "victory," through his "perceived" mishandling of the 9/11 crisis, up to its "liberally biased" criticism of his assertions of the need to attack Iraq in the name of US national security. This was all part of an inherently liberal media's conspiracy to make the embattled leader look worse than he really was, contended Coulter, motivated by disdain for "common people" and their "traditional" American values, and their freedom to express and defend such notions. In light of the mid-term election results of 2002, when Republicans regained control of both the House and Senate chambers of Congress, Coulter seemed to have found a ready audience for her point of view.

And while there may have been nothing new in many of Coulter's observations, positions, and arguments expressed in her book, they would frequently be taken to absurd, mean-spirited, extremes as part of the ensuing "publicity wave." An example can be found in the *New York Observer* interview she granted, following her on-air complaints on an NBC TV appearance, that she was frequently mischaracterized and misquoted. After making sure that she was "on the record," and in fact being recorded, she stated that her only regret regarding Oklahoma bomber and mass murderer Timothy McVeigh's deadly activities was his choice of target, suggesting that the *New York Times*, an unrelenting critic of the Bush presidency, would have made a more fitting and useful target. When various media figures expressed shock at such a callous statement, particularly following 9/11, Coulter "spun" her remarks on the conservatively biased Fox News Channel's *Hannity and Colmes* show, claiming that what she had said was merely satirical, and no different from equally offensive remarks made about conservatives on *Saturday Night Live* and *The Daily Show*, and that she would continue to make similar remarks in the future.

Coulter wasted little time before releasing her third, provocatively titled, partisan tome, *Treason: Liberal Treachery from the Cold War to the War on Terror* in June 2003. In it, she defends the notoriously "troubled" presidency of Richard Nixon, claming that the liberal media and Democratic politicians had undermined US foreign policy by being less than co-operative or sympathetic to his policies and goals. The book spent 13 weeks on the bestseller list, and firmly established its author as a partisan defender of all things Republican and Conservative, who, she argued, were the only "true" Americans.

The 2004 presidential election was shaping up to be one of the most divisive and contentious in at least a couple of generations, and Coulter certainly tried, as a loyal partisan, to do as much media damage to her perceived enemies as possible. After an initial misstep with the cancellation of a *USA Today* article as part of proposed "opposition coverage" of the Democratic National Convention, (allegedly due to issues of readability and clarity), Coulter rebounded nicely with appearances in *Feeding the Beast* (a documentary critical of 24-hour news channels,) and *Farenhype 9/11* (a "counter-documentary" about film-maker and activist Michael Moore), before taking center-stage in the bio-documentary, *Is it True What They Say About Ann?*

Having clearly "arrived" as a media spokesperson for the GOP "base" constituency, Coulter crowned these achievements with the release of her fourth book, *How to Talk to a Liberal (If You Must): The World According to Ann Coulter*. The volume, notable for its "cheesecake" author's cover photo, and pseudo-instructional writing tone, essentially argues that conservatives needn't bother to do *anything* to ease differences of opinion with their liberal fellow citizens, and that anything *resembling* such behavior, represents a caving in to the pressure created by "liberal guilt." Combined with the re-election victory of her chosen candidate, President Bush, a few weeks later, her bestselling books added to what had already been a "banner year" for the GOP's new "Queen of Mean."

As such, in 2005, Coulter cut a much lower media profile than usual, probably due to the "business as usual" tone set by the Bush Administration after the inauguration in the first half of that year, and then due to its obvious mishandling of the Hurricane Katrina disaster and the ensuing political fall-out that dominated the second half. While occasionally appearing on Fox News programs, or as a known partisan commentator in "round table" discussion shows, she remained largely hidden from public view, refusing even to take the bait of caricatures and parodies on popular TV comedy and cartoon shows. She was also chastised from an unusual source in August that year, when her syndicated column was dropped by the *Arizona Daily Star*, citing complaints from "many readers" who found her "shrill, bombastic, and mean-spirited. And those words [were] from readers who identified themselves as Conservatives."

Still, in 2006, Coulter seemed to outdo herself with her new book *Godless: The Church of Liberalism*, in which she attacked the entire adversarial ideology as "anti-religious," yet ironically having as many "religion-like" beliefs and tenets supposedly as irrational and beyond questioning as any within the so-called Christian Right. In addition to making this assertion, and questioning the validity of the Theory of Evolution and those who "believe" in it, Coulter also made several critical remarks about the so-called "Jersey Girls," four "9/11 widows" who were known for being "liberal media-friendly" critics of the Bush Administration, and therefore "enemies." Characterizing them as self-obsessed harpies, reveling in the media attention and "cashing in" on their well-publicized grief, Coulter pointedly advised them to "hurry up and pose in Playboy," as their media shelf-life was dwindling.

For many, the remarks seemed particularly vicious, absurdly timed, and largely out of line with the other "points" in her book, which was otherwise enjoying great commercial success, having debuted as a number-one bestseller. Coulter refused to apologize during a *Today* show "response" interview, in which she was asked to "clarify" her remarks, insisting instead that any sympathy the group might garner as "9/11 widows" was now and forever tainted by their use of that status to pursue liberal political agendas and goals. This only generated further media controversy, which, in turn, caused further cancelations of her syndicated column in newspapers across the country, making many observers wonder if the continued presence of controversy in Coulter's career would be a blessing or a curse.

Coulter herself seemed to have no such concerns, making quasi-homophobic remarks about the alleged "secret" sexual orientations of first Bill Clinton, and then Al Gore later in 2006. While she hid behind a quickly delivered "Just kidding" when pressed about the validity of her assertions and her use of words like "fag," Coulter showed no signs of tiring in her role as a figure of controversy for its own sake. Indeed she wasn't, as 2007 and the run-up to the 2008 Presidential elections would make completely clear.

Addressing the 2007 Conservative Political Action Conference, she stopped just short of calling Democratic candidate John Edwards a faggot, not, she would insist, because it was necessarily inaccurate in describing the happily married and seemingly straight former Senator, but because of public disapproval of the word "faggot." The event was misconstrued by the media-conscious public as Coulter calling Edwards the dreaded "F word," and was even used by Edward's campaign website to generate campaign funds in the name of combating "the politics of bigotry." Eventually, as gay rights groups of many different political persuasions increasingly condemned the remarks, Coulter again hid behind her now standard defense of having been "only joking."

Regardless, every new outraged response from the Edwards Campaign usually resulted in an even more insulting comeback from Coulter. Eventually, the presidential candidate and his family took the moral "high road" and simply refused to talk about Coulter, whom Elizabeth Edwards summed up as a "she-devil." Coulter moved on as well, making a point of refusing to apologize for her remarks, instead holding them up as an example of her right to free speech.

She also made use of the first amendment to publish her sixth book, *If Democrats Had Any Brains, They'd Be Republicans,* which was not only a number-one bestseller, but has become, since the time of its publication, the number-one bestselling non-fiction book on the topic of political parties for major internet book retailer Amazon.com. Such sales are probably attributable to Coulter's by now practically built-in fan base, rather than the book's content, which seems largely concerned with pointing out a hodge-podge of any remaining differences between the two ideologies left unmolested by Coulter in her previous writing. Be that as it may, incidents immediately following the book's release again raised questions of how far even a controversial and openly partisan political commentator could go in expressing his or her knowingly divisive views.

During an interview on CNBC's *The Big Idea* program with interviewer Donny Deutsch (an observant Jew), Coulter suggested that Christians viewed themselves as "perfected Jews." The remark led to an on-air argument between the two, with Deutsch claiming such a concept was both insulting and antisemitic. And while defended by Dennis Prager, a noted conservative and Jewish talkshow host, Deutsch's sentiment was later echoed more loudly by the Anti-Defamation League, who, along with the American Jewish Committee, said they had found the remarks poorly reasoned and insulting.

While Coulter has been largely quiet for some time, that silence will surely not last forever. Facing an election year in 2008, the Republican Party was still smarting from its 2006 mid-term election defeat, as an unpopular war in Iraq ground on, and the US domestic economy stagnated and floundered. A perfect time for Coulter to re-surface with yet another screed about the evils of Liberals and Democrats, even as everyone else wonders how they could possibly be to blame for the tragedies, crises, and failures of leadership of a US government which has been dominated by the Republican Party for the last eight years. One can be sure the explanation will be infuriating, hilarious, and very well publicized. KD

Simon Cowell

I Don't Mean to Be Rude, but . . .

Born on 7 October 1959, Simon Phillip Cowell, the man who wears his trouser waistband so high it grazes his armpits, achieved his current level of fame by insulting people on popular reality TV shows *Pop Idol*, *The X Factor*, *American Idol*, and *Britain's Got Talent*. Cowell's fame, or infamy, developed during these TV appearances, in which he developed the catchphrase "I don't mean to be rude, but . . ." He later used this as the title of his December 2003 autobiography. In the same year he was number 33 on UK TV Channel 4's list of the all-time "100 Worst Britons." A lot of his witty one-liners have been rumored to be the product of coaching that Cowell received from well-known UK publicist Max Clifford. Whether this is true or not, they often appear contrived and ultimately predictable. However he continues to pull huge audiences for his shows, who perhaps see him as a human version of "The Grouch" from *Sesame Street*.

Cowell's first assault on the music business ended in bankruptcy when Fanfare Records, a company which he had formed with record-producer Pete Waterman, folded. Deep in debt, Cowell was forced to move back in with his parents. However, later that year, he rebounded and became an A&R consultant for record company BMG. In that role Cowell signed up a number of terrible acts to S-Records and made his first grubby marks on the world of trashy pop music. He signed acts that included Curiosity Killed the Cat, Sonia Evans, Five, Westlife, Robson & Jerome, and Ultimate Kaos. He is also guilty of releasing several novelty recordings featuring the likes of wrestlers of the World Wrestling Federation, children's TV characters The Teletubbies, Zig and Zag, and the Mighty Morphin' Power Rangers. Unfortunately for those with delicate aural sensibilities, these were huge successes.

Once he'd hit the big time in the desolate world of bottom-rung performers, Cowell moved on to create, and became a judge on, the first season of *Pop Idol* in 2001, and on the first season of *American Idol* in 2002. In 2004, along with Sharon Osbourne and Louis Walsh, Cowell was a judge on the first series of the British talent show *The X Factor*, which became an instant success with viewers, and has returned each year since then. In 2006, Cowell was voted the tenth most terrifying celebrity on TV in a UK *Radio Times* poll of 3,000 people, although what is so terrifying about this pantomime villain is hard to say. One worries that the viewers of his programs share the low level of intelligence as some of the performers. Still, it is his "bitingly critical" comments and attitude for which he is best known. In fact, so famous has he become for his attitude that, on countless occasions, audiences on *American Idol* have hardly given him a chance to speak, booing him even before he's made his opinions known – the pantomime perform-ance *par excellence*. He seems to enjoy the role, appearing to be at home with this cartoon-like personality, which is clearly carefully crafted to hone its impact. Cowell must be delighted that in the United States he is likened to TV personalities such as Judge Judy (aka Justice with an Attitude).

His reality TV singing competitions draw millions of viewers world-wide. The hopeful contestants turn up to mass auditions which are televised for our entertainment. Just as people used to laugh at the village idiot, court jester, or inmates of the asylum, modern viewers laugh at – certainly not with – the wannabes. During the auditions, Cowell sits smugly as judge. The performances are followed by an unsparingly blunt appraisal of the contestant's talents, personality, or even physical appearance. Contestants are frequently told that they can't sing, look terrible, and must be mad to have even considered turning up to the audition. The sad thing is, the audience at home are often forced to agree with his appraisals. It is pitiful to watch some of the no-hopers giving performances that would frighten a cat, throwing themselves into it body and soul, yet still making the viewer ask, "What were you thinking?" It's a terrible thing to judge, and a terrible thing to do, but extremely funny to watch, and Cowell, on the lowest, most cynical path to making big bucks knows this. He revels in his power, like a Roman Emperor giving the thumbs up or thumbs down signal which determined whether a defeated gladiator would be allowed to live or not after a bout in the Colosseum. Cowell's doesn't restrict his insults and wisecracks to the contestant's singing performance; his attacks are often spitefully personal. Contestants from all walks of life have been offended by what he has had to say to them. In the 2006–7 season of *American Idol*, Cowell said that one of the contestants "looked like a bush baby," causing a major outcry at what was perceived as potential racism. In the course of the same season he was also criticized for seeming to roll his eyes at a reference to the US Virginia Tech shootings, although, to be fair, video evidence proved that he was rolling his eyes at his fellow judge, Paula Abdul, not at the Virginia Tech massacre.

Of course, Cowell has earned the right to look smug. He is not just the presenter of these popular TV talent shows; he owns the company that makes them and the record company to which the best contestants are signed. Some of his comments would certainly get a hired presenter sacked, but that is unlikely to happen in his case because he is his own boss – the perfect deal! In 2002, Cowell set up the TV production and music publishing house Syco Records, which releases records by contestants from *The X Factor* and *America's Got Talent*, a win-win situation for Cowell. All these reality TV talent competitions are produced by Syco, which earns big money for Cowell in both the UK and the United States. He is in complete control and is determined to make sure that everyone knows it. He has become a multi-millionaire, gorging himself on this frenzied, egotistical media circus. In 2003,

Cowell also appeared on the one-off *World Idol* program. It became apparent that each country's version of the original *Idol* show had attempted to come up with its own Simon Cowell-type personality, their very own national pantomime villain to encourage audiences to boo from the safety of their sofas.

In conclusion, Cowell is not only an asshole, but also a rich asshole, and, perhaps even more annoyingly, he's become rich by being a caricature of an asshole. In the United States, he stayed on as a judge on *American Idol*, earning an estimated $40 million per series for another five years. He reportedly also has a deal with Fox, allowing his production company to broadcast *Got Talent* and *American Inventor* on other networks, but with no personal obligation to appear in the shows. Meanwhile, back in the UK, he signed a deal with ITV, apparently worth around $13 million a year for three years, which gave ITV the rights to the hit UK talent show *The X Factor*. He's a fantastic figure to hate, and yet also a very irritating one, because that's exactly the reaction he's hoping for.

Surprisingly, while seeming callous and insulting to the unfortunates who appear on his shows, he is a strong supporter of animal rights and has appeared in a video for PETA in which he reminds drivers of the cruelty, and dangers, of locking pets in hot cars in the summer. Clearly, cruelty to humans is another matter altogether. DL

Endemol and Reality TV

The Golden Cage

The name may sound like a laxative brand, but Endemol is the TV company that invented reality TV, at least as we know it. The company was founded in 1994 when the TV production companies owned by Joop van den Ende and John de Mol merged. The name came from the combination of the two men's surnames. Endemol has produced many TV game shows and children's TV programs, but it is best known internationally for *Big Brother*, the breakthrough reality TV show, with versions being broadcast worldwide, modeled on the initial Dutch version. Although there were earlier experiments with documentary-style reality TV, many see Endemol's *Big Brother* as the real source of the new phenomenon of "Reality TV." Endemol is thus chiefly responsible for the myriad TV programs in which hapless members of the public volunteer to become lab monkeys, while being observed by millions. They usually do this in the hope of achieving the paltry level of fame that comes from having one's name and face in the downmarket tabloid newspapers and magazines.

The idea for *Big Brother* supposedly came about during a brain-storming session at the production house of John de Mol Produkties (an independent part of Endemol) in 1997. The working title was "*de Gouden Kooi*" ("The Golden Cage" – the original working title of George Orwell's novel *Nineteen Eighty-Four*, in which Big Brother is the all-seeing leader of the dystopian Oceania). The first *Big Brother* went on the air in the Netherlands in 1999 on the Veronica TV channel. Since then it has been a prime-time hit in almost 70 different countries. *Big Brother* may be awful, but it is undoubtedly mindlessly addictive, in the same way as biting your nails, cracking your knuckles, or picking at a scab. Each series lasts for around three months, with a number of people (normally fewer than fifteen at any one time) living together full-time in a "Big Brother House", isolated from the world outside but beneath the continuous gaze of television cameras. The housemates try to win a cash prize by avoiding the regular evictions, which are usually voted for by the public.

These programs are generally referred to as "Reality TV," but it could be argued that they are anything but "real." Endemol's peculiar format has twisted our perception of "reality" so that the viewing public are now complicit in this "life-enhancing" or "self-destructive" spectacle, depending on how the participants are perceived.

Endemol is particularly to blame for the type of show where the producers design an enclosed, prison-like environment and control the day-to-day activities, creating a fabricated world in which the competition plays out. Like a tiny version of our increasingly authoritarian societies, these environments can give the viewer a bland foreboding. While watching it dawns on us that future real-world tyrants might not control us with cattle-prods and barbed wire, but might instead choose to sedate our minds with mindless entertainment and pointless tasks. The producers have become mini-world dictators with previously unheard of broadcasting control. They specifically select the participants and use carefully designed scenarios, challenges, events, and settings to encourage particular behaviors and conflicts. These scenarios are often highly deliberate in their editing strategies, able to portray certain participants as heroes or villains, and to guide the drama through whatever chronology and selective presentation of events suits their current "script." We are not watching a fly-on-the-wall reality show so much as becoming involved in a laboratory experiment where the producers act as scientists who manipulate a group of knowing subjects. The subjects play with the producers at the same time as the producers play with them.

Endemol has created a new breed of gameshow contestant. Some participants of reality shows have later admitted that they changed their behavior to seem more erratic or emotional in order to hog camera time. Even a toddler knows that they get more attention when they have a tantrum. Former contestants have spoken publicly about the strategies they used on reality shows. Most of these strategies involve going into character as "the stupid one," the "jolly one," "the aggressor," "the diplomat," "the flirt," and so on, with each contestant attempting to create a persona for him- or herself that is different from all the others. The shows are paradise for voyeurs, but do very little to help our understanding of the world around us. In fact, worryingly, according to the UK's Learning and Skills Council, one in seven UK teenagers hopes to gain fame by appearing on reality TV. Endemol, in attempting to create a new viewing experience, has created a new lifestyle where the quest for even "fifteen minutes of fame" has become an acceptable career path for otherwise talentless youth. Endemol has created a monster. "Reality TV" shows can turn their participants into national celebrities, but they can also destroy them. They are often derided as "Z-list celebrities" once the TV program is over, and the general public rapidly turn their backs on those who they perceive have done nothing to warrant their new-found fame. The road from hero to zero is very short in the new world of fame.

What is the legacy of Endemol? There are currently at least two TV channels exclusively devoted to reality TV: Fox Reality in the United States, and Zone Reality in the UK. As well as this, several other cable channels, such as Viacom's MTV and NBC's Bravo, feature a large chunk of original reality programming. On any given day one could watch 24 hours of "Reality TV." Fat teenagers are sent to boot-camps to run ten miles a day, there are confessional talk shows, dating shows, talent competitions, combatants on rival islands, even has-been celebrities trying to re-launch stagnant careers – the list goes on and on. Thank Endemol for letting us know what reality is really like, and for giving our children something concrete to strive for. Bravo (cue applause) – well done! DL

James Frey

A Million Little Pieces (of Bullshit)

Don't believe everything you read . . .

James Frey's book *A Million Little Pieces* became a bestseller after he claimed it was a true memoir . . . except it wasn't. It was a complete fabrication (if actually not a bad piece of fiction). The mistake Frey made was to threaten to sue investigative journalism site the *Smoking Gun* after they investigated some of his claims and found them to be unsubstantiated. Rather than own up to what could be described as a brilliant piece of post-modernist fakery, he attempted to defend his position, which consequently began to unravel, as he quickly became known as a fraud.

Let's start with the book itself. It's actually a great read. Frey tells a detailed, warts-and-all story of his life as a young crack addict, alcoholic, and all-round asshole, told through his recovery and redemption in a Minnesota rehab clinic. The memoir became a huge hit after Oprah Winfrey selected it for her book club, championing its bravery and, er . . . honesty.

Website the smokinggun.com investigated Frey's book in detail, and came up with some surprising information. They concluded that Frey had hugely exaggerated his past, and had made inflated claims about his criminal record and his involvement in an accident which had claimed the lives of two high school students.

"Police reports, court records, interviews with law enforcement personnel, and other sources have put the lie to many key sections of Frey's book," according to an article posted on the *Smoking Gun*. It began to seem that everything about Frey's story was, at best, embellished, and, at worst, completely made up. His worst criminal convictions seemed to be for driving under the influence of alcohol. He had never been investigated by the FBI for selling cocaine. No mafia and federal judge buddies he met in rehab had leaned on hillbilly Ohio prosecutors to get him out of a long jail sentence. And, in the most shameful fiction, contrary to his claims, he had nothing to do with a train accident in his hometown that killed two young women. In his book, Frey claimed that he had been with one of the victims on the night of the accident. In fact, it is reported that another student, Dean Sperlik, had asked Sanders out, but, fearing that she wouldn't be allowed to go out with Sperlik, Sanders told her parents that she was going to the movies with Frey. At the movies, Frey recalls, Sanders met up with Sperlik, who drove off with Sanders, only to be crashed into by an oncoming train at the railroad crossing. Sanders was killed, and Sperlik was seriously injured. Frey claimed that he had been questioned by police, as the person responsible for Sanders being out that night, and recalls being blamed for the tragedy by Sanders' parents and by her friends. "I took a lot of punches . . . and every time I threw a punch back, and I threw one back every single time, I threw it back for her," he writes. His memories were contradicted by the police report, by the chief police investigator and by Sanders' parents, none of whom could recall his being close to Melissa, being with her that night, or being blamed for the accident.

Frey was subsequently interviewed by the *Smoking Gun* and "did, for the first time, admit that he had embellished central details of his criminal career and purported incarceration for 'obvious dramatic reasons' in the non-fiction work," according to the publication. He also reportedly admitted to taking steps, around the time *A Million Little Pieces* was published in hardcover in 2003, to legally expunge court records related to the most apparently egregious criminal activity of his lifetime. But it seems that Frey's whole crazed past as a dope-addled, violent criminal was also a piece of fiction.

As the issue gained notoriety, the book's hardcover publisher,

Doubleday, and paperback publisher, Anchor, issued a joint statement to the effect that they stood by James Frey, when asked for comment by the Associated Press. To dig his own grave even deeper, Frey dismissed the story on his website, bigjimindustries.com, as "the latest investigation into my past, and the latest attempt to discredit me." The rebuttal continued, "So let the haters hate, let the doubters doubt, I stand by my book, and my life."

Eventually, however, the unveiled faker had to do the rounds to explain his position. One of these "confessionals" took place on the *Oprah Winfrey Show*. Winfrey had included Frey's book in her book club, and now she announced that she felt that she had been duped. What we can't know is if it was because she had actually been moved by the book, because she had believed it all to be true? Or was it because she felt that she was sharing Frey's shame, having recommended his book in her book club in the first place? No-one likes to be seen as a sucker, after all. Frey also appeared on *Larry King Live* to defend himself. In his public appearances, he showed little sign of the flamboyant persona that had appeared in his book. Maybe he really does live in a world of pure fantasy.

Of course, other memoirs have been disputed in recent years, including *Fragments of a Childhood 1939–1948*, a Holocaust memoir by Binjamin Wilkomirski, and Tony Hendra's *Father Joe*, about the author's troubled past, and the priest who helped him recover. Publishers have acknowledged that they don't fact-check memoirs, relying instead on their authors. Still, the scandal doesn't seem to have destroyed Frey's career as an author, even though his integrity as a memoirist has been destroyed. He should probably have owned up to the fraud at the first opportunity, had some fun with it, and turned the whole business to his advantage. Frey has signed a two-book deal with Riverhead Books, an imprint of the Penguin Group (USA). Another memoir, *My Friend Leonard*, concerning Frey's relationship with another recovering addict from rehab, is also published by Riverhead. As an author of fiction, rather than a teller of truth, he clearly has a future. DL

Paris Hilton

Best Scream

The debutantes of all previous eras were seemingly "simpler" public figures, whose activities occupied the deliberately rarefied atmosphere of charity events and high-profile, but carefully orchestrated, "social functions." Press coverage, if there was any, was strictly from the society columns of the local newspapers, and scandal and controversy were openly shunned as antithetical to the notions of what constituted "high class" behavior in US culture. The idea that discretion is a necessary tool of an obviously privileged lifestyle seems charming and "classy," at least when compared to the high-profile antics of so-called "celebutante," Paris Hilton.

Already heir to the considerable Hilton Hotel fortune, Paris has seemingly made it her life's work to transform herself into a self-proclaimed, and heavily self-promoting, "celebrity" through her involvement in modeling, reality TV shows, film cameos, pop music, an autobiography, and several lines of diverse, but related, "couture" items, such as perfume and shoes. Conversely, however, her attention-seeking "adventures" have also had a controversial side, such as her well-publicized "home sex video" and her repeated legal problems related to a well publicized drink-driving conviction, which have come to define her shameless multimedia persona almost as much as her clearly more calculated efforts to achieve and maintain fame.

Those efforts first took the form of a modeling career, in 2000, when the bi-coastal and practically straight out of school Hilton began working for self-promoter Donald Trump's agency, T Management. Besides working for "The Donald," she also booked work through Ford Models, Models 1 Agency, and Nous Models, appearing in campaigns for GUESS, Tommy Hilfiger, Christian Dior, and Marciano, establishing a reputation as "New York's leading It Girl." Using the leverage of this notoriety, Paris easily found a cameo role in the movie *Zoolander*, related to modeling and requiring minimal speech on her part.

This comparatively limited exposure ended in 2003, with the premiere of *The Simple Life*, a reality show on Fox Television. The premise was that Paris and fellow Beverly Hills "problem child" Nicole Richie would attempt to live with a family of "regular people" in rural Arkansas, and the candidly comic results would be shared with the public. This did seem to have a certain superficial charm, and the initial ratings were strong. However, what became clear after a few episodes was that Hilton and Richie saw the show more as an opportunity to behave like buffoons in public than to interact in any real way, or try to understand, the working people with whom they lived. As a result, the ratings slowly but steadily declined over the course of that season and the following two.

If Paris didn't seem to notice, it could have been because she had numerous other projects to keep her busy. In 2004, she started a record label, Heiress Records, wrote autobiographies of both herself and her dog, Tinkerbell, and launched her own fragrance. But it was her appearance in a very different kind of media that earned her the most notoriety that year.

On 15 June, Paris's ex-boyfriend, Rick Salomon, released a private video of the couple having sex, days before the debut of the second season of *The Simple Life*. Amazingly, Hilton weathered the media scandal with nothing more than a shrug, and a well-aimed lawsuit at the video's distributors, as well as Salomon. Adopting a devil-may-care attitude, Fox broadcast the new season of *The Simple Life* without seeming to wonder whether such a controversy might have a negative impact on ratings. Like the show's "star," all Fox seemed to care about was capturing the public's attention, regardless of the reason why.

Following the scandal, Paris cut a lower profile, limiting her activities to her TV show, another film cameo, and her almost made-for-publicity engagement to Greek shipping heir, Paris Latsis. By the fall, though, the engagement was off, the cameo had won her a dubiously assigned Teen Choice award for Best Scream, and the TV show was in free fall due to public disagreements between Paris and co-star, Nicole Ritchie. Paris' solution to these potential career problems? Project!

In early 2006 it was announced that Paris had found several well-known producers willing to record her musical debut, and she had booked studio time to create an eponymously titled album. With all the other types of media outlets or markets that Paris was plugged into, this was the peak of her media exposure, her "saturation point." There really didn't seem to be *anything* this girl would not do to get attention, and, so far, she had not yet shown any talents to justify such attention in the first place. The public was growing increasingly irritated at her talentless grandstanding.

As a result, the album's release, late in the summer of 2006, was met with underwhelming public apathy. While critics claimed that the album was better than they had expected it to be, its relative mediocrity could not be obscured by Paris' promotional abilities and efforts, and it failed to produce a hit single, or even reach gold sales. If this lack of success bothered Ms Hilton, she did not have to dwell on it for very long.

In September, Paris was arrested for driving under the influence of alcohol, and reckless driving, resulting in her licence being suspended by the court two months later, and a $1,500 fine and 36 months' probation when her plea of no contest was finally entered on the second charge on January 2007. Less than two weeks later, however, she was pulled over for driving with a suspended license, and, as a result of the offense, even signed a document acknowledging that she was not supposed to be driving. Before this most recent charge could be addressed by the court, she was pulled over *again*, this time for doing 70 mph in a 35-mph zone, still on a suspended licence, and without the benefit of headlights, even though it was well after dark at the time of the incident. These actions were deemed by Los Angeles City prosecutors to be in contempt of the previous rulings of the court, and were used as the basis for their decision to declare Hilton to be in violation of her probation status.

On 4 May, Paris was sentenced to 45 days in jail, for violating her probation status. The sentence immediately sparked an internet petition, allegedly initiated by fans, which was circulated, imploring Governor Schwarzenegger to pardon Paris. When the petition created a backlash, in the form of a counter-petition, Paris gave up the effort, as well as plans for an official, legal appeal against her sentence.

On 5 June, Paris reported to the Century Regional Detention Facility to begin her jail time. Within hours of beginning her incarceration, however, she is alleged to have fallen into a despondent and non-responsive state, which led to her being sent to the jail's infirmary for medical supervision. This medical emergency was used by LA County Sheriff Lee Baca, the following day, to re-assign Hilton's sentence to 40 days of home confinement with electronic monitoring.

This reprieve from the jailhouse was to be short-lived, however, as on the day of her release, the judge presiding over her case, heard about the re-assignment of sentence, and demanded Hilton re-appear before him on the morning of 8 June. At that time, he reiterated the terms of her sentence, explicitly stating that she *had* to serve jail time, with no work furlough, release, or electronic monitoring, and ordered her back to jail to continue her sentence. Despite throwing a temper tantrum in response to the judge's orders, Paris was then taken back into custody, first to the medical wing of Twin Towers correctional facility, then back to Century Regional five days later.

When released on 26 June, Paris claimed to be a changed woman. As she related on *Larry King Live*, her incarceration had led to her speaking with the chaplain Marty Angelo, who had encouraged her to lead a more purposeful life. To that end, she announced she was visiting Rwanda in November 2007 to gain some much needed perspective on her life, but, so far, she has yet to venture forth on this pilgrimage.

So what new ventures *has* Paris been busy with since her ordeal, and the maturity and insights it supposedly afforded her? A new line of shoes bearing her name came out a couple months after her release, followed by her newest fragrance Can Can, with another album, and a cartoon series about her, her sister Nicky, and, of course, her dog Tinkerbell, going into production. She has also, apparently, become an animal rights spokeswoman, recently having realized that fur is "gross."

In the end, though, the endless self-promoting, and profit-driven thinking might not have been such a bad idea on Paris' part. While her heiress status might have been the initial spark that led to her becoming a full time "celebrity," it was recently largely eliminated by her grandfather's decision to change his will. Embarrassed by her antics, most notably, allegedly, her jail time, Barron Hilton has decided that 97 per cent of his estimated $2.3 billion fortune will be donated instead to the charitable Conrad H. Hilton Foundation, rather than risk approximately $60 million being squandered by his errant granddaughter. While seen as harsh punishment by some, to those who remember the discreet charm of "Old Money," it seems a fitting lesson in the importance of maintaining one's respectability, though whether it will be understood that way by its intended beneficiary remains to be seen. KD

Don Imus

Shock Jock

"Shock Jocks," for the uninitiated, are radio broadcast personalities, who may or may not play music like conventional radio disc jockeys, and are noted for their reliance on sketches, pranks, interviews, and guests of a sensational or shocking nature. This is usually an attempt by the broadcaster to ensure maximum listenership figures, which determine the rates that can be charged to advertisers. One of the first "shock jocks" was Don Imus, who, along with longstanding rival Howard Stern, helped pioneer the deliberately controversial format, and whose success, along with Stern's, virtually guaranteed a perpetually growing legion of imitators in morning radio markets nationwide. In time, the two men turned their initial regional broadcasting success into multi-market, syndicated simulcasts, seemingly governed by the ethos of "how low can you go?" While Stern's on-air antics were more overtly sensational, depending largely on crude sexual humor, unapologetic sexism, insulting interviews of guests, and a seemingly limitless supply of women willing to take their tops off in public, Imus chose to rely more on character-driven sketches and low-brow "social commentary," largely based on stereotypes and clichés about the appearance and mannerisms of anyone outside his white, male "key demographic." This controversial, but commercially successful choice of content, became first a trademark, and then, eventually, a liability, in a career based on pandering to the lowest common denominator.

Don Imus was born in Riverside, California, in the summer of 1940. He followed an uneventful childhood with a two-year stint in the Marine Corps in the 1950s, before beginning work in a series of unremarkable jobs until 1968, when he convinced the owner of KUTY radio station in Palmdale, California, to hire him as a morning DJ, claiming that he would do an infinitely better job than the station's current "drive time" announcer. He moved to KJOY in Stockton in 1969, until he was eventually fired for saying "hell" on air – no big deal compared with some of what he would have to say later in his career.

When Imus began work at KXOA in Sacramento shortly thereafter, he seemed determined to attract more listeners through outrageous behavior, most notably in the form of on-air pranks, such as ordering 1,200 hamburgers to go from a restaurant worker who was unaware that he was being listened to by a huge radio audience. The ratings garnered by such antics propelled Imus into larger radio markets by the early 1970s, first to Cleveland's WGAR, and then to New York City's WNBC, where he quickly gained an even bigger reputation for erratic behavior and crude humor. During this time he recorded three comedy albums of sketch material – *1200 Hamburgers to Go*, *One Sacred Chicken to Go*, and *This Honky's Nuts* – but with limited success. Ultimately, he returned to Cleveland after he was let go from WNBC for being potentially more trouble than his ratings at the time merited.

During this period in Cleveland, Imus took the opportunity to move into a TV interview format, with the advent of his talkshow on WHK. As the station was part of a conglomerate, a freshly sanitized Imus was enabled to return to New York broadcasting via WNEW station. This new exposure lead to the new, revised version of Imus regaining his job as drive-time host for WNBC in 1979, where both his popularity and commitment to controversy as a component of his career were to be tested by the arrival of another future innovator of "shock" radio.

Howard Stern worked at the same station as Imus for three years, from 1982 to 1985, but in that time their almost instantaneous mutual dislike for one another quickly became one of the deepest and longest-lasting feuds in the entire "shock jock" community. Motivated by Imus's alleged off-air rudeness, Stern, who was less well known at the time, quickly and repeatedly turned the senior broadcaster's every snub and slight into the basis for numerous harshly worded diatribes and sardonic parodies fired back at Imus on a sometimes daily basis from Stern's show. While Imus never publicly responded to Stern's on-air taunting, his off-air confrontations, comments, and behavior towards Stern and his staff are the stuff of broadcasting industry legend. When Stern was fired in 1985 for one of his many brushes with the Federal Communications Commission (FCC) over the content of his show, many, including Stern himself, believed that he was removed by WNBC Executives to placate Imus, who was more popular at the time.

In the years that followed, despite Imus's very public hatred for Stern, the two rivals' careers paralleled each other. Like Stern, Imus became nationally syndicated in the early 1990s, and began simulcasting on television during the established morning show in 1996. Despite their equivalent levels of media exposure, Imus' sketches and commentary regained their previously narrow-minded, low-brow tone, as though he had been vindicated, or sanctioned by like-minded media commentators, because the content of his shows was considered far less offensive than the continually deteriorating behavior on Stern's. Even so, one should consider the following examples when assessing the character of this alleged "lesser evil":

- Repeated references to lesbians and gays as "lesbos" and "faggots."

- Repeated references to Arabs as "ragheads."

- Referring to Stern in a 1984 interview as a "Jew bastard" who "should be castrated" and "put in an oven."

- Referring to TV journalist Leslie Stahl as a "gutless lying weasel."

- Referring to conservative media commentator Rush Limbaugh as a "fat, pill-popping loser."

- Referring to fellow MSNBC broadcaster Tucker Carlson as "a bow-tie-wearing pussy."

- Referring to African-American sports columnist Bill Rhoden as "a *New York Times* affirmative action hire."

- Referring to publishers Simon & Schuster as "thieving Jews."

This is not to say that there has been no public outcry as a result of such crass public commentary; it's just that by comparison with so many deliberately aggressive, vulgar, and/or rude broadcasters since the advent of Imus, who have gone out of their way to be increasingly offensive, the man credited by many as having "originated" the concept, has gone for being more *consistently* offensive, while staying within range of the average middle-class, suburban bigot. While the expression of such narrow-minded views in public has become commonplace, they remain deeply offensive to those who have to endure them as part of their daily existence. More recent events have certainly illustrated such subtleties to Mr Imus, if he failed to grasp them in the past.

On 4 April 2007, during a discussion with the cast of his show, Imus characterized the Rutgers University women's basketball team as "rough girls." When an on-air member of the group, McGuirk, characterized them as "hardcore hos," Imus responded that they were, in fact, "nappy-headed hos," with McGuirk further commenting that the upcoming match between Rutgers and Tennessee would be reminiscent of the "jigaboos versus the wannabes" in the Spike Lee film *School Daze.* When made aware, the next morning, of the initial public outrage the comments had created, Imus attempted to dismiss the incident in typically blunt style as "some idiot comment, meant to be amusing." Given the controversy that followed, it was obvious that he had been only half successful in his previous effort, leaving him little choice but to start back-pedaling as fast as he could.

On 7 April, Imus issued a formal statement of apology, agreeing that the remarks had been inappropriate and that they were understandably offensive. He followed this on 9 April with an appearance on civil rights leader Al Sharpton's radio program to further address the controversy, answering Sharpton's charges of racism and sexism and his demand that Imus be fired, with the defense of acknowledging that he had gone too far, and had allegedly learned from the incident, not to make fun of people who don't deserve to be made fun of. Meanwhile, Rutgers coach Vivian Stringer went on record with possibly the deepest question raised by the entire incident, "What has society come to that anything is acceptable today?"

Attempts to answer the question were made by a variety of sources, beginning, the following day, with MSNBC, who announced that they were suspending Imus and his friends indefinitely. Other media commentators weighed in quickly, with the likes of Pat Buchanan, Bill Maher, and Rosie O'Donnell supporting Imus' right to make inflammatory remarks as a comedian, claiming that he was protected by the first amendment, and other journalists, such as MSNBC media analyst Steve Adubato and *New York Times* reporter Gwen Ifill, pointing out that such comments had been a longstanding feature of Imus' program, regardless of the current controversy and Imus' apology. Meanwhile, Coach Stringer announced that Imus had agreed to meet with her and her team to discuss his comments and for him to get a better understanding of their impact on the team.

Whether the discussion would have had any effect remains a moot point because the following morning, on 11 April, MSNBC announced that it would no longer be simulcasting the television portion of *Imus in the Morning*, effective immediately. MSNBC's decision was made on the same day that numerous sponsors had threatened to pull their advertising, and numerous NBC and MSNBC television personalities had made their opposition clear, effectively eliminating the possibility that Don Imus might return to regular broadcasting. The following day, CBS radio, which syndicated Imus, followed suit, seemingly ending the controversial career of the original "shock jock," for the same kind of sophomoric "humor" that had made him "successful" in the first place.

But this was not the end, of course. On 2 May, Imus announced his intention to sue CBS for the remaining portion of his $40-million contract with the company, alleging it had been wrongfully terminated, in light of the fact that the contract in question had clearly stated that Imus had been hired to be "irreverent" and "controversial." By the summer of 2007, it had become clear that Imus would be returning to the airwaves soon, in all likelihood to one of CBS's competitors, and that his suit with the company had enough legal merit for there to be widespread rumors of an early settlement. By 14 August, the rumors became fact when it was announced that CBS would settle the dispute out of court, but remained steadfast in their decision not to rehire Imus.

On 1 November, CBS competitor Citadel Broadcasting announced its plans to sign the *Imus in the Morning* show with a multi-year, multi-million dollar contract, in exchange for a nationally syndicated radio show. On 14 November, the *New York Times* reported that cable network RFD-TV had agreed to simulcast the video portion of the new program. On 3 December, Imus returned to both radio and TV airwaves, drawing a clear and public warning from Al Sharpton that he and other civil rights activists would be watching him closely. One can't help but wonder if such concerted and ongoing scrutiny might result in the shock jock's final disappearance from the airwaves, though the outcome is more likely to be a brief interruption before Imus returns to his place as the lowest of lowest common denominators in public discourse. KD

Rush Limbaugh

Chief Ditto-Head

Rush Limbaugh is the most popular syndicated radio broadcast host in the United States, with an average of just over 20 million listeners a week. Broadcast on over 650 stations across the country, the majority of them AM stations with a so-called "news-talk" format, the consistently highly rated "infotainer" is also one of the loudest media voices for so-called "conservative causes," as well as for the Republican Party. While admired by many for reviving AM radio listenership, as well as for being an unswerving advocate of right-wing issues and agendas, he is equally criticized by media watchdog groups, late-night comedians, Democratic politicians, and more liberal media commentators for factual inaccuracies and vicious partisan bias.

Named after a grandfather from whom he acquired his unusual first name, Rush was born in mid-January 1951, in Cape Girardeau, Missouri. The men of the Limbaugh family were mostly lawyers, from his grandfather on down to his brother, David; both an uncle and a cousin are federal judges for the state of Missouri. In stark contrast, Rush proved to be a mediocre student, preferring to seek opportunities in radio broadcasting and sports, to the point of dropping out of college after attending only his freshman year. Luckily for the young Limbaugh, he had an extremely high draft number, and was also 4-F status, due to a high school football knee injury, or he might well have served in the Vietnam War, or experienced the consequences of evading it.

Rush spent most of the 1970s as a disc jockey under a variety of assumed on-air names, starting out in Pittsburgh as Jeff Christie in 1972. He ended up in the Kansas City area, and, in 1979, he took a break from broadcasting, where he'd been only marginally successful in smaller markets, to work as the promotions director with the Kansas City Royals baseball team. Though he returned to radio in 1984, from that time onwards he only worked as a commentator in the emerging "news-talk" format, and never again as a disc jockey.

Starting out at Sacramento's KFBK, where Rush had originally been brought in to replace the recently fired Morton Downey Jr, Rush began as a radio call-in show host with a notably conservative agenda, and unremarkable ratings. When the Federal Communications Commission (FCC) repealed the Broadcast Fairness Doctrine in 1987, which required broadcasters to provide equal air time to anyone with a view opposed to one expressed by any station, its staff, or their guests on-air, Limbaugh took full advantage of this newly obtained privilege, and adopted an openly partisan, conservative on-air persona. By August of the following year, the show's ratings and attendant controversy, as a result of the views it espoused and its tone, were brought to New York City, and national syndication, with station WABC acting as a flagship for what was beginning to emerge as a media phenomenon.

Since then, the Rush Limbaugh Show has been broadcast from noon till 3 p.m. (Eastern Standard Time) each day. The show is a free-form radio call-in show, on which topics are frequently drawn from recent news stories and other current events. What makes the show unique is its nakedly partisan, conservative political slant, and Rush's so-called humor, which he uses to underscore the talking points. As a result, all opinions in opposition to the show's bias are treated with obvious disdain; environmentalists are regarded as "wackos," feminists as "feminazis," and those with a political conscience as "politically correct." With equally predictable jests and jabs at Democrats and liberals on divisive issues such as abortion, AIDS, gun control, police brutality, nuclear disarmament, and the plight of homeless people in the United States, the show's vaudeville tone has clearly struck a chord with its built-in niche market, the self-proclaimed "ditto heads," since its inception during the presidency of George H. W. Bush.

When Bush Snr was succeeded by Democrat Bill Clinton in the election of 1992, this reversal of fortune for the Republican Party was met by rabid resistance from the Limbaugh program and its host, resulting in a surge of new listeners and in the number of affiliate radio stations carrying the program, and a ratcheting up of Rush's partisan rancor. Every aspect of the new administration was criticized or lampooned by Limbaugh and his loyal "ditto heads," from Hillary Clinton's allegedly un-First Ladylike behavior, to Chelsea Clinton's supposed ugliness as First Daughter, as well predictable resistance to such early Clinton policy iniatives such as the treatment of gays in the military, and proposed legislation for a national healthcare system. When the GOP took control of Congress during the 1994 mid-term election, it is unsurprising that the Republicans awarded Rush the title of "honorary member of Congress," while referring to themselves openly as the "ditto-head caucus," openly acknowledging the show's help with galvanizing Republican resistance to the "evils" of Democratic national policy agendas.

With the appointment of Kenneth Starr by the Office of Independent Counsel that same year, Rush frequently found himself acting as a mouthpiece for the so-called Republican Revolution. His unwavering support for House GOP Leader Newt Gingrich added to almost day-by-day coverage of Starr's constant fresh investigations spun off from his original brief, saw Limbaugh's media profile continue to rise throughout the Clinton Era. Limbaugh used his notoriety to publish two books, host a short-lived syndicated television version of his radio program, produced by future Fox News CEO Roger Ailes, from 1992 until 1996, and even launched a series officially licensed neckties. His prestige within the circles of the Republican elite at the time was such that when he got married for the third time in 1994, the marriage was presided over by none other than Clarence Thomas, who had befriended Limbaugh after the latter's on-air defense of Thomas' controversial Supreme Court nomination.

It should be noted that while this was a particularly successful period of Rush's career, he was not without opponents or critics. Liberal comedian Al Franken went so far as to publish the bestselling book *Rush Limbaugh Is a Big Fat Idiot*, and the commentator was also a frequent, if predictable, target of sketch comedy shows and prime cartoons, given his rotund appearance and defiantly partisan rhetoric. Less amusingly, Rush was also criticized for 50 different inaccuracies and distortions within the course of a year by the media watchdog group Fairness and Accuracy in Reporting. He was later similarly censured by the non-profit Media Matters for America for similar conduct.

By the end of the decade, Rush seemed to be on top of the world. The Monica Lewinsky scandal had all but toppled the Clinton Presidency, and tainted the prospective Presidential campaign of Al Gore by association, which, together with a booming economy, virtually guaranteed a return to the White House of the GOP, in the form of George W. Bush. Limbaugh would, of course, offer partisan commentary throughout the drawn-out and contentious election, and, like many of his partisan Republican allies, he seemed very enthusiastic to "undo" the perceived "damage" of the Clinton presidency. When the United States was attacked nine months later by al-Qaeda, on 11 September, Limbaugh wasted no time in blaming liberal contempt for the military and the weak foreign policy of the previous administration, holding them directly responsible for the attacks, instead of blaming the inaction of the current commander in chief, who, it seems, had failed to heed numerous warnings about an imminent terrorist attack.

Predictably, Rush focused most of his post-9/11 rhetoric on consolidating Republican efforts to reclaim control of Congress during the 2002 mid-term election, as the presiding Democratic majority had been understandably hesitant in its support for the White House policy of expanding the "War on Terror," into a ground war in Iraq. Despite his somewhat ironic public acknowledgment that he was struggling with increasing hearing loss, for reasons unknown, Limbaugh vowed that he would soldier on, with the help of a stenographer, for the good of his party and the United States, before eventually solving the problem with cochlear implant surgery. When the election provided the desired results, and Iraq was invaded by US forces, Limbaugh shifted his career focus.

In an attempt to broaden his public appeal and profile, Limbaugh took a job as a commentator on ESPN's *Sunday NFL Countdown*. He first announced the "good news" to the public in July 2003, and began his job as analyst, on the 7 September premiere of the weekly sports round-up show. He lasted only three weeks on the job before racially charged comments about the competency of black Philadelphia Eagles' quarter-back Donovan McNabb, specifically, and black quarterbacks in general, forced him to resign on 1 October as a result of the massive public outcry over what were perceived as overtly racist remarks.

Even before the dust had settled from his widely reported resignation, Rush had appeared on the cover of the 3 October issue of the *National Enquirer*, allegedly for being under investigation for having illegally obtained the prescription drugs oxycodone and hydrocodone, a story which was quickly confirmed by other more mainstream media sources. To his credit, in response to the growing swell of accusations that he was a drug addict, Limbaugh stated on-air, a week later, that he would enter rehabilitation treatment immediately after the broadcast, for an "ongoing drug dependency problem." While Rush successfully completed his rehab therapy within the prescribed 30 days, the ensuing investigation as to whether he had broken any laws to maintain his addiction, lasted for close to two years, eventually requiring the assistance of previous on-air adversary, the American Civil Liberties Union, to help block Florida investigators from seizing confidential medical records in order to determine the extent, if any, of Limbaugh's guilt.

When the State of Florida was denied this legal access in late 2005, Limbaugh was indicted shortly thereafter on charges of "doctor shopping." Through a final plea bargain in April 2006, Rush was allowed to plead "not guilty," in exchange for paying for the cost of the court's investigation, and agreeing to 18 months of continued treatment for his addiction. The entire protracted legal fiasco was viewed as especially ironic by most non-ditto heads, given the host's supposedly longstanding and vocal hatred of drugs, as shown on an episode of his show, when he asserted, "We have laws against selling drugs, pushing drugs, using drugs, importing drugs . . . So if people are violating the law by doing drugs, they ought to be accused and they ought to be convicted and they ought to be sent up."

Since then, very little has been heard from Rush apart from his continued commentary on his so-called, self-owned Excellence in Broadcasting network. Aside from being publicly criticized for claiming that actor Michael J. Fox "plays up" his debilitating Parkinson's disease for the sake of his advocacy on behalf of the disease, Limbaugh has been careful to keep his more divisive or partisan preaching for his pre-biased choir, or for like-minded viewers of the Fox News cable channel. How his career is likely to be affected by the public's dislike for the Republican Party, following George W. Bush's presidency, is uncertain, but rest assured that as long as Mr Limbaugh is still of sound mind and body, he will continue to provide vocal opposition to any Democrat unfortunate enough to be elected by the will of the US people, whether anyone but ditto heads likes it or not. KD

Norman Mailer

The Spooky Artist

When your prime character is a man, the key choice is not how bright he is, because however smart, he can't be more intelligent than you are. That's easy. You dumb him down to taste or bring him up to your level.
Norman Mailer, *The Spooky Art*

Many people have mixed feelings about Norman Mailer. He was politically outspoken, unpredictable, and uncontrollable. He was great in panel discussions and in front of audiences, but it's hard to get past his rabid sexism.

In *The Spooky Art*, Mailer collected his thoughts on the art of writing. He comes across as unapologetically macho and regressive in his attitudes. The book is a strange read. His distinction between male and female authors is hilarious, as he insists that men can create a god-like hero, tougher than the author is, but a woman, rather than being tough, needs only to be more sensitive (toughness, of course, being unnecessary for a woman): "She could write about a woman who uses her sensitivity and sensibility more than herself, because she can then key on all the frustrated times in her existence when the sensitivity and sensibility she possessed were not appropriate to a harsh occasion." He even gives a bit more of his view of women by writing, "Or a woman who's colder than herself? Without doubt." Cold-hearted bitches one and all. It is no secret that Mailer spent the age of women's liberation denouncing and rejecting any move towards greater equality between the sexes.

In a 1960s' interview with Paul Krassner in *The Realist*, the subject turned to masturbation, and Mailer declared that masturbation was misunderstood to be healthy, when it is, in fact, traumatic and damaging to men, because it is an essentially isolating act. He suggested that men shoud do anything necessary to avoid having to masturbate, even if they had to commit rape. Yes, that's right, a casual recommendation of rape. One can accept that he was being deliberately incendiary, but even so it is one of many times when he has overstepped what most people would regard as being the boundaries of decent behavior.

There is also the inescapable fact that Mailer actually stabbed one of his wives, Adele Mailer, in 1960, at a Manhattan party. Presumably he was trying to provoke a reaction, rather than actually attempting murder, an act for which most prefer to avoid having an audience. Acting out his emotions at a party meant that he would be guaranteed to be the center of attention.

His book *Marilyn: A Biography by Norman Mailer with Pictures by the World's Greatest Photographers* is another example of his sexism. With *Marilyn*, Mailer once again overstepped a few ethical boundaries that, if they weren't legally or morally clearcut, did nonetheless put his professionalism and judgment in doubt. Mailer noted in his introduction that the problem with trying to write a biography of Marilyn Monroe was that public knowledge of her story was rooted in a string of newspaper gossip column lies. These had become more ingrained in the public consciousness than the more sedate facts. He proceeded on to use the very newspaper articles he was criticizing as the foundations for his biography. He reportedly confessed that he had at one time had the sexual fantasy that he would have been man enough to satisfy Marilyn. Mailer recast her life in his own terms, suggesting that no man could equal her self-regarding ambition. The book is a repugnant masterpiece of misogyny. Mailer's interviews and limited newspaper research, combined with his own guesswork and sexist viewpoint are mostly worthless. He hadn't met her, or spoken to her, so he treated her merely as an object of fantasy rather than as a real person. He pictured her as a Napoleon of publicity, meeting her death on Fifth Helena Drive, in Brentwood; a sex siren who made being a star seem as though it was as easy as "ice cream." He saw in her a combination of opposites, soft as a lamb's wool, yet as cruel as steel. His conclusion was that she had sexual power greater than any man she ever met. In his fantasy version of the star, she went through progressive fantasy kingdoms, from the muscle of Joe DiMaggio to the brains of Arthur Miller, and on toward a magical state of "Princessdom."

Mailer's *Marilyn* is purportedly a work about sexual legends, but Mailers innuendo and dirty jokes reduce it to the level of boorish locker-room chat. He allowed his full personality to shine through in the book, even trying to discredit Arthur Miller, in one of his characteristically macho moments which seems to reveal more about his own jealous disposition and vanity than it does about Miller himself.

Still, as an old, white, male writer who spoke in such an unreconstructed male voice, one can't deny that he was in touch with his true emotions, and with the collective heart of man at his least appealing. In this respect at least his writing was truly revealing. DL

Piers Morgan

Sophisticated, Self-Balancing

Piers Morgan once broke three ribs after falling off a Segway, a two-wheeled, motorized, gyroscopically balanced scooter, while traveling at 12 mph, in California. This was only three days before he was due to be making the biggest TV appearance of his life, as judge on the grand final of reality show *America's Got Talent*. While that fact is not necessarily funny in itself, it became more amusing when this fact was juxtaposed with his own words in his column in the UK newspaper the *Daily Mail* after George Bush had had a similar accident. "You'd have to be an idiot to fall off, wouldn't you, Mr President?" Morgan had written, "If anyone can make a pig's ear of riding a sophisticated, self-balancing machine like this, Dubya can".

Quite what he was doing riding on the geek machine known as the Segway, Morgan has never explained. Apparently he was cruising comfortably along the promenade at Santa Monica beach, when, inexplicably, his sense of balance failed him. Writing subsequently, in *Live* magazine, Morgan clearly regretted his previous comments about George W. Bush. Morgan wrote, "Since only he and I appear to have ever fallen off one, I think the makers of the Segway can probably still justifiably claim the machines are "idiot-proof." For many, though, "karma" would be the word that comes to mind.

Becoming a judge on *America's Got Talent* was one more step down in Morgan's long fall from grace after being sacked from his job as *Daily*

Mirror editor over the publication of faked photographs. The *Mirror* was renowned, during Morgan's period as editor, for its strong opposition to President Bush and his "War on Terror" and the war in Iraq.

Things began to fall apart for Morgan, when, in early May 2004, he paid for, and subsequently published, photographs, which were supposed to depict Iraqi prisoners being abused by UK troops. Morgan was the youngest national daily newspaper editor when he started at the *Mirror* and had survived previous controversial incidents, such as being sued by supermodel Naomi Campbell, but this time, his demise was inevitable. One of the photographs published appeared to show soldiers of the Queen's Lancashire Regiment (QLR) urinating on an Iraqi captive with a bag over his head. In another photograph the same hooded man is being hit in the groin with a rifle.

There was an immediate uproar, and some commentators suggested that the photographs may have led to revenge killings of UK and US troops. Morgan loves the limelight and seems to revel in the opportunity to take a controversial stance. He always defended his decisions vociferously in the face of the resulting outcry. The furore over the faked photographs was no exception. Morgan agreed to be questioned by Members of Parliament about the publication of the photographs. At first, Morgan had seemed entirely convinced that the photographs were genuine, but it soon became clear that neither he nor his staff had done enough fact-checking. Once again, the need to achieve notoriety and to sell newspapers had over-ridden sufficient consideration of potential pitfalls. Inadequate consideration had been given to the possible fall-out if things went wrong, as they did in this case.

Following intense pressure from various quarters, the Mirror Group sacked Morgan as editor of the *Mirror*, in May 2004. It is fair to say that his actions had been reckless and irresponsible, and might have led to retaliatory attacks on US and UK troops, resulting in loss of life – a stupid outcome, given his anti-war standpoint.

The Queen's Lancashire Regiment (QLR) later held a news conference where they pointed out several anomalies in the photographs which proved, categorically, that they were fakes, that could not have been taken in Iraq. The shirt that the "Iraqi prisoner" was wearing was in pristine condition; the truck in which the photographs had been staged had never been deployed in Iraq, and was, in fact, to be found at a Territorial Army base in Lancashire, England. Nevertheless, the QLR's reputation had been damaged by Morgan's decision to publish the photographs. He was even accused of helping to recruit for al-Qaeda by publishing the images. In spite of all the criticisms, he was unrepentant to the end, insisting that his source (known as Soldier C), had told him that captured Iraqis were being abused. Soldier C, a member of the part-time Territorial Army, was questioned by Royal Military Police after he had given this information to the *Mirror*.

So Morgan moved on to seek attention elsewhere, getting himself a column in right-wing UK tabloid newspaper the *Daily Mail*, and appearing on TV, as a pundit on current issues. How he ended up sitting next to Simon Cowell on *America's Got Talent* is anybody's guess; perhaps Simon's obligatory sniping comments were beginning to look a bit tired, and it was time to recruit a new bully to the show. Morgan's appearance did, however, bring fresh notoriety. At one stage he is reported to have made a nine-year-old girl cry, provoking Sharon Osbourne to threaten to quit the show. *America's Got Talent* is not the only reality show in which Morgan has appeared to maintain his media profile. While taking part in *Celebrity Apprentice*, he is said to have noted that the women on the show had blamed each other for their team's shortcomings, thereby giving men the advantage. What a sad comedown: from youngest ever mainstream UK newspaper editor to reality-TV wannabe, picking on women and children. DL

Bill O'Reilly

Spin Zone

Of all the conservative voices on the partisan, pro-Republican Fox News Channel, none speaks more loudly, nor more combatively than Bill O'Reilly. Besides hosting the channel's top-rated *The O'Reilly Factor* program, the high-profile political commentator also hosts a nationally syndicated radio program with an audience of 3.25 million, and is the author of six bestselling books, as well as a weekly syndicated political column in newspapers with a national reputation, such as the *New York*

Post and *Chicago Sun-Times*. A self-proclaimed straight talker, who refers to his program as "the no-spin zone," O'Reilly is often the subject of public criticism and controversy, which he tends to dismiss or disparage.

Though born in New York City in 1949, O'Reilly moved with his family to Levittown, Long Island, in 1951. After attending a local Catholic high school, he studied at Marist College, graduating with a BA in History in 1971. After an unsuccessful try-out for the New York Mets, O'Reilly taught English and History in Miami for two years, before attending Boston University and earning a Masters degree in journalism in 1976.

O'Reilly spent the rest of the 1970s as a regional reporter and anchor for local news programs in Scranton, Pennsylvania; Dallas, Texas; Denver, Colorado; Portland, Oregon; Hartford, Connecticut; and Boston, Massachusetts, before taking an anchorman position with WCBS in New York in 1980. Based on his previous related experience, he was promoted to network news in 1982, when he joined the *CBS Evening News* team as a war correspondent, reporting from El Salvador, and later Buenos Aires when he covered the war between the United Kingdom and Argentina over the Falkland Islands. O'Reilly's tenure as a war correspondent was brief, however, as a dispute with CBS News executives over uncredited use of riot footage shot by O'Reilly's crew in Buenos Aires lead to his resignation the same year.

By 1986, O'Reilly had resurfaced as a correspondent for *ABC World News Tonight*, where he stayed for three, largely uneventful years. In 1989, he joined the nationally syndicated tabloid news program *Inside Edition*, starting first as Senior Correspondent and later anchorman, after original host David Frost was fired. During that time, O'Reilly gained minor distinction as one of the first broadcasters to cover the dismantling of the Berlin Wall, and as the first host of a national current events program on the scene to cover the 1992 LA riots.

In 1995, O'Reilly was replaced as anchor by former NBC and CBS anchorwoman Debra Norville, in an attempt by *Inside Edition* to improve its image. O'Reilly used the time to earn a second Master's degree, in Public Administration, from the Kennedy School of Government at Harvard University. On graduating, he was recruited and hired by Fox News Channel chairman and CEO, Roger Ailes, to anchor his own news commentary program, *The O'Reilly Report* (later *The O'Reilly Factor*), in 1996. Like the conservative channel itself,

O'Reilly was a largely unknown media presence throughout the remainder of the 1990s, gaining greater public attention, along with the rest of Fox News, during the 2000 presidential election campaign, and the fiercely contested, media-saturated, and endlessly drawn-out victory of George W. Bush that followed.

While a self-professed political "independent," O'Reilly has frequently defined himself as a "traditionalist" in terms of his deeper social values, defined by the host as being based on "certain fundamental things that this country was founded upon that I respect and don't want changed. That separates me from the secularists who want a complete overhaul in the way the country is run." From such an obviously reactionary and socially conservative starting point, *The O'Reilly Factor* has become a media filter for those with similar values. Partisan debate is practically guaranteed by the shared attitude of host and viewers with regard to both the subjects for on-air "discussion" and the identity of occasional guests, who are carefully chosen for their adherence to opposing points of view, all but guaranteeing partisan debate.

The O'Reilly Factor is divided into separate, labeled on-air segments, and is broadcast every weekday at 8 p.m. as a summary of recent and ongoing news stories. A series of Talking Point Memos, which frequently underscore Republican issues and agendas, on the leading news of the day, are followed by Top Story and Impact segments focusing on specific news stories which may or may not conveniently coincide with the previous "talking points." These are followed by the Unresolved Problem segment, in which O'Reilly discusses news stories which he feels are not getting enough attention in other media – usually "good deeds" performed by groups or individuals favored by conservatives, or concerning conservatives accused of wrongdoing by liberals and democrats – before moving on to the most controversial segment, the Personal Story.

This segment takes the form of an interview in which the guest is usually the author of a recently released non-fiction bestseller, a contemporary "newsmaker," a witness or participant to a major recent news story, or a journalist who has recently interviewed a significant figure in the news. The guest, having been "pre-interviewed" by O'Reilly's producers, is interviewed with significant partisan bias from the outset, with O'Reilly enthusiastically endorsing the points of guests with whom he finds himself in agreement, or aggressively and reflexively refuting all opinions and assertions, no matter how reasonably presented, or cogently expressed, if they differ to any extent from his own view, and that of his loyal viewers. Within such a tightly controlled context, O'Reilly has been known simply to shout down his more assertive on-air opposition, at times even going so far as to cut a guest off mid-sentence, and demand that his staff turn off the guest's microphone, and escort him or her off camera, if he deems the guest's point of view too "inflammatory" to the host and his viewers' sensibilities.

The next item in the show is Factor Follow-Up, in which O'Reilly revisits an issue or guest from a previous program, frequently making use of the occasion to make negative comments about any recent guests or media figures who have made critical remarks about himself, conservative and Republican causes, or Fox News and its notorious right-wing bias in covering news. Back of the Book is a grab bag of unrelated items, ranging from serious smaller stories to human-interest fluff, and is followed by the more controversial Pinheads and Patriots segment, devoted to publicly praising anyone whom O'Reilly feels has been good to or for the United States, and criticizing anyone who has done anything perceived as harmful to the United States. The final segment, Factor Mail, is O'Reilly's on-air response to viewer mail, in which he frequently selects letters and e-mails from opponents which he subjects to a vigorous counterattack, before signing off quickly, with an invitation to the audience to e-mail the show. While there are occasional segments, like "Friday's with Geraldo" and "Factor Investigation", the show tends to adhere strongly to its basic structure, which seems to be reinforced by viewer loyalty, as is apparent in *The O'Reilly Factor*'s Nielsen ratings.

This popularity does not mean that O'Reilly and the show have not attracted criticism and controversy, however. O'Reilly and his program have drawn repeated fire from such diverse public figures as Al Franken, Bill Moyers, George Clooney, Chamillionaire, Ludacris, Joe Scarborough, and Keith Olbermann, as well as "refusals to appear" by the likes of such prospective interviewees as Hillary Clinton, Nicholas Kristof, and Tony Blair. And while he has been a subject of parody on numerous cartoon and comedy sketch TV shows, and criticized by numerous legitimate media watchdog groups, O'Reilly's greatest controversy has been a public scandal of his own, which he has never brought onto his program's No Spin Zone.

On 13 October 2004, it was reported that O'Reilly had pre-emptively filed a lawsuit against former *The O'Reilly Factor* producer Andrea Mackris, as well as her legal representation, for allegedly attempting to extort $60 million from O'Reilly, in exchange for not filing a sexual harassment lawsuit against him. Mackris' suit, filed the same day, claimed the incidents forming the basis of the recently resigned producer's motion, were repeated, unwanted comments and questions from O'Reilly regarding such topics as phone sex, vibrators, threesomes, masturbation, the loss of his virginity, and his sexual fantasies. The references to specific comments and incidents contained in the suit, allegedly attributable to O'Reilly, gave considerable and immediate merit to the allegations, and the suit was quickly settled by O'Reilly's attorneys for an undisclosed sum, believed to amount to millions of dollars, in exchange for Mackris' total silence about the matter. Since then, O'Reilly has never discussed the suit either on air or off, with any member of the media, news-related or otherwise, leading many critics to wonder, loudly and publicly, what "No Spin" actually means.

Something else that might have deflated O'Reilly's public profile shortly thereafter was the premiere of the Comedy Central cable network's *The Colbert Report*, in 2005. Following that network's enormously popular faux news program *The Daily Show*, *The Colbert Report* was an almost point-by-point parody of *The O'Reilly Factor*, spoofing everything about the Fox News program, from its patriotic graphics and bombastic theme, to its segmented format and its host's "blustering" persona. After being viewed as mean-spirited by much of the US public for his on-going media feuding with liberal comedian and commentator, Al Franken, O'Reilly, in an uncharacteristic move, publicly invited the deadpan Colbert onto his own program, and also appeared on Colbert's show. Such crossover appearances looked for all the world like an ideological lovefest involving two like minds, even though one of them, at least, was clearly joking. Together with the US public's growing dissatisfaction with the Bush Administration and its defenders, Colbert has, in the view of many, muzzled the man he obsequiously refers to as "Papa Bear O'Reilly," if not totally defanged him, leaving him to preside over a "bully pulpit" which seems increasingly at risk of failing to provide fresh victims to browbeat before the Fox News faithful. KD

Gordon Ramsay

Hellish Chef

There's never been a better time be an asshole on TV. *Hell's Kitchen* is a reality show presented by Gordon Ramsay, a highly successful and skilful English chef who chooses to behave like a boorish bully. A selection of hapless contestants compete for the opportunity of taking over a restaurant and perhaps aping his aggression, while Ramsay subjects them to taunts, challenges, and verbal putdowns.

One contestant is eliminated each week, often apparently on a whim (for example, Ramsay told one loser that he was "too fat and he'd always be dropping things"). Like much of reality TV we are given the uncomfortable feeling that we are participating in a modern-day version of the Stanford Prison Experiment, in which students play-acting as warders and prisoners took on the real attributes of the roles they were asked to act out. The contestants who most fully conform to the outrageous demands of the producers and presenters flourish, independence of spirit is crushed, and meanwhile we sit on our sofas being entertained by this horror show.

Ramsay's insults and machismo rise above the norm, even for reality TV. One occasionally feels that only the rules of TV prevent him from actually assaulting a junior chef who has not lived up to his expectations. If not actually a sociopath, he appears to be being paid to portray one. Much of the show revolves around how much the contestants can take of what Ramsay is dishing out, in almost cartoon-villain style.

It is easy to be entertained by Ramsay and similar figures on TV – reality show contestants are chosen for being the kind of people who desire fame badly enough to put up with a high level of abuse, so on one level we feel that they can't complain. But *Hell's Kitchen* often makes for uncomfortable viewing as contestants are condemned for their appearance, their politics, or even their sexual orientation. In one episode of a celebrity version of the show a male contestant was constantly derided by another contestant for being gay, in a way which was emblematic of the bullying tone of the show, even if Ramsay was not personally involved.

In another of Ramsay's programs, *Ramsay's Kitchen Nightmares*, broadcast on the United Kingdom's Channel 4, Ramsay has been accused of deliberately feeding meat to a vegetarian. In this reality show, owners of failing restaurants invite Ramsay to help them turn their businesses around, by first observing and then making changes to menus, staff, procedures, and so on. In one episode, broadcast coincidentally during National Vegetarian Week in the United Kingdom, Ramsay invites passers-by to sample pizzas from a struggling Italian restaurant, La Lanterna, in Hertfordshire, England. One of the passers-by, named Bob, tells Ramsay that he has been a vegetarian for eight years. Ramsay responds by telling Bob that the restaurant's chefs have prepared a special vegetarian pizza, and he gives some to Bob try. After Bob has eaten some of the pizza, Ramsay tells him, "Unfortunately, that pizza has got a lot of mozzarella and tomatoes, but underneath all that there is parma ham."

Bob objects to Ramsay that he has played "a mean trick" on him, but Ramsay responds by saying that Bob hasn't "come out in a big rash," laughing, and offering the vegetarian some more pizza. He also tells the chefs that they have "converted a vegetarian." Bob runs out of the restaurant looking very upset as Ramsay calls out after him, "Good luck with the Vegemite!" By tricking a vegetarian and laughing at his discomfort, Ramsay reveals his complete disregard for people's feelings.

Infuriated by this incident, vegetarians denounced Ramsay's behavior as both offensive and unethical. Tina Fox, chief executive of the Vegetarian Society of the United Kingdom, commented, "I am amazed that Gordon Ramsay can find the discomfort of a fellow human being so amusing. It can be deeply upsetting for vegetarians to find they have eaten any part of an animal in error. Would Gordon find it equally amusing if an anaphylactic customer died at the table due to eating nuts?" Ramsay seems to have minimal respect for the sincerely held moral beliefs and ethical choices of others. Some vegetarians choose not to eat meat for serious dietary or religious reasons. Only a true asshole would feed meat to people who feel that eating meat is wrong. There is certainly nothing amusing about it.

A Channel 4 spokesman responded to complaints by stating that the producers believed that Ramsay had made a genuine mistake, that he had not deliberately set out to feed meat to a vegetarian. However, in an interview to promote the BBC's Comic Relief program in 2003, Ramsay was asked what had been his most recent lie, to which he replied, "To a table of vegetarians who had artichoke soup. I told them it was made with vegetable stock when it was chicken stock." It would seem that he enjoys upsetting people who live according to rules which differ from his own, especially vegetarians.

Ramsay has also admitted that he is not a stay-at-home dad. Clearly, he works hard, what with the cooking and the TV shows and dreaming up new insults with which to abuse restaurant staff, guests, and contestants. However, instead of at least pretending that he wished he could spend more time with his children, Ramsay boasts of his absentee parent credentials. In an interview he told Larry King, "The time I have with the family is little. But it's quality. I've never been one to be home, I've never been a hands-on dad. I'm not ashamed to admit it, but you can't run a restaurant and be home for tea at 4:30 and bath and change nappies." He went on to say that he doesn't feel he has neglected his children, Megan, twins Jack and Holly, and Matilda. A busy man, he doesn't seem to have much more time for his family than he does for some of the poor souls who appear on his various shows.

An asshole? You decide. DL

Judith Regan

If she Did it

Judith Regan has been described as "the Angriest Woman in Media." She describes herself thus: "I was the perfectionist manager who wanted everything better. My author's book covers had to be perfect . . . the title had to be changed 20 times . . . the sales goals had to be revised. The content had to be reconstructed. I was never happy unless it was done and done right" (*Harper's Bazaar*, 2007). She has apparently inspired several books and screenplays about what a hilariously evil boss she is seen as. It is also rumored that several prominent agents will not take their projects to her, and that even some of her admirers won't talk on the record, because they don't want to show up on her radar.

She is one of the most successful woman in publishing history, yet she enjoys little respect. Fear and loathing might be closer to the mark.

Regan's name has also become a byword for sex, with books like *She Comes First: The Thinking Man's Guide to Pleasuring a Woman*, porn star Jenna Jameson's memoirs, and Legs McNeil's oral history of the porn-film industry, *The Other Hollywood*. "I don't publish pornography," she told the *New York Times*, "I publish smart books about sex. A lot of people try to imitate what I do, but they don't do it well."

In the most infamous episode of Regan's career she was unceremoniously sacked over the planned publication of the O.J. Simpson book *If I Did It*, in which the former US football star discusses hypothetically how he would have killed his wife Nicole and her friend Ron Goldman. Simpson, who was acquitted of murder in a 1994 criminal trial, agreed to an "unrestricted" interview with book publisher Judith Regan. Initially, Regan defended the controversial book project in public, despite urgent requests from the families of the deceased not to go ahead. A Fox TV program was planned, in which O.J. Simpson would tell "how he would have committed" the slayings. The whole event was advertised as "O.J. Simpson, in his own words, tells for the first time how he would have committed the murders if he were the one responsible for the crimes."

Nicole Brown Simpson's sister, Denise Brown, released a statement to the media protesting against publication of the book, pointing out how it would affect Nicole's children and subsequently a large furore developed about the ethics of publishing such a book. Tabloid headlines targeted Regan for consorting with the prime suspect in the most notorious murder case of the past decade. Finally, News Corp., the parent company of book publisher HarperCollins and the Fox network canceled publication of the book and the television special when it became clear that the controversy had got out of hand. "I and senior management agree with the American public that this was an ill-considered project," News Corp. Chairman Rupert Murdoch said. "We are sorry for any pain that this has caused the families of Ron Goldman and Nicole Brown Simpson." At the same time a brief statement from HarperCollins CEO Jane Freidman, the publishing house's boss, stated, "Judith Regan's employment with HarperCollins has been terminated, effective immediately. The Regan publishing program and staff will continue as part of the HarperCollins General Books Group."

However, if the firing of Judith Regan as head of her book publishing imprint ReganBooks, a unit within HarperCollins, by the top brass at Rupert Murdoch's News Corporation was brutal, the defamation lawsuit she brought by way of revenge promised to be at least the equal of it. In her lawsuit Regan accused News Corp. of seeking to smear her. She contended that company executives had urged her to lie to federal officials about a former New York police chief, Bernard Kerik, with whom she had had an affair. The suit also claimed that executives were determined to undermine her reputation because they feared the damage she might inflict on Mr Kerik, and, by proxy, his former mentor, Rudy Giuliani, once New York's mayor and now running to be the Republican Party's nominee for president. "Because of the damaging information that defendants believed Regan possessed, defendants knew they would be protecting Giuliani if they could pre-emptively discredit her," the lawsuit said. A spokesman for News Corp. responded by stating that Regan's claims against the company were "preposterous."

In her own words, in a *Harper's Bazaar* profile, Regan wrote, "The media went on a rampage, blaming me for the whole OJ book debacle. They came out, guns blazing, and tried to kill me. I felt like Faye Dunaway's character in the final scene of *Bonnie and Clyde*. Bullets flying in every direction." In fact, she used this metaphor of execution several times. At one point she writes that something happened "after a month of taking the blows without protection," as if her sacking was an attempt on her life. Publishing is after all the business in which it becomes hard to distinguish fact from fiction. She also writes, "They tried to hurt me, and maybe they did, but I know this much is true: You can take your punches, and you can take everything away from me, but no one will ever hijack my imagination, my drive, my creative spirit, or my dignity." Strong words indeed. Her behavior as a boss has been well documented to the point of mythology, but Judith seems less happy to be the one on the receiving end of aggressive behavior. "People were afraid to come to my defense . . . it disappointed me to the bone and broke my heart . . . It was a vulnerable moment for me." Do we believe her or not? DL

Jerry Springer

Freak Show Host

Jerry Springer (born Gerald Norman Springer, on 13 February 1944) a British-born US celebrity and former Democratic mayor of Cincinnati, Ohio, has become a byword for "trash TV." On the surface, *The Jerry Springer Show* is a talk show on which troubled and dysfunctional families discuss their problems before a studio audience before the audience and host offer suggestions on what should be done to resolve their situations. In actuality, the show's main focus is on tabloid topics such as adultery, bestiality, incest, homophobia, homosexuality, divorce, infidelity, pornography, racism, pedophilia, and transvestism, and the show takes pride in its own notoriety. In 2002, the show proudly boasted that it had been voted the "Worst TV Show Ever" by *TV Guide* magazine.

How did this intelligent Democratic politician come to front a show known worldwide for its apparent disregard for moral boundaries or limits? The show started as a politically oriented talk show. Early guests included Oliver North and Jesse Jackson, and topics covered included homelessness and gun politics, beefing up the commentary for which Springer had gained local fame as a reporter and anchor. However, in the money-led and ratings-oriented world of television, low ratings led to a reality check – an overhaul of the show and its structure by a new production team ensued.

The search for higher ratings led the program towards increasingly tawdry and controversial topics, it became increasingly successful. It still dealt with some sensitive issues, but the show's success came about mainly because it was the sort of television that stare open-mouthed, unsure whether to be entertained or appalled. The researchers dug up an endless parade of families and their friends who didn't seem to care at all about the general public's opinion of them. It became, as Springer himself apparently admitted, a "freak show" on which guests sought their 15 minutes of fame through proclamations and demonstrations of increasingly bizarre, and occasionally criminal, behavior. Despite Springer's calculated and patronizing "dumbing down" for the guests and the audience, its huge success has led to it being broadcast in many countries around the world. At one stage, following the addition of a stripper named Angie, and a pole for her to dance around, the show gained so much popularity that it was the top-rated daytime talk show in the United States. Complaints led to the stripper being dropped after a few months, but the pole remained for a while, with willing members of the audience being invited to perform with it.

Springer closes each show with the words, "Take care of yourselves . . . and each other," but the participants clearly aren't listening, and don't follow either piece of advice. Federal Communications Comission (FCC) regulations regarding the broadcast of indecency and obscenity led to profanities and other explicit language on the program being bleeped, while Jerry chuckled into his microphone and the audience whooped with pleasure. As the search for ever more outrageous stories went on, the producers resorted to muting to edit out explicit language. In fact, the muting sometimes removes a number of words, and even entire sentences, making passages of speech incomprehensible, but allowing the imagination to run riot. The fact that he was making TV that couldn't even be understood by its viewers seemed not to be a problem for Springer though. In later episodes, as guests began to strip their clothes off for attention, nudity and the partial exposure of breasts or buttocks have been blurred out. Such indecent exposure is generally followed by a wry or provocative comment by Springer himself.

The Jerry Springer Show has received extensive criticism and created many controversies for a variety of reasons, including prurience, foul language, and exploitation of the vulnerable. One doesn't have to be upset by nudity, bad language, or violence to be concerned by some of the issues raised by the show. It has been reported that a London rabbi referred to Jerry Springer's show as "a kind of pornography" and saw him as an inappropriate selection for a speaker at a major Jewish fundraiser. The rabbi is supposed to have commented that when a person like Jerry Springer is the speaker at such a function, it is time to stop and ask ourselves what has gone wrong. However, Springer apparently hit back at these comments, replying that a rabbi shouldn't be watching the show in the first place, and that he wouldn't want his own rabbi to watch the show. These comments suggest that he has little respect for the show's real audience. The phrase "Jerry Springer Nation" has also been used by some who see the program as being a bad influence on the morality of the nation. The phrase associates Springer with any form of "lowbrow" entertainment. The accusation is that the way that Springer knowingly capitalizes on the disadvantages of his guests and the stupidity of his audience has become a new paradigm for the lowering of standards in TV. For instance, much has been made by the media of the controversial episode about a man who had married his horse.

Regardless of such criticism, Springer continues to be a genial host. At times he seems to enjoy pretending to be dumber than his guests and audience, by claiming not to understand a topic, a ploy which encourages the show's participants to elaborate even further, to the raucous delight of the studio audience. The obscenity, blasphemy, and offensiveness are used as entertainment, but the result sends a disturbing message about the decline of US popular TV culture.

As participants and audiences of Jerry Springer's show continued to "take care of themselves and each other," questions began to be asked in the general media. There were claims that there was a "fight quota" for each episode, and that guests were encouraged to fight each other. Other allegations suggested that the fights were staged, as choreographed as the most staged wrestling match, and that the security guards knew before a show began when they were going to get involved. At one stage Chicago City Council suggested that if the fistfights and chair-throwing were real, then the guests should be arrested for committing acts of violence in the city.

The worst possible outcome of the show's progressive desensitization to violence occurred in May 2000. A married couple, Ralf and Eleanor Panitz, were guests on a "love triangle" episode of the show entitled "Secret Mistresses Confronted" along with Mr Panitz's ex-wife, Nancy Campbell-Panitz. The couple had been divorced since 1999 but had continued to cohabit for periods even after Panitz secretly married Eleanor, in March 2000. Ralf Panitz was angry at having been barred by a judge from living in his ex-wife's house. The couple also complained about Ms Campbell-Panitz's behavior, and accused her of stalking them. Hours after it was broadcast on 24 July 2000, Ms Campbell-Panitz was found dead in the very home that the three had been fighting over, and Florida police soon confirmed that they were treating the death as homicide.

In August 2000, Springer appeared on CNN's *Larry King Live* to talk about the incident, asserting that it "had nothing to do with the show" and claiming that his talk show did not glamorize deviant or criminal behavior. On 27 March 2002, after 18 hours of deliberation by the jurors at the end of a ten-day trial, Mr Panitz was convicted of his ex-wife's murder and sentenced to life in prison.

It was subsequently reported that Mr Panitz, having been issued a first-degree murder warrant for the death, was attempting to flee to Canada to avoid prosecution. Upon news of the 52-year-old woman's murder, a spokeswoman for the program issued a statement saying it was "a terrible tragedy."

Future television executives, how low can you go? DL

Corporate Assholes

Collateralized Debt Obligations

Ponziesque

The credit crunch that engulfed the world financial system in 2007 has been widely blamed on irresponsible sub-prime lending in the United States, lending that created a bubble in the housing market.

That is part of the truth, but a large part of the blame for the problems lies with the financial institutions which invented and peddled new financial products such as Collateralized Debt Obligations (CDOs). These new products enabled mortgage lenders to sell on, and theoretically to spread the risk, of the loans they were making. The loans were effectively chopped up into small pieces, distributed into CDOs with various levels of risk rating, and sold to other agencies.

This made a lot of people a lot of money. The loan companies were able to take far greater risks as a result, while mortgage brokers and media shills encouraged more and more risky lending practices. The financial institutions that traded CDOs and other paper securities made huge profits, mega-bonuses were paid to traders, and the ratings agencies who gave these CDOs their optimistic risk ratings also profited from the overall process. The problem was that, rather than eradicating risk as advertised, the CDOs merely created a situation where the risk was intensified. If something unexpected, for instance a fall in house prices, ever came along, then huge numbers of these CDOs would be simultaneously downgraded or even rendered completely worthless.

And since the risky lending was driving prices up into a bubble, it was all the more inevitable that the "unexpected event" of a fall in house prices would materialize. When this finally happened in 2007, huge amounts of value and paper wealth went up in smoke, the credit markets were paralysed, and the world economy faced a pronounced risk of recession. At this point, the traders and city whizzkids who had helped to create the situation, and who had profited from the boom, started to cry out for the government to bail out the financial institutions, something that central banks around the world were forced to do in an attempt to limit the risk to the system as a whole.

In any other context it would be clear that this whole process was a dishonest scam. Economies, livelihoods, savings, and businesses were put at risk by a process that falsely claimed to abolish financial risk while actually increasing it. In the *Alice in Wonderland* world in which we live, the banks have to be rescued from their own follies, and it is unlikely that anyone will be put on trial for the scam, which can be fairly compared to a Ponzi scheme: a fraudulent investment scheme which pays unusually high returns to investors, but only from money paid in by subsequent investors, rather than from profits generated by any real business. Inevitably, there are insufficient funds for later investors to be reimbursed even their original investment. Charles Ponzi, who emigrated from Italy to the United States in 1903, was not the first to run such a scheme, but managed to take in so much money that his scheme became known throughout the United States.

Will we learn from the stupidity of this episode, and the way in which we have been fobbed off with illusory prosperity while the bankers transferred money into their own pockets? That remains to be seen. One can only pray that next time a financier suggests that the banking system is capable of regulating itself and behaving in the interests of everyone, he or she is met by incredulous laughter and firm regulation. Is it too much to hope that governments have finally learned never to trust bankers again? DL

Conrad Black

As he's Painted

The basic details of Conrad Black's rise and fall are well known – his wealthy background, his spell in charge of Hollinger, and his final downfall when convicted of mail fraud and obstruction of justice in the United States. The reason that Black rises above the froth of ordinary scandal is the sheer scale of his hubris and pomposity.

A businessman who got into newspapers in the 1960s and built up a personal empire, Black was always fond of the trappings of power and wealth. One of the issues that dogged him in the years leading up to his trial was the level of expenses he charged back to his corporation that appeared to relate to personal extravagances. His second wife Barbara Amiel is blamed by some for encouraging his hubris in this respect, a suggestion that is supported by reported "business" expenses such as $2,463 on handbags, $2,785 on opera tickets, and $140 for "jogging attire" for Barbara. Hollinger money was allegedly used to refurbish one of the couple's homes, and the company jet was used to fly them on holiday. Their lavish parties and wealthy abodes in several countries probably did inspire some envy in observers, but Black made the mistake of assuming that this was the only motivation for criticisms of his financial conduct.

In 2003, an internal inquiry at Hollinger found that Black had received over $7 million of unauthorized payments. Black was accused of having presided over "corporate kleptocracy." This was the start of the convoluted process that led to Black's eventual conviction and sentence of up six-and-a-half years in a US jail.

While he was in charge of Hollinger, Black had spent years trying to get round the rules that prevented him from accepting a British peerage, eventually resorting to giving up his Canadian citizenship. The irony is that this pursuit of a title has cost him dearly in the end – after his conviction he is no longer eligible to reclaim Canadian citizenship, nor can he be transferred to a Canadian jail, something which would have significantly increased his chances of an early release.

Black is paying for his errors, so it is perhaps harsh to throw more opprobrium at him, but there is something in all of us that enjoys a story where pomposity and greed lead eventually to someone's downfall. And the sheer scale of Black's pomposity makes his fall from grace all the more gratifying as an ending to the story. DL

Blackwater

Soldiers of Fortune of the Great Dismal Swamp

Until the beginning of the twenty-first century, mercenaries in the United States were considered largely a fringe-dwelling oddity, a small but occasionally troublesome element, along with militias, survivalists, or even overt racial separatists, who made up what some called the extreme right of the political spectrum. Notable for strongly worded views concerning a narrowly defined notion of patriotism, "liberal" interpretations of Second Amendment gun ownership rights, and a preference for rural camps and compounds, such individuals and groups were closely scrutinized by both Attorney General Janet Reno and many mainstream news media outlets, even as they were defended and sometimes championed by conservative talk radio personalities and strenuously sympathetic publications such as *Soldier of Fortune*. The year 1997 saw the establishment of one more such operation in the form of Blackwater USA, which describes itself as a "private military company," with a state-of-the-art, 6,000-acre training facility and headquarters located in North Carolina's Great Dismal Swamp.

Its founder, Erik Prince, is a former Navy SEAL, a one-time White House intern under President George H. W. Bush, and a recent veteran of covert operations in Bosnia, under the auspices of the Clinton Administration and its efforts to bolster UN peacekeeping efforts in the former Yugoslavia. After leaving the military, Prince used inherited wealth to start Blackwater, with fellow former SEAL, Gary

Jackson acting as president of the company, which, in its earliest form was largely concerned with "survival" and "executive training" instruction, provided by an allegedly elite staff, comprising mostly former special operatives and law enforcement veterans. Both the nature and scope of the company were to be profoundly changed by the 2000 election victory of George W. Bush, and the 9/11 terrorist attacks in 2001.

In 2002, Blackwater created a subsidiary, Blackwater Security Consulting, in anticipation of the perceived need for private security providers in the recently declared "War on Terror." After the fall of the Taliban later that year, Blackwater was utilized, along with other military "contractors," to provide protection for US State Department "assets" in the fledgling democracy of Afghanistan, and managed to do so without noticeable incident, functionally anonymous, visible only as heavily armed figures in civilian dress, constantly flanking figures of importance to US foreign policy in the slowly recovering country. Meanwhile, the Bush Administration, along with its recently elected Republican majority allies in both houses of Congress, were busy with the run-up to the eventual war in Iraq, a conflict which would significantly raise Blackwater's public profile, often in controversial ways.

In the spring of 2003, following the fall of Saddam Hussein's government, Blackwater was awarded a $21-million, no-bid contract to provide security for recently appointed Administrator of the Coalition Provisional Authority, Paul Bremner, who used the company to provide security for all government interests and agents under his considerable authority. For almost a year, the company retained its trademark anonymous presence, only occasionally identified by the media, usually as part of the larger news story about the record number of no-bid contracts won by US firms engaged in the reconstruction of the recently "liberated" country. For the time being though, the media was more concerned with the seemingly endless chaos of the unanticipated level of Iraqi resistance to what was perceived as an occupation, or else focused on the lucrative price tags and questionable selection procedures for recently granted no-bid contracts.

Blackwater's media anonymity came to an abrupt halt on the last day of March 2004, when Sunni insurgents killed four Blackwater personnel who were providing security for food service ESS's convoy through the city of Fallujah. The four men became media symbols of the increasingly emboldened insurgency when their dead bodies were dismembered and burned literally to a crisp, before being hung from a nearby bridge over the Euphrates river, all to be captured and replayed endlessly in video coverage of the war by mainstream news media. This ambush led to a concentrated US attack on the city during the so-called First Battle of Fallujah, and it would not be the last time that Blackwater appeared in the media.

In fact, 2005 was a year in which Blackwater was utilized for the first time in a "domestic capacity," when it was contracted by the embattled Department of Homeland Security, to provide law enforcement, relief aid, and protection for government facilities, in New Orleans following the ravages of Hurricane Katrina, at an estimated cost of $240,000 a day. It was also the beginning of a two-year period during which Blackwater contractors were involved in 195 "shooting incidents" in the Iraqi combat theater, in which Blackwater contractors allegedly fired first in 163 cases. Some of the more noteworthy examples include the following:

- On 6 February 2006, a Blackwater sniper opened fire from the roof of the Iraqi Justice Ministry, killing three guards working for the state-funded Iraqi Media Network. Thirteen witnesses alleged that the shooting had occurred without provocation; the Iraqi police report described the shootings as "an act of terrorism," but despite all this the State Department took the word of fellow Blackwater guards and ruled that the contractor's actions "fell within approved rules governing the use of force."

- During a 2006 collision with a US Army Humvee in Baghdad, Blackwater guards were alleged to have disarmed the soldiers and forced them to lie on the ground at gunpoint, until they had disentangled their own SUV from the wreckage.

- On 17 December 2006, Blackwater is alleged to have been instrumental in helping allegedly corrupt Iraqi politician Ayham al-Samarie escape Iraqi police custody (having been contracted privately to guard him, prior to his arrest) and aiding his flight, first to Dubai, then later Chicago. Their client apparently feared that he would be killed in jail, and has received assurance from US officials that he will not be extradited back to Iraq.

- On 24 December 2006, Blackwater employee Andrew Moonen is alleged to have shot and killed a security guard of the Vice-President of Iraq, while obviously drunk. Although fired by Blackwater for violating their alcohol and fire arms policies, an investigation by the US Attorney's office remains ongoing.

- In May 2007, Blackwater is alleged to have opened fire on Iraqi Interior Ministry commandoes, leading to a protracted stand-off according to both Iraqi and US officials investigating the incident.

- On 30 May 2007, Blackwater employees shot an Iraqi civilian deemed to be "driving too close" to a State Department convoy.

- Most notoriously, on 16 September 2007, Blackwater is alleged to have opened fire on Nisour Square in Baghdad, killing 17 civilians, in what numerous witnesses called an unprovoked attack, which continued even as those in the crowd attempted to flee. There are further allegations that the attack was aided by two Blackwater helicopters in the area at the time. The conclusions of an ensuing FBI investigation ruled that at least 14 of the killings had been unjustified.

The Nisour Square shootings and their high-profile media attention proved to be the last straw as far as the Iraqi government was concerned. They revoked Blackwater's licence to operate in the country, following yet another shooting less than 24 hours later on 17 September. In the face of a second FBI investigation, brought about by the latest allegedly unprovoked shootings, Blackwater's top executive, Erik Prince, was called before the Congressional Committee on Oversight and Government Reform to answer charges concerning his company's perceived reckless behavior and seeming contempt for the safety of Iraqi civilians.

The hearings began on 2 October 2007, centering on Prince's testimony and documents obtained from the State Department and Blackwater. Prince objected to the use of the term "mercenaries" in his testimony, and largely defended his company's practice of shielding seemingly reckless employees due to an absence of other infractions on their part, and fears that local Iraqi authorities would be too punitive if allowed to prosecute his employees. He also declined to provide financial information about his firm, unless it could be submitted in writing at a later date.

When the committee issued its report, shortly after the hearing and the testimony of Prince, they concluded that Blackwater was "staffed with reckless, shoot-first guards who are not always sober and do not always stop to see who or what was hit by their bullets." They also questioned the cost-effectiveness of continuing to use the firm, observing that Blackwater was charging an average of $1,222 per day, per guard, "equivalent to $445,000 per year, or six times the cost of an equivalent US soldier." Such conclusions were unlikely to be good news for Blackwater's management.

On 5 October, the State Department announced new rules, requiring all Blackwater operatives in Iraq to be escorted by State Department Security, as well as requiring video cameras to be mounted in all Blackwater vehicles, and all their radio communications to be monitored. The Iraqi government, still angry about the company's seeming disregard for its authority, also imposed new laws, ending any immunity from prosecution for all foreign military contractors. Despite such setbacks, Blackwater, like any other private company which has experienced a period of sustained profitability, continues to grow in new directions, even as it faces the fresh challenge of tighter regulation.

To date, Blackwater has been involved in two long-term projects clearly designed to expand the scope and variety of their global operations, alluded to by their rebranding as Blackwater Worldwide towards the end of 2007. One project is the ongoing construction of two new training facilities, in Illinois and California, designed to provide better settings for police and military training in many different types of environments. The other is Blackwater's acceptance of a Department of Defense contract, as part of its Counter-Narcotics Technology Program Office's efforts, valued at up to $15 billion. There have also been rumors that Blackwater's leadership has been acting in a "foreign policy advisory capacity" for presidential candidate, Mitt Romney, although the extent and compensation for such "advisement" is unknown at this time.

If there are any potential obstacles to Blackwater's ongoing success, aside from new guidelines from their "top client," the US federal government, they may be related to the initial incident that made the public aware of their existence. The families of the so-called Fallujah Four, whose relatives were so gruesomely killed and displayed during the early days of the Iraq war, have been in a protracted legal battle with Blackwater, not for any monetary damages, but merely for the details concerning their sons' and husbands' well-publicized demise. Blackwater has gone to the trouble and expense of hiring former Special Prosecutor Kenneth Starr – who achieved prominence in the 1990s with his relentless investigation of Bill Clinton and the resulting impeachment proceedings – to counter-sue the grieving families for a total of $10 million, on the grounds that their lawsuit is contractually prohibited by documents signed by their deceased loved ones.

Perhaps this underscores the observation that the primary trouble with mercenaries is that while you can frequently pay them enough to kill for you, even without hesitation or question, you can rarely pay them enough to die for you, regardless of the nature of that "compensation." And when mercenaries have the gall to present themselves to a critical public as "patriots," it is perhaps this which gives their claim such a hollow ring, especially in the light of such supposedly military virtues as loyalty and honor, so respected by the public, especially in those servicemen and women who embody them. A hard point to make to those with an attitude of "Kill 'em all, let God sort 'em out." KD

Clippit

The Late, Unlamented
Microsoft Office "Assistant"

Since the concept was first mooted, humanity has been suspicious of anything resembling "thinking machines" or "artificial life." One need only witness the malevolent behavior of the HAL 9000 computer in *2001: A Space Odyssey*, or the title character in any of the *Terminator* movies, to see that this fear is still alive and well in modern life, even as this kind of technology becomes an increasingly common part of it. Still, one can't help but doubt that humanity's technophobes could have conceived that artificial intelligence would take the form of a pest as intrusive and banal as Clippit.

Officially designated the Microsoft Office Assistant by its creators, Clippit has bothered and annoyed Microsoft Word users for over ten years, but has finally – many would say mercifully – been retired in recent editions of MS Office, due to its widespread unpopularity. If you find yourself asking why, you've clearly never had to deal with this cybernetic interloper, and your nerves are probably better off for it. However, to give such fortunate readers an idea of the problem, the following are examples of Clippit's exasperating advice and "assistance":

• Any user who types the date at the top of a new document, and follows it with the word "Dear" will cause Clippit to appear, unbidden, with a cartoon talk-bubble that reads "Looks like you're writing a letter. Want help?" The user must then stop what she is doing, and answer yes or no with the appropriate buttons below Clippit's question, or he will remain on the screen, blocking the user's view of the text, while seemingly smirking and staring off into space.

• If the user clicks on Clippit to request advice on a simple topic like, "How do I format a newsletter?" Clippit will sit there giving the appearance of taking notes on a steno pad, before answering by giving multiple options, including many which barely address the user's enquiry, let alone clarify it. For example, the options listed as answers to the above question include the following: "Lay out text in a newsletter style document," "Ways to lay out text in a newsletter style document," "Force the start of a new newspaper column," "Remove newspaper column," "Create newspaper columns," and "Create newspaper columns to continue story in the next column on the same page." Clearly, only the first answer has any direct bearing on the question asked, and the rest are fairly superfluous.

• Should an increasingly irritated user be foolish enough simply to "hide" Clippit on more than one occasion, he or she will actually receive the prompt, "You've hidden me several times now," and be given the option to hide Clippit yet again, which the user has already asked to do, or to deactivate him altogether, a real come-on to an understandably annoyed user.

- Ironically, when accessed to generate these examples, the offensive Office Assistant Clippit "volunteered" numerous options on how to use "bullets" in an MS Word document, even though no help had been requested and the Spelling/Grammar checker had indicated no format-related "typos."

With such examples of intrusiveness, poor design, and redundancy, one could almost believe that this function had been invented by a group of comedians. And, while this may not be the case, Clippit has certainly been the butt of many jokes. He has been parodied on animated shows like *The Family Guy, Drawn Together,* and *The Simpsons* (twice, no less). He has also been ridiculed frequently on the BBC's *The Now Show,* and referred to on the Demetri Martin comedy album *These Are Jokes.*

With all this negative exposure, one can't help but wonder at Microsoft's tardiness in removing Clippit from its widely distributed product. However, from the time of Clippit's creation in 1997, until the XP edition of Windows in 2003, the Office Assistant has survived as the default help option for all too many frustrated Microsoft Word users. The XP edition, for reasons known only to Microsoft, still featured Clippit in its Help section, but at least the Office Assistant was no longer the default option for users struggling with their documents.

This decision to terminate Clippit was greeted wtih great joy by the public, even inspiring a short-lived website, officeclippy.com, which reveled in the iconic paperclip's apparent demise. In animated shorts, the creators of the site imagined Clippit's unemployment woes, made all the more hilarious by the use of deliberately annoying comedian Gilbert Gottfried's voice for the ill-fated clip. Public approval of these animated shorts was high enough to get them uploaded to YouTube.com, at least until its acquisition by litigation-shy Google. With lines like "X . . . XP . . . as in, ex-paperclip?" one can only imagine the delighted response of MS users everywhere, something that not even Microsoft could ignore any longer.

When Microsoft Vista, the latest version of the Windows operating system made its debut in the spring of 2007, there were many new features the company touted. Oddly, a better selling point might have been the first edition of the MS Office and Word programs devoid of Clippit, even as a *non*-default option. And while there may have been many complaints about various new functions and processes in Vista, there was at least, finally, a normal Help menu, devoid of the obsequious animated paperclip. That alone may well have increased sales by several million units.

Now if we could just find a way to do away with every other form of pop-up. KD

Enron

America's Most Innovative Company

Enron has become a byword for accounting fraud and dubious corporate practices. But it didn't start out that way. The entity that eventually became the Enron corporation started out as the Northern Natural Gas Company, in 1931, and was, for many years, a profitable, highly respected company. A series of mergers and acquisitions resulted in the business being renamed Enron under the chairmanship of Kenneth Lay in 1985.

By 2001, Enron claimed to have revenues of $111 billion, it employed 22,000 people, and had been named "America's Most Innovative Company" by *Fortune* magazine on numerous occasions. *Fortune* was right. Enron was an extremely innovative company. Unfortunately, as the 2001 Enron scandal revealed, many of these innovations had been of dubious moral and legal status.

The first cracks in the Enron edifice started to show on two different fronts. Firstly, the company spent huge amounts of money developing the transaction system Enron Online, and, as a result, its accountants started to use increasingly questionable systems to shuffle money off the balance sheet and between companies within the corporation. Secondly, Enron's behavior with regard to the California energy system came into doubt.

The California deregulation plan, enacted in the late 1990s, allowed Enron to make huge profits. They used a series of business practices with macho names such as "Death Star" and "Fat Boy" to profit from the deregulated system by, for instance, manufacturing energy shortages, and then claiming to have relieved the problem. In the wake of deregulation, California was plagued by rolling power cuts. In part, these were caused by Enron employees, who were intentionally manipulating supply and prices to make profits for their corporation.

Meanwhile, the corporation's accounting practices became ever more elaborate, leading observers to comment that Enron's finances were obscure to the point of incomprehensibility. In October 2000, Daniel Scotto, a respected Wall Street analyst chose to suspend ratings on Enron as a result of his observations. From that moment onwards, the edifice that was Enron started to crumble, in a steady but nevertheless spectacular fashion.

In August 2001, Jeffrey Skilling, the CEO, resigned, using the old standby of "personal reasons" as his excuse. He had sold nearly half a million shares in the run-up to his departure, which didn't fit too well with the official message that the company was basically sound. Ken Lay took over as CEO, making reassuring noises, but investors were starting to get spooked.

In October of that year, Enron announced a $1-billion markdown in its profits, which it claimed was due to investment losses. Analysts and regulators were by now taking an increasing interest in the corporation, and the Securities and Exchange Commission announced an investigation. As shares continued to fall, a white knight appeared on the horizon in the form of Dynegy, a rival energy company which proposed a takeover and rescue bid. But in the face of increasing concern about Enron's liquidity, and a downgrading of the company's ratings, the takeover bid failed.

On 30 November 2001, Enron filed for bankruptcy in Europe, and two days later followed the same course in the United States. At the time, it was the biggest bankruptcy in US history, and thousands lost their jobs as a result. Many also lost their pensions, and this was a source of particular bitterness given the final settlements and alleged insider trades which had enriched many of the company's bosses during Enron's final months.

Many of the details of the frauds and dubious business practices took a while to come out, as the investigation was complex, but gradually the pigeons came home to roost. Several of the executives at the top of Enron were put on trial for their parts in the company's downfall. Arthur Andersen, the major accountancy firm which had failed to regulate Enron's accounting excesses in their audits was dissolved as a direct result, and the resulting legal action also led to the collapse of another corporation with questionable accounting techniques, WorldCom.

After an extended trial, Kenneth Lay and Jeffrey Skilling had the highest profile of the 21 employees found guilty of charges including securities and wire fraud. Lay died before sentencing, but one can imagine that his sentence would have been even longer than the 24 years and four months that Skilling was sentenced to.

It is tempting to mock the Enron executives who were directly responsible for the crimes and bad business practices which destroyed Enron. But perhaps one should cast the net wider in searching for culprits. It has been observed that the modern corporation is legally defined in such a way that it is prone to act psychopathically in its own interests, regardless of the consequences for individuals and nations.

Enron was an extreme example of a corporation run amok, but, in some respects, the convicted individuals had simply taken what they had learned from corporate culture one step further. They tweaked balance sheets to show profits, they used multiple companies to project the figures that were required. They concealed wrongdoing and exploited loopholes to generate profits for the company. In the process, as individuals, they made fortunes from bonuses, payoffs, and share profits. Part of the shock felt throughout the business world was at the things Enron had done; but equally shocking, surely, would have been the recognition of how essentially similar some of Enron's practices had been to those of other corporations in pursuit of profits, or, sometimes, simply survival.

How many corporate bully-boys watched the trial of Lay and Skilling with a certain sense of "There, but for the grace of God, go I?" Perhaps the biggest assholes in this instance are those corporate leaders who are still getting away with similar practices and crimes? DL

Rupert Murdoch

The Master's Voice

Sometimes a public figure is more disliked for what he represents than for who he is. From Rupert Murdoch's point of view there is no problem with his hugely successful media empire – he has become extremely wealthy by doing something that he is very good at. He is one of the wealthiest people in the world, and controls a hugely successful business.

However, for those who observe that the media is becoming ever more narrowly focused and more condescending in its approach to the news, there is a serious problem created by the fact that more and more of the mainstream media is owned by fewer and fewer people. Murdoch's News Corporation owns newspapers and television stations across the United States, the United Kingdom, Australia and the Far East, including the *New York Post*, the *Times*, Fox TV and the Sky television network. Politically, Murdoch is a long-term Republican supporter (he has described televangelist Pat Robertson, for example, as being right on all the issues in the 1988 election) and was close to the Thatcherites in the United Kingdom.

The channels and newspapers owned by Murdoch don't slavishly follow their owner's instincts at all times. But at key moments, Murdoch's media power can be hugely influential – for instance, in the United Kingdom, it has become New Labour mantra that the party must stay close to Murdoch, especially since a last-minute *Sun* headline was seen as being partially responsible for the Labour Party's failure to win the 1992 election. There are also concerns about the degree to which the various parts of News Corp. support one another, creating a monolithic structure of information distribution which, to a large degree, controls the terms on which news is conveyed to the public.

For those who oppose the war in Iraq, the fact that all 175 of the newspapers Murdoch owns editorialized in favor of the war in the run-up to the invasion may be enough to condemn him. But even for those who support the war, it must be of concern that such a huge chunk of our media can be controlled by one individual at such a key moment in history. DL

Northern Rock

Solid as . . .

The story of Northern Rock is perhaps best viewed as a black comedy, something like the 1950s' films produced in the United Kingdom's Ealing Studios. The Rock was originally a small local building society based in Newcastle, England. However, from the late 1990s, it took advantage of new, laxer banking regulations to expand massively. The plucky little local company took on the big boys of the banking world, and seemed to win. By offering cheap mortgages on excellent terms, the Rock's share of the mortgage market grew until it was one of the market leaders, taking the fifth largest share of the market. It was led in this remarkable crusade by Adam Applegarth, a balding, assertive businessman from the North-East region of England, who had been appointed CEO in 2001. The business was hugely popular in its local area, well known for its charitable contributions, and for its sponsorship of Newcastle football team.

However, in September 2007, the Rock became the first UK bank in over a century to suffer a bank run. Grannies, young mums, and white-haired gentlemen were pictured queuing in their thousands outside Northern Rock branches across the country to withdraw their money, afraid that the bank was about to become insolvent. So where did it all go wrong?

It became apparent that Northern Rock's miraculous growth under Applegarth had been rather less solid than it had appeared. One of his first mistakes had been to decide that savers were not that important, closing local branches and doing little to reward the prudent. This was because the Rock's business model had become increasingly dependent on borrowing short-term from the money markets in order to fund their long-term mortgage book. As a result, their fractional reserve of assets was far lower than that of a conventional bank or building society.

This all worked fine in a period of gung-ho growth and easy credit. But, in the early autumn of 2007, a credit crunch finally arrived, following problems with the US sub-prime mortgage markets, and the whole model of debt repackaging that had become standard practice over the preceding years. Warren Buffet, the Sage of Omaha, once pointed out that it is only when the tide goes out that you can see who has been swimming with no clothes on. The Rock provided a perfect illustration of this maxim. When the money markets seized up, the Rock was forced to apply to the Bank of England for an emergency loan. When the bank made this loan public, as they were legally required to, Northern Rock's shares plummeted, and the public panicked, and started to withdraw their money by the wheelbarrow-load.

After an excruciating period of dithering, the Chancellor of the Exchequer (the UK equivalent of the US Secretary of the Treasury), Alistair Darling, stepped in and guaranteed all depositors' savings. He assured the public that the Rock was a fundamentally sound business, but many disinterested observers concluded that the government had effectively been forced to nationalize an insolvent business. Full nationalization duly followed, following the failure of extended attempts to find an acceptable private rescue package.

Who are the assholes in this whole charade? There are a few possible culprits.

The Northern Rock board was clearly ridiculously blasé and overconfident, and failed utterly to assess properly the risks of their expansion. In the aftermath of the debacle, Adam Applegarth claimed to the Treasury Committee that no-one could possibly have predicted the problems that had engulfed his company. Applegarth is clearly a reasonably intelligent man, having become CEO at the age of 39, yet he could brazenly claim that no one in his position could have been expected to wonder if his business model would stand up to a change in global conditions, or evaporate in a puff of smoke at the first hurdle.

His behavior is roughly the equivalent of driving a car with no brakes and, after the inevitable crash, claiming that no-one could have been expected to know that he might actually have to stop the car at some point. Only in a dumbed-down world, in which political spin and advertising slogans have replaced serious discussion, could a CEO make such a ludicrous statement in the expectation of it being taken seriously.

But there are other assholes, too, implicated in this sorry business. The entire financial community had for years been operating a system which rewarded high risk-taking with massive bonuses, thereby discouraging responsible banking. While the likes of Northern Rock

were taking massive gambles with depositors' money, it became
necessary for even the most staid banks to compete, and the whole
industry had become riddled with carelessness.

The UK government, led by newly anointed Prime Minister Gordon
Brown, also came out of the affair with little credit. They allowed the
Rock to twist in the wind while they delayed and prevaricated, before
coming up with a series of non-solutions to the problem, which created
more risk and dangers. They also seemed to try to pin the blame for the
fiasco on the Bank of England governor, Mervyn King, who had been
the most sensible actor throughout. Indeed, it had been Gordon
Brown, who, as Chancellor, had taken the role of banking regulation
away from the central bank and given it to the Financial Services
Authority, a quango staffed by ex-bankers who generally rubber-
stamped even the riskiest of their erstwhile colleagues' endeavors. The
result had been a complete failure to see the risks that the Rock was
taking.

The bank run also showed up bad practice in the media. The
immediate reaction of several financial writers to the news of the
emergency loan was sensationalist reporting, which failed to mention
the extensive guarantees already in place for depositors. TV journalists were sent to hang around Northern Rock branches to see if a
bank run resulted. In several cases it was rumored that the crowds
filmed queuing to take out their money had actually been rounded
up by journalists, to pad out their story. Although, if this were true,
it soon became a self-fulfilling prophecy, as other depositors felt
obliged to follow suit. As the bank run developed, more than one
financial journalist may well have taken a queasy look in the mirror
and wondered if they had just bitten the hand that fed them
overpriced, expense-account lunches.

But in the final analysis, the story of Northern Rock's downfall was
an old-fashioned morality tale, with hubris as its defining sin. The
plucky little regional company had never really had the money it
needed to support its expansion. And when the chips were down, the
mouse that stood up to the lions turned out to be a rather feeble little
beast.

For years, bankers had been telling the world that the only people
who could regulate financial services were bankers themselves, because
no-one else could possibly understand the complexities involved. The
Northern Rock bank run was the moment when the curtain was pulled

back and the UK public realized that the mighty Wizard of Oz of the banking sector was just an old gentleman in threadbare clothing pulling a few rusty levers and praying that he'd get away with it. DL

Donald Trump

Towering, Infernal Ego

There has never been a bigger or better businessman than Donald Trump – according to Trump, at any rate. The billionaire real estate developer, hotel and casino owner, bestselling author, and reality show host would have us believe that his name is synonymous with luxury, style, and shrewd dealing in business, regardless of evidence to the contrary, like feeble profits, unexpected losses, and even the occasional bankruptcy. None of these factors, however, is allowed to detract from the alleged opulence, prestige, and glamor supposedly inherent in the Trump "brand name."

Born to real estate developer Fred Trump, Donald spent his early years attending the Kew-Forest School in Queens, followed by four years in the New York Military Academy, which was supposed to teach the boy how to be "assertive." The young Trump then attended Fordham University for two years, before transferring to the Wharton School at the University of Pennsylvania, to take advantage of that institution's strongly business-oriented curriculum. He graduated in the spring of 1968 with a BSc in Economics, a "concentration" in Finance, and a strong desire to make as big a mark, as rapidly as possible, in his newly chosen career.

Donald began his career by working for his father's company, overseeing the elder Trump's middle-class rental properties in Brooklyn, Queens, and Staten Island. While proving himself surprisingly adept at filling vacant units in struggling family holdings, the younger Trump's eye for higher end operations initially took the form of the redevelopment of the bankrupt Commodore Hotel, and his steering of the Javits Convention Center construction project onto property he had recently optioned. Despite such ambitious goals, he drastically underestimated the cost of these initial projects; the final cost of the Javits Center, for example, was easily 600 or so million dollars over the projected $110-million bid by Trump. While Trump offered to take the project over at cost, the offer was finally declined by New York City Government, probably on account of the developer's initial massive miscalculation.

Such a setback did not deter Trump from continuing to expand his property holdings, in which he showed a noticeable preference for high-end hotels, convention centers, luxury condos, and, from the late 1970s to the late 1980s, casino resorts. Seemingly having learned the lessons of his past, by the mid-1980s Trump had achieved some local celebrity in the New York tabloids, when he took over the troubled restoration of the Wollman Rink in Central Park, completing the by then six-year-old project in six months, and $3 million dollars under budget. He gained more national exposure around this time with the publication of his bestselling autobiographical memoir, *Trump: The Art of the Deal*, in the fall of 1987, which he used as the basis for high-profile cameo appearances in TV and film throughout the 1980s and early 1990s.

Despite such profitable and notable successes throughout this period, by 1990, Trump had experienced some setbacks, both in terms of public notoriety, and the financial bottom line. Just as he was encountering debt-related problems with his third casino, the Taj Mahal, he was simultaneously caught up in a messy and public divorce from his then wife Ivana, due to an alleged adulterous relationship with model Marla Maples. The divorce provided fodder for the tabloids for weeks on end, and the Taj Mahal filed for bankruptcy, and Trump avoided litigation with his bond-holders by ceding them a 50 per cent stake in the restructured venture.

The year 1992 was equally unkind to Trump, as a recession impacted on the profitability of the Trump Plaza Hotel to the degree that it filed for Chapter 11 bankruptcy in November of that year. By 1994, however, "The Donald" had rebounded nicely with the liquidation of under-performing assets, like his airline, Trump Shuttle, and by refocusing on his remaining assets, like the Trump Tower, and his casinos, which were by then more solvent. A year later, he combined those same casino holdings into a single, publicly owned company,

Trump Hotels and Casino Resorts, and used its initial success story as a stock offering to flirt with running for President as a potential candidate of the Reform Party, in 1996. By the end of the decade, however, this venture, too, was in decline, with stock in the company trading at single-digit prices, even as the rest of the market ran at a decidedly more bullish pace, and as its seemingly oblivious founder and public spokesman continued to look to further expand his national property holdings, his national media exposure, and his officially licensed product lines.

The earliest years of the new millennium found Trump uncharacteristically quiet, as the country was momentarily distracted by other issues such as the much contested 2000 election, and the beginning of the "War on Terror." Nevertheless, by 2003 Trump had rewarded the public's patience with the premiere of his own "reality" TV show, *The Apprentice*, produced and hosted by "The Donald" himself. On the show, aspiring tycoons compete for a high-level management job at an appropriate Trump enterprise, with the worst performing contestant each week being dismissed by the host, with a dramatic, "You're fired!" The show was an instant hit as a result of its high-tension antics, and blunt dismissals, and breathed new life into the glory that is Trumpness.

Meanwhile, back in the "real world," Trump Hotels and Casino Resorts was continuing to hemorrhage money, and needed restructuring to satisfy its increasingly unhappy bondholders. In 2004, Trump announced that he would cede an additional 29 per cent of his 57 per cent controlling interest in the company to those investors, in an attempt to quell their anxieties about the under-performing investment. Despite those concessions, the company still filed for Chapter 11 bankruptcy by the end of that year, and Trump relinquished his title of CEO, and rebranded the venture as Trump Entertainment Resort Holdings in the spring of 2005.

Ironically, even as Trump the "actual businessman" was suffering his latest commercial setback, Trump the "media businessman" was enjoying increasing success with his TV show *The Apprentice*. As a result of its strong ratings, the show had increased its host's fee from a mere $50,000 an episode to an estimated $3 million an episode, as befitted a show with such impressive Nielsen ratings. This enhanced media profile, however, while clearly profitable, combined with his reaction to a scandal within one of his many entertainment enterprises to create The Donald's highest profile tabloid media feud yet, in December 2006.

That fall, Miss USA Pageant title-holder Tara Conner almost lost her crown when it was revealed that she had been engaging in underage drinking, despite strict pageant rules forbidding such behavior. The Pageant is co-owned by Trump and NBC, and while Conner ultimately retained her title by entering rehab for alcohol abuse, many were critical of Trump for having been too sympathetic in allowing Conner to retain the title due to her willingness to come clean and seek treatment. One critic, talkshow host Rosie O'Donnell, aired her complaints about Trump's handling of the situation in the course of an appearance on the ABC talk show *The View*, and, in so doing, stirred up a cross-media feud which lasted for weeks, in which both camps made increasingly over-the-top criticisms of the other's purported lifestyle and allegedly irresponsible behavior, until declining public interest finally brought the bickering to a halt.

If such media shenanigans didn't, in some ways, spell out that Trump had officially "arrived" as a media figure, the addition of his star to the Hollywood Walk of Fame in early 2007 surely did. He made high-profile appearances during a World Wrestling Entertainment (WWE) pay-per-view, backing his own wrestler against WWE owner Vince McMahon's in a Hair vs Hair match, and in an episode of the NBC gameshow *Deal or No Deal*, in which he wrote a personal check for the sons of a losing contestant to the value of $25,000 as a consolation prize, before he finished the year with a seemingly deliberately controversial appearance on *Larry King Live*. In the interview with Larry King, Trump extensively criticized the Bush Administration and its handling of the war in Iraq, predicted that Hillary Clinton and Rudy Giuliani would be the respective presidential candidates for their parties, and said that the supposed beauty of film star Angelina Jolie was a matter of opinion (clearly, his opinion differed from most others). The Donald has plans for a future reality show, in which he will adjudicate in financial disputes between people. Given his vast experience of renegotiating financial settlements in real life, and his media image as a shrewd dealmaker, it seems likely to a be a truly Trump-worthy success. Undoubtedly, it will be hailed as such by its host, regardless of how well it actually does in the world in which the rest of us live. KD

Wal-Mart

Costly Bargains

Wal-Mart department stores are large, discount-driven establishments that form the largest retail chain in the world, making Wal-Mart the largest publicly owned corporation on the planet, according to the Forbes 2007 Global 500 business rankings. Known to the public consistently to have the lowest advertised sale price for a wide variety of retail items, the corporation accounts for 20 per cent of US domestic retail grocery sales, and 22 per cent of retail toy sales. Wal-Mart is the largest private employer in the world, and also the fourth largest global employer overall, behind the People's Liberation Army of China, the National Health Service of the United Kingdom, and the Indian National Railways.

Much of the company's astronomical size and unparalleled success is credited to its founder, the late Sam Walton, for the development of supposedly sound retail philosophies, which, in turn, have produced the store chain's record profits. Detractors of the late retailer, would point out that Walton also provided the philosophical basis for many of the chain's often unfair, and frequently illegal, business practices. Regardless of one's position on the retail giant and its founder, it is universally agreed that Wal-Mart's runaway success, first in US and then global retail markets, has a strong foundation in the policies and practices of its founder, and his early business experiences which helped to mold these.

Walton was born in 1918, in Kingfisher, Oklahoma, to rural, middle-class parents. Growing up during the Great Depression, the young Walton was well-known for the large number of chores and odd jobs he undertook to help his family make ends meet. Following college and a job as a munitions maker during the Second World War, Walton opened his first retail store, a franchise outlet of the Ben Franklin variety stores, in Newport, Arkansas, in 1945.

As the owner of the operation, Walton made it a habit to engage in extremely competitive business practices, in an attempt to consistently court maximum commercial success. He purchased large volumes of fast-selling products from the cheapest wholesalers he could find, and then used the lowered wholesale cost as the basis for charging consistently low prices to his customers. He also made a point of staying open later than most of his competitors, with extended shopping hours during the Christmas season, all of which, when combined with the store's well-chosen, central location for numerous rural communities, resulted in notable success and steady profits for the enterprising young franchiser.

His first real challenge as a successful retailer came when Walton's landlord, assuming his tenant's success had mostly to do with the location of his store, refused to renew Walton's lease, despite the business's consistent payment of an outrageous five per cent of store revenue under the original lease contract. Walton was to use the incident as a lesson in his future business dealings, from then on seeking maximum personal advantage in terms of store placement, and lease conditions, as he opened other retail franchises for the Ben Franklin chain, and later his own company, Wal-Mart, which launched its first store in Bentonville, Arkansas, in 1962. As Walton applied his aggressively competitive business practices without the constraint of Ben Franklin's business guidelines and the established supply chains of a franchise, his company flourished, being incorporated on Hallowe'en 1969, and being publicly traded on the New York Stock Exchange by 1972. To outside observers, such initial success seemed an almost textbook example of hard work, shrewd competitiveness, and the desire to provide goods and services at fair prices, adding up to an ideal success story of classic American capitalism, but later, closer examination of Wal-Mart was to prove that there were also far more sinister reasons for the chain's success.

The enormous number of allegations against the firm have taken over two decades to be investigated fully, partly as a result of company efforts to suppress public knowledge of its business practices, and partly because of public apathy in the face of the substantial savings to be made by shopping at the retailer. Nevertheless, when fully uncovered and compared with similar practices of an equally ethically questionable, or simply flatly illegal, nature, the overall pattern suggests a profoundly aggressive and competitive business model, intended to achieve nothing less than the total domination of the entire retail market sector. Such practices are known to include, but may not be limited to, the following:

- Selecting centrally located rural towns with established shopping districts to guarantee a retail customer base and guarantee competition without comparable wholesale buying power.

- Demanding concessions such as tax cuts from the local governments of prospective host cities and towns, while threatening to site shops just outside those governments' jurisdictions and tax bases if such demands are not met.

- Using so-called predatory pricing: selling specific, popular items at a loss, to draw business away from smaller, non-corporate retail competitors in the same market.

- Paying employees the lowest average wages of any US-based retailer and keeping the number of full-time employees, who are legally entitled under federal labor laws to be given benefits such as healthcare and overtime pay, to an absolute minimum.

- Violating child labor laws by assigning illegal shift times and through non-payment of overtime for work performed after scheduled work hours.

- Violating US immigration laws by knowingly hiring illegal aliens, frequently for lower wages and longer hours of work than are legal under US labor laws.

- Using just about any means possible, including surveillance, disinformation campaigns, and threats of possible termination, to keep employees from attempting to unionize or bargain collectively in labor relations with the company's corporate management.

- Outsourcing work, primarily to China, to produce low-price Wal-Mart brand products, ensuring a healthy profit margin despite low retail prices.

- Demanding special price concessions from "name brand" product wholesalers in return for their purchase and sale by Wal-Mart.

- Instructing underpaid and uninsured employees on how to apply for social welfare programs such as food stamps, welfare, and Medicaid to gain benefits and payments the company cannot or will not provide for them.

• Deliberately ignoring "lesser problems" such as the localized environmental impact of specific outlets, or the security of store parking lots, if they affect in any way corporate profitability.

The basis for these allegations comes primarily from the record number of lawsuits brought against Wal-Mart by city and state governments, labor organizations, and individual employees and customers. A fuller account of the details of these allegations is given in films such as *Wal-Mart:The High Cost of a Low Price*, released in 2005, as well as in numerous books concerned primarily with matters such as global trade, labor rights, and responsible corporate governance. An ever-increasing number of anti-Wal-Mart groups can also be found on-line on websites such as hel-mart.com, walmartwatch.com, wakeupwalmart.com, and walmartsucks.org. While it remains to be seen whether the company will ever suffer any financial impact as a result of such efforts to curtail its relentless profiteering, one can be fairly certain that Wal-Mart, and the Walton heirs, who make up most of its top corporate officers, will fight such efforts in any conceivable way they can. KD

Film Assholes

Woody Allen

The Heart Wants What the Heart Wants

When it comes to assholes, sometimes it is the quality of a single, defining transgression, rather than the quantity of smaller ones, that earns them public disdain. Furthermore, sometimes that transgression, while of a deeply personal nature, can be so essentially vile, that, once revealed, it has a nullifying effect on all the previous public accomplishments of the transgressor, no matter how grand or seemingly well deserved. Like his fellow, formerly celebrated, but now notorious filmmaker, Roman Polanski, Woody Allen is decidedly guilty of just such an extraordinary lapse of judgment, and flaw in conduct, and character. Like Polanski, Allen's lapse involved a questionable liaison with a significantly younger woman, under highly dubious circumstances.

Until that "liaison," Allen was viewed by the public with considerably more sympathy. He was seen as a highly insightful, yet deeply funny, comic "genius." His career and achievements served as the foundation for a beloved film persona of a neurotic, but well intentioned, intellectual, overwhelmed by the conflicting social mores of "modern life." Informed by an unflinching emotional honesty, his often ironic observations about romantic relationships had even earned him the status of an unlikely "sex symbol," as he was viewed as a sterling example of the "nice Jewish boy" cultural cliché, a plain but sincere alternative to smooth-talking "ladies' men."

The reality of Allen's life by 1980 was only slightly out of line with those perceptions. While he had seemingly remained the long-suffering and average-looking "mensch" he played in his films, he had been romantically linked to several attractive and accomplished actresses, among them Louise Lasser and Diane Keaton, and had started dating actress Mia Farrow. Given that Farrow had several children, both from her previous marriage to André Previn and through adoption, Allen, who had been publicly and comically suspicious of such extensive emotional commitments, seemed finally to have accepted the inevitability of a domestic partnership, and the "child rearing" it is intended to support. Throughout much of the often publicized relationship, Farrow and Allen seemed surprisingly grounded at the head of an otherwise unorthodox, but completely functional "blended" family.

This is not to say that the relationship didn't have its quirks. The couple never legally married, nor even cohabited, despite eventually having a child together, a son, Ronan Seamus, in 1987. Nevertheless, regardless of the obvious logistic challenges, and difficulties of parental "labeling" that such a domestic arrangement would create, the Farrow–Allen household was largely typified in media "photo ops," as an ordinary family, "bonding" while engaged in normal activities. By 1992, however, the internal dynamics of the household had shifted in dramatic, shocking, and very public ways.

During that year, Mia found several nude pictures of her adopted daughter, Soon-Yi Previn, in one of Allen's books. When confronted with them by Farrow, Allen admitted to having taken the photos, and further, to a sexual relationship with his 22-year-old, common-law stepdaughter. News of the affair and the dissolution of Farrow and Allen's relationship shortly thereafter, completely stunned just about everyone.

It didn't matter to many that Woody and Mia had never been married, or that Soon-Yi wasn't a minor, or that she had never referred to Allen as her stepfather in any way. The nature of their roles was supposed, by most, to be implied by Allen's sexual relationship and romantic partnership with Soon-Yi's adoptive mother, and his presumed efforts to help support Soon-Yi's healthy development, based on that partnership. Woody's behavior was considered by many to be at the very least "spiritually incestuous," even if it failed to meet any legal definition of incest.

In fact, incest is so universally despised as a crime, that along with wanton murder, rape, and cannibalism, it is widely regarded as deeply taboo, and therefore seen by almost the entire human species, as antithetical to basic decent conduct, or even long-term survival, at least at the societal level. The core reason for the taboo's existence may be to prevent genetic inbreeding, but it also underscores another basic human principle, that one should not violate the implicit trust of the parent–child bond. And not only had Woody Allen violated that particular trust, but he had also violated the trust of the child's mother. For by becoming sexually involved with a child that Mia Farrow was still in the process of raising, Allen clearly betrayed his relationship with her as well. These ethical and moral observations were not lost on any sane person who heard of the scandal, and as a result public sympathy rested firmly with Farrow.

The couple's public and ugly separation sparked disturbing press reports for months to follow. Soon-Yi was the only family member to side with Allen, for obvious reasons, and broke off all contact with her former adoptive mother and siblings without much additional public comment. Meanwhile, during custody hearings concerning Farrow and Allen's remaining children, Mia made credible, though unsupported, allegations that Woody had inappropriately touched their adopted daughter Dylan. Based on this, and taking into account Allen's relationship with Soon-Yi, the judge granted sole custody, with supervised visitation allowed to Allen, to the children's mother, in the hope of preventing potential abuse without overstepping the judge's narrowly defined authority, at least with regard to a father's rights under the law.

Following the couple's separation, Woody struggled to regain his reputation as a film-maker, but he found it tough going due to public sentiment surrounding the recent scandal, at least initially. He often became frustrated, and refused to comment when asked about the split from Farrow, or else defended his actions with simple, but dismissive, comments like, "The heart wants what the heart wants." Interestingly enough, it was noted at the time of his affair with Soon-Yi that he had stopped going to psychoanalysis, after having been a public and longstanding devotee of such therapy for most of his adult life.

He and Soon-Yi married in 1997, and later adopted two daughters, Sidney and Manzie, without incident. Though his career has rebounded to some extent since the time of the scandal, largely due to the critical acclaim his subsequent films have enjoyed, he retains a large "negative following" of people who both remember the scandal, and remain sickened by it. KD

Warren Beatty

You're So Vain

"He also revels in his life. Having no strong family ties, he goes wherever he wants, whenever he wants. Having no strong compulsion to work, he takes off months to hop around the world, read, dabble in politics, and consort with beautiful and interesting women. While other stars hang out with one another in Malibu, Beatty moves and mingles with the 'right' people. He has numbered among his friends the likes of Lillian Hellman, Robert F. Kennedy, Hubert Humphrey, George McGovern, and Jerry Brown." (*Time*, 1978)

For the above description read womanizing, shallow, self-involved, and solipsistic asshole. Warren Beatty was the classic Hollywood dilettante, living a life of self-absorption. At his prime, he seemed simply too egotistical and childlike to consider others when he made decisions. He achieved great power in Hollywood quite early in life, after the huge success of *Bonnie and Clyde,* and was subsequently able to pick and choose his projects while living the life of a Beverly Hills playboy. His personal life was lampooned in one Doonesbury cartoon, where a female character is asked why she dated him and replies, "Well, it was the '70s. It was kind of like cocaine...you'd meet a girl in the bathroom who'd say, 'So, have you tried Warren Beatty?' "

Before his marriage, Beatty was a famous womanizer, regularly sleeping with his co-stars, who have included Natalie Wood, Julie Christie, Diane Keaton, and Madonna. He is also rumored to have had relationships with Joan Collins; Leslie Caron; Liv Ullmann; Brigitte Bardot; Carly Simon – who, it is said, wrote the song "You're So Vain" about him; Elle Macpherson; Goldie Hawn; Candice Bergen; Cher; and Britt Ekland.

Madonna taped Warren Beatty's telephone calls when they were dating (during the filming of *Dick Tracy*). Madonna was going to put the taped telephone calls in her movie but Beatty sued to prevent her from doing so. There's not much good that can be said about her, but Madonna did manage top make Warren Beatty look like such a fool that he realized it was finally time to settle down and married Annette

Beining.

There is little schadenfreude to be found in contemplating Beatty's life, movies, and conquests. But even the most successful lives can yield a few gems for those who are bitter enough to hope to hear bad things about the rich and famous. The Madonna calls debacle provides one such moment. And infamous for his "love 'em and leave 'em" attitude, an aging Warren had also had the tables turned on him by supermodel Stephanie Seymour, who unceremoniously dropped him to pursue Axl Rose of rock band Guns N' Roses. Hah! DL

Tom Cruise

Sofa-Jumper

Bouncing around on Oprah's sofas yelling about Katie Holmes, slagging off new moms with post-natal depression, actually *believing* in and promoting Scientology! Where to start?

Tom Cruise is a short man with a big idea of his own importance. He was apparently diagnosed as dyslexic when he was seven, but claims that Scientology has helped him to overcome this disability. His reading still can't be that good, though, or he'd be able to read accounts of his absurd behavior and take steps to get help. In 1997, Cruise and other big-time Hollywood entertainers took out an international newspaper ad denouncing Germany for resorting to tactics against Scientologists that the compared with the totalitarian tactics that the country had used against the Jews under Hitler during the 1930s. He is said to have lobbied politicians in France and Germany, where the legal systems regard Scientology as a business and cult, respectively. In 2005, the Paris city council revealed that Cruise had lobbied officials Nicolas Sarkozy and Jean-Claude Gaudin, describing him as a spokesman and militant for Scientology, and barred the council from having any further dealings with him. For his various services, David Miscavige awarded Scientology's Freedom Medal of Valor to Cruise in late 2004.

Cruise's strong advocacy for Scientology has led to the reporting of some strange behavior. It has been alleged that he has tried to introduce a number of his co-stars to Scientology. Cruise also co-founded and raised donations for Downtown Medical to offer New York 9/11 rescue workers detoxification therapy based on the works of L. Ron Hubbard. This drew criticism from the medical profession, as well as firefighters.

Another controversy erupted in 2005 after Cruise openly criticized actress Brooke Shields for using an anti-depressant, which Shields believed had aided her recovery from post-partum depression after the birth of her first daughter in 2003. Cruise asserted that there is no such thing as a chemical imbalance in the brain, and that psychiatry is a form of pseudoscience. This led to a heated argument with Matt Lauer on the *Today Show* on 24 June 2005. Brooke Shields responded to Cruise's comments by calling them "irresponsible and dangerous." Cruise also said in an *Entertainment Weekly* interview that psychiatry "is a Nazi science" and that methadone was actually originally called Adolophine after Adolf Hitler, a story which is just about universally accepted to be an urban myth. In an interview with *Der Spiegel* magazine, Cruise is quoted as having said, "In Scientology we have the only successful drug rehabilitation program in the world. It's called Narconon . . . It's a statistically proven fact that there is only one successful drug rehabilitation program in the world. Period." While Narconon claims to have a success rate of over 70 per cent, the accuracy of this figure has been widely disputed.

Oh, and one interesting fact. Each of Tom's three wives has been younger than the previous one by eleven years: Mimi Rogers, born 1956; Nicole Kidman, born 1967; Katie Holmes, born 1978. Actresses born in 1989, beware! DL

Mel Gibson

Not in his Right Mind

Why is Mel Gibson an asshole? Where does one begin? There were accusations of antisemitism leveled at him when his film *Passion of the Christ* was released, from observers concerned at the way in which Jewish involvement in Christ's death was depicted. When his father suggested that the Holocaust had been exaggerated, not everyone was fully convinced by Gibson's attempt to distance himself from his father's views on the subject. Mel dismissed accusations of antisemitism as nonsense, but later went on to provide a certain amount of corroborative evidence when he was pulled over for drunk-driving and started screaming about the "fucking Jews."

"Fucking Jews," Gibson is reported to have said, ". . . the Jews are responsible for all the wars in the world." He then asked the deputy who had pulled him over, "Are you a Jew?" It is rumored that the deputy was ordered by his superiors to rewrite his report, eliminating references to Gibson's bad conduct and antisemitic remarks.

Gibson himself reportedly said that he was "not in his right mind" when he made the comments. Nice work, Mel, blame the drink! Alcohol may bring out the uglier elements of one's personality, but it won't completely transform a person's political viewpoint. It's a pretty poor excuse.

Gibson is simply another rich star who believes that his power excuses him from ordinary constraints on public behavior. If he weren't a star, he wouldn't be of much concern to anyone, but the makers and shakers of Hollywood have huge power because of their money, and their access to the mythmaking media of the modern world.

There's a simple solution in a case like this. Hollywood stars need our attention to survive. So don't listen to him, don't watch his films, in the cinema, on DVD, or on television. DL

George Lucas

Jarring

George Lucas is a genius, no doubt about it. So what is he doing in this book? You can pretty much sum it up with three damning syllables: Jar Jar Binks.

The original *Star Wars* trilogy was a great cinematic achievement. It revitalized the science fiction movie, it more or less created its own genre, and it told great stories in three pieces of stunning film-making. If that was all there was to the story, Lucas would be a hero.

But the *Star Wars* films were also a malign influence on modern US cinema. The films of New Hollywood, from *Easy Rider* and *Bonnie and Clyde* to *Five Easy Pieces* and *Taxi Driver* had established a serious, adult form of cinema, with complex narratives and cinematography. Lucas' own *American Graffiti* showed that he could make intelligent films too. However, *Star Wars* – along with *Jaws* – more or less blew classy film-making out of the water. By triumphantly and unapologetically using B-Movie sensationalism and mega-budget effects, Lucas delivered the era of the blockbuster. Blockbusters had to be big, stupid, and child-like in their filmic approach. They had to appeal to the lowest common denominator in order to make the millions that their bloated budgets demanded. Ideally they had to make as much money from merchandising as from ticket receipts.

But intelligent cinema struggles on regardless, and we might have forgiven Lucas if he hadn't eventually returned with further episodes of the *Star Wars* series. From the first glimpse of Jar Jar Binks in the risible *Episode One: The Phantom Menace,* long-term *Star Wars* fans knew that Lucas had blown it, and defiled his own legacy. Jar Jar Binks wasn't the only dreadful thing about the new movie – Ewan McGregor's awful performance was one of many other embarrassments. The new films weren't entirely without merit, but after the long wait, they were a horrible, horrible disappointment. And, to add insult to injury, fans also had to get used to the sacrilege of referring to the original films as merely episodes four to six.

If Lucas ever wins one of those worthless lifetime movie awards it should be awarded by someone dressed in a giant Jar Jar Binks suit who should yell in George's face and beat him over the head with the award until he breaks down and weeps for forgiveness for besmirching his own classic series. DL

Guy Ritchie and Madonna

Mr and Mrs Madonna

They make terrible films. Well, he always makes terrible films, but they're curiously even worse than terrible when she's in them. She has bulging muscles on her forearms that make her look like an aging transvestite, and he looks like a drunken football hooligan who's run out of beer. *Swept Away* is best forgotten. When Madonna tries to act she almost always displays a weird inability to get inside the mind of a character. She can only ever be Madonna playing at acting. The result is generally absolute rubbish. Meanwhile, Ritchie's career continues to go from strength to strength. When he turned up at the premiere of *Revolver* with his wife in tow, according to London's *Extra* newspaper, the crowd booed them . . . and that was *before* the show! Apparently they were too busy to sign autographs.

They're into Kabbalah, which is some funny pseudo-Jewish religion which involves tying bits of string around one's arm. Perhaps Madonna does it to work her muscles, by trying to make the string snap when she clenches her fist. They even had a Kabbalah ceremony to renew their wedding vows four years after the original wedding. Apparently only Gwyneth Paltrow and Chris Martin turned up. No need for a free bar then.

When they're not busy tying bits of string, Madonna and Guy Ritchie like to tour the developing world looking for little children to take home with them. Sometimes this seems to lead to problems, when rumors emerge that the original family wants their child back. Still, it sounds like fun at Madonna and Guy's house. No TV, an hour of disco dancing every night, and macrobiotic food (no wheat, no dairy).

Guy is beginning to look more and more downtrodden as the media is awash with tales of Madonna's supposed control-freakery. He's often referred to as Mr Madonna. Even Christmas is controlled, with the children apparently getting only three presents each and no celebrations. What is it with these rich people? DL

Michael Moore

Partial Asshole

Michael Moore is not always an asshole. In fact, he has some good ideas and makes films which offer interesting new perspectives on his subjects. However, sometimes in his work, he is perhaps guilty of twisting the truth in small ways in his attempts to provide a balance to the distortions of the mainstream media.

Moore's 2004 film, *Fahrenheit 9/11*, criticised President George W. Bush's close connections to the family of Osama bin Laden and came up with an array of reasons why the justifications offered for invading Iraq were dishonest. Moore's film won the *Palme d'Or* at the Cannes Film Festival, although Moore's insistence that it be considered under the Best Picture and not Best Documentary meant that it was excluded from the Academy Awards. In retrospect, Moore was more right than wrong. The Iraq War was sold to the public on the basis of false claims. However his excessively confrontational stance gave his right-wing enemies a great deal of ammunition, sometimes to the point where his message became obscured. For example, Michael Moore borrowed the title to his film *Fahrenheit 9/11* from author Ray Bradbury, who, in 1953, wrote the dystopian science fiction classic *Fahrenheit 451*. Bradbury is reported to have called Moore a screwed asshole and a horrible human being, among other things. Bradbury, a well-known right-winger, apparently insisted that politics had nothing to do with it, saying that he was simply angry because Moore's movie had aped his own title. It's a typical Moore moment in that a dramatic, inflammatory move ended up detracting from the issues covered in the film. Bradbury had apparently called his publishers hoping to get Moore to explain himself, but never heard back from them.

Others blame Moore for ruining General Wesley Clark's hopes of becoming the Democrat's presidential candidate. Several US commentators have commented that Moore's support for Clark proved the kiss of death when Clark failed to distance himself from Moore's claim that George Bush had evaded military service. Moore is seen by many to have slandered the president, and Clark, by allowing him to do so, may have said goodbye to his chance to become president.

Moore's examination of gun violence and American culture's infatuation with weapons in his documentary *Bowling for Columbine* won him the Oscar for Best Documentary in 2002. The awards ceremony was just weeks before the United States' 2003 invasion of Iraq. The organizers were perhaps understandably dismayed when Moore seized the moment to deliver a lecture to the TV audience. He invited the other nominated filmmakers to accompany him to the stage, and made his acceptance speech into another Michael Moore tirade. It is at such moments that one tends to despair of Moore's timing and tact levels. He doesn't seem to know when to choose not to shove his message in people's faces, and has probably alienated more supporters than most as a result. He received for his behavior, and he even turned this into another controversy, reportedly claiming that CNN artificially boosted the volume of the booing to suit the station's political bias. It's perfectly possible that the different sound level may simply be a result of CNN's microphone being closer to the booing audience members than other station's microphones or that there is another simple explanation. But regardless, the problem caused by this kind of nitpicking is that it merely encourages his numerous critics to continue in their endless quest to find minor distortions in Moore's own films, and to use these as a stick with which to beat him.

In 2003, James Nichols, the brother of one of the Oklahoma City bombers Terry Nichols, filed a suit against Moore, alleging that he was tricked into appearing in *Bowling for Columbine*, and accusing Moore of libel, defamation of character, invasion of privacy, and intentional infliction of emotional distress. A judge dismissed the suit in July 2005. More grist to the critics' mills.

Moore's critics tend to see him as anti-American. Huge numbers of words have been devoted to deconstructing the words he's spoken on film, or to attempting to prove that certain scenes have been recreated after the fact. His critics also accuse him of setting up and editing interviews to give himself an easy victory.

And some of these criticisms may hold water. However there is very little in the way of distortion in Moore's films that isn't matched or surpassed by distortions in the mainstream media. Moore is in the business of making emotive movies, not dry legal documents. He is expressing his own views and doing so rather powerfully. Those who set out to debunk him have their own agendas, and are usually far more forgiving of those who agree with them.

For all the acres of paper and webspace that are devoted to debunking Moore, no-one has yet won a lawsuit claiming he had his facts wrong. The infuriating thing about observing him in action is that he gives his critics too much encouragement on the minor details and thus allows the big picture to become obscured. DL

Gwyneth Paltrow

The Princess

Gwyneth Paltrow? One defining memory of her is that weeping and wailing Oscar speech. The necklace she wore that night was called the "Princess" which more or less sums up her public image. There is something infuriatingly superior about her attitudes, at least as they come down to us through the media. This is an actress who never really had to graft her way to the top. She was born into an extremely well-connected Hollywood family. Her godfather Steven Spielberg cast her in her first movie. She dated Brad Pitt, which brought more media attention and boosted her career at an early stage. It wasn't the hardest road to stardom.

Possibly the most irritating thing about Paltrow is the contrast between her claims about her life and the reality we see. She moans about the pressures of fame, but appears on a string of magazine covers. That tearful, rambling Oscar acceptance speech only went to drive home the point that she cares a great deal about her career.

Here is a woman who complains constantly about the intrusive press but seems ever-ready to strike a pose for *Vogue* or *Vanity Fair*. She is also someone who seems to have a sense of her own supreme importance. The story that she had demanded (and failed to get) a five-mile exclusion around her villa on the Mediterranean island of Mallorca did nothing to contradict this perception.

Paltrow speaks with the air of a serious actress who thinks deeply about her artistic choices. But coming from a wealthy Hollywood family means that she achieved this luxury the easy way rather than working her way up to it as an achievement.

She is teetotal and has expressed distaste for seeing drunken women, which in itself is somewhat of a condescending attitude. But she has also made adverts for Martini Rosso. She dislikes intrusions into her private life. But she made the film *Sylvia*, (about the poet Sylvia Plath) in spite of Plath's sister making a plea for the film not to be made. One value for me, a different value for everyone else?

Paltrow also insulted working mums everywhere by expressing her disapproval of going back to work after having a child. Apart from the fact that this is easy for an extremely rich woman to say, it seemed that princess Gwyneth was going to devote her life to caring for her daughter, Apple. Her resolve only lasted eight months before she agreed to appear in *Running With Scissors* alongside Annette Beining, presumably as she came to realize that sitting languidly around on a film set is a much easier task than full-time, unassisted parenting.

An insipid, simpering hypocrite. DL

Roman Polanski

High-Profile Fugitive

Possibly the most despicable kind of "asshole" is someone who has been wronged deeply by others, but who, rather than choosing not to engage in any form of abusive act resembling his own mistreatment, instead uses the ordeal as a justification to commit abuse himself. Film-maker Roman Polanski certainly seems to fit such a description. As both a young survivor of the Holocaust and a man who lost his pregnant wife, Sharon Tate, to a Manson Family murder spree, he would probably have received greater public sympathy, had he not chosen arbitrarily to victimize an adolescent girl, for no reason other than his personal gratification, and then to flee the ensuing legal charges to live as Hollywood's most notorious fugitive. In fact, it is these actions alone that make Polanski the infamous figure he is still considered by many to be, second only to Woody Allen as a predatory transgressor, who is still regarded with mixed feelings, due to his previous and ongoing work as a film-maker.

Polanski was born a Jew in Poland, shortly before the Nazi invasion and occupation of that ill-fated country, which was swiftly followed by attempts to exterminate the Jewish population. During the early days of the occupation, members of his family were sent to separate concentration camps, while the young Polanski lived out the conflict in hiding, working under rough conditions, as a farmhand for sympathetic fellow Poles. By the time the conflict ended, he had lost both his sister and his mother in concentration camps and seen his father all but destroyed by his internment.

The horrors of this extreme injustice were not lost on the young Polanski and, in many respects, influenced his later film career, as he tried to make sense of the human capacity for treachery and evil, and the often devastating effects of such choices on all concerned. Even his earliest efforts as a fledging film-maker, first in Poland, and then in England, were concerned with characters making questionable choices, with profound consequences for themselves, as well as for the often unwitting victims of such frequently underhanded choices, or transgressions with dark motivations. With his unflinchingly direct visual style, Polanski was soon considered an edgy and innovative talent, openly embraced as an up-and-coming maverick on his eventual arrival in Hollywood in the spring of 1968, with his new bride, the actress Sharon Tate.

His first US film, the horror movie *Rosemary's Baby*, was both a critical and commercial success, for its disturbing depiction of a naïve young woman deceived and betrayed by a Satanic cult with a blasphemous hidden agenda. It earned Polanski his second career Oscar nomination, and served as an almost darkly ironic counterpoint to events which were to occur a year later.

In August 1969, the pregnant Sharon Tate, and four of her and Polanski's friends, were murdered by members of the Manson Family in a particularly horrifying and bizarre fashion. The attack had been intended for the former occupant of the house, Terry Melcher, a record producer who had declined to record the music of cult leader Charles Manson. In revenge, Manson had ordered his followers to go to what he believed to be Melcher's current address, and "kill everyone there," and his followers had done so with utter savagery, not even sparing the life of a pleading pregnant woman.

Polanski was in the United Kingdom at the time of the killings, and was immediately questioned by police on his rapid return to Los Angeles. As there were no other likely suspects at the time, Polanski was subjected to extremely close scrutiny by the LAPD, but was ultimately eliminated as a suspect due to a lack of motive and having been abroad at the time of the grisly and sensational crime. When Manson and company were later arrested on unrelated charges and linked to the mass murder, Polanski returned to Europe, having given away all possessions that he said reminded him of Tate. He would later say that his greatest regret in life was not having been at home with his pregnant wife on the night of the attack.

Through the 1970s, Polanski released four films, noteworthy both for their technical skill, and their dark subject matter. *Chinatown*, Polanski's third film, was nominated for eleven academy awards and won the Oscar for Best Original Screenplay. While that film, as well as Polanski's subsequent works, is notable for its violent and disturbing content, such on-screen depictions would, in some ways, pale by comparison with the real-life actions of the by now celebrated director, shortly thereafter.

In 1977, Polanski became embroiled in a scandal involving his alleged drugging and rape of a 13-year-old girl he had been contracted to photograph, for an upcoming edition of French *Vogue* magazine. The initial shoot was said to be unremarkable, until the director asked the model to change her outfit in front of him. While she agreed, she later said, in a 2003 interview that she hadn't felt that such behavior was appropriate, and that it had made her very uneasy about posing for a second photo shoot, which was supposedly necessary to complete the project. Her unease would prove to be well founded.

That second shoot, on 10 March 1977, was a series of photos of the clearly underage girl drinking champagne. At some point during the shoot, the model claimed to have realized Polanski's less than professional intentions for the meeting, but had had no idea, due to her inexperience in such matters, of how to extricate herself from an increasingly uncomfortable situation. What she also didn't know was that the champagne had been spiked with Quaaludes, a powerful sedative, and, after the drug took effect, Polanski is alleged to have raped her.

When arrested by the police following the incident, Polanski was charged with rape by use of drugs, furnishing a controlled substance to a minor, and committing a lewd and lascivious act upon a child under the age of 14. He eventually plea bargained these crimes down to a single charge of unlawful sexual intercourse with a minor, a significantly lesser charge. However, unwilling to face even this lesser charge, Polanski instead chose to flee the United States, seeking refuge in France, where he retained citizenship.

To be fair, Polanski's version of events at the time, later recounted in his autobiography, were, and are, decidedly different from those of the court and public record. He claimed that the infamous modeling shoot had been part of a "casting couch" blackmail scheme orchestrated by the girl's mother. He further claimed that his flight to avoid prosecution had been spurred by an anonymous tip-off, that the judge presiding in the case had decided to disregard his plea agreement, and was planning on sentencing him according to the original indictment, which could have resulted in a sentence of up to 50 years in prison. In the light of such "unfair" treatment, he claimed that he had had no choice but to become a fugitive, specifically to France, in part because of that country's unwillingness to extradite its citizens for crimes committed in other jurisdictions.

Over thirty years have passed since the ill-fated and "illuminating" photo shoot, and in that time, both the suffering of the victim and the nature of the perpetrator's crime have largely passed from public consciousness. Because of the relatively minor nature of the charge from which Polanski is supposed to have fled, many members of the public still believe that the nature of the actual crime was "simple" statutory rape, perceived by most to be a crime of poor judgment, rather than deception or force. Since then, Polanski has made a number of films, several of which have gained either critical acclaim or awards from either the Cannes Film Festival or the Academy of Motion Picture Arts and Sciences, the governing body behind the Oscars, or both, signaling that much of the professional film-making community has forgiven or forgotten the film-maker's brush with the law and his international flight to escape justice.

In fact, his 2002 awards at both the Cannes Film Festival and the Academy Awards, for the film *The Pianist,* might have been what broke the longstanding, and almost anonymous silence of his former "alleged" victim. In a 2003 interview, the woman in question, by then in her early forties and identified as Samantha Geimer, reiterated her story in detail, along with its aftermath for her and her family, as well as offering candid insights into both Polanski, and the incident itself. To her credit, Ms Geimer claimed to have "moved on" from the attack, but was disappointed by Polanski's inability to deal with its consequences and accept some responsibility for his actions. In a powerful display of forgiveness, she further asserted that she felt Polanski probably would not have done the same thing again, if he were capable of going back to that point in time, and has paid for any mistake he may have made back then, presumably in terms of what the incident has cost his reputation and career. Clearly, such statements are far more of a testament to the psychological resilience and basic decency of the victim than any reflection on the seemingly remorseless character of her former perpetrator.

It is uncertain what the future holds for the besmirched director. While many still hail his film work as original, intense, and even groundbreaking, there remains an equally loyal group of feminists and victims' rights advocates who view him as a successful and high-profile fugitive from justice. While he will undoubtedly continue to make works of art that challenge our perceptions of human behavior, it is almost equally indubitable that he will never challenge his own

Sporting Assholes

Tonya Harding

Fallen Angel

Tonya Harding is quite possibly the most controversial athlete the sport of figure skating has ever produced. While even her detractors would admit that she was one of the strongest "jumpers" and "spinners" so far witnessed in the sport, her unpolished personal style, inconsistent performances, and aggressive demeanor towards competitors made her a controversial performer, and may, ultimately, have come together in a shocking manner to end her career. Still, love her or hate her, one has to acknowledge that she generated more publicity for the sport of figure skating than any other performer to date, even if it was for some of the worst reasons, and showed the sport in the worst possible light.

Harding was born into a blue-collar family in Portland, Oregon, and began skating at an early age. Despite being asthmatic, she was a strong, natural performer who landed her first triple Lutz at the age of 12. Her talent was strongly supported by her mother, Lavona, who sewed many of her daughter's first costumes, and supported her decision to leave high school during her sophomore year, when she had already been invited to take part in international skating competitions. While a little rough around the edges, no one could deny the powerful, raw talent which Tonya Harding brought to the rink.

During the 1980s, Harding improved gradually, but steadily, as a skater in competitions on the national level. She took sixth place in the 1986 US Championships, her debut year, fifth in 1987 and 1988, and third in 1989. However, it was the turn that her career took in the 1990s that was to make her notorious.

In 1990 itself, Tonya did poorly, finishing seventh at the US Championship, due to flu exacerbated by her asthma. It was at this time that she married Jeff Gillooly, who was to be an important element in the controversies that were to dog Tonya through the 1990s and beyond.

Tonya experienced something of a reversal of fortune in 1991, when she landed her first triple Axel at the US Championships, garnering her first 6.0 score of her career, and taking second place behind Kristi Yamaguchi. This was the second triple Axel ever landed by a woman, and the first by a US competitor. She completed two triple Axels at the Skate America competition that same year, and, in a later competition, she set a world record by combining a triple Axel with a double toe loop. However, 1991 was to prove the climax of her career, for she would never again land a triple Axel in competition again.

In 1992, Tanya came third at the US Championships, after twisting her ankle during practice, and fourth at the Winter Olympics that same year. Even worse, she only took sixth place at the 1992 World Championships, despite a weak field of competitors. No one could have known this at the time, but Tonya was at the beginning of a downward spiral.

During the 1993 regional qualifying competition for the US Championships, someone telephoned in a bomb threat against Tonya to the organizing committee, which excused her from that competition. In a later round, during her short program, she asked to be allowed to start over when her dress became unhooked. At that year's Skate America competition she stopped midway through her free skate, complaining of a loose blade, and resumed skating only after an examination by a skate technician. However unusual, petty, or annoying these incidents may have been, they were to prove as nothing compared with what happened next.

On 6 January 1994, at a practice session for that year's US Championships, a masked assailant struck rival skater Nancy Kerrigan on the knee with a metal pipe, injuring her, preventing her from taking part in that competition, and making it unlikely that Kerrigan would compete in the Winter Olympics at Lillehammer later that year. Within days, the investigation into the attack led to one Shane Stant, who confessed that he had been hired by Harding's now ex-husband, Jeff Gillooly, and friend, Shawn Eckhardt, to attack and injure Kerrigan to improve Tonya's chances at the US Championships. Funnily enough, Tonya ended up "winning" more or less guaranteeing herself a place on 1994 US Olympic Team. While Harding admitted

Tonya Harding* 213

to having helped to cover up the attack on Kerrigan, she maintained that she was innocent of having helped to plan it, and, when threatened with expulsion from the Olympic Team, she threatened legal action, thus retaining her place on the team.

The sensational nature of the story drew more publicity to the Olympic Figure Skating event and the two skaters involved than anything the public had ever seen. Tonya made the cover of both *Time* and *Newsweek*, and reporters and news crews attended her practices in Portland, as well as camping out in front of Kerrigan's home. CBS assigned Connie Chung to follow Tonya's every move at Lillehammer, and over 400 press members routinely thronged the practice rink, speculating on the rivalry, as well as the likely winner of the actual competition. When it was finally all over, Tonya had finished eighth, Nancy second, and the ratings for the female figure skating event at the Winter Olympics had never been higher.

On 1 February 1994, Jeff Gillooly accepted a plea bargain in exchange for his testimony against Harding. To avoid the further prosecution in which this new testimony would result, as well as the likelihood of a jail sentence, Tonya pleaded guilty to having hindered the investigation into the attack. She was sentenced to three years' probation, 500 hours of community service, and a $160,000 fine. Strangely, she continued to maintain that she had played no role in planning the attack, despite the testimony of all the other conspirators, and even went as far as to get an angel tattooed on her back, to symbolize her innocence.

The United States Figure Skating Association (USFSA) was apparently unimpressed, however, and, after conducting its own investigation, stripped Tonya of her 1994 win, banned her for life from all the association's sanctioned events, and even banned her from coaching. As part of her plea bargain agreement she had already resigned from the USFSA, and had given up her spot on the team for that year's World Championships. However, it was clear that the association was making its opinion of Tonya Harding known to the entire skating community and was effectively banning her from participating in anything that could be construed as the "pro skating circuit." Harding's career as a figure skater was now officially over, even as the sport enjoyed a vastly increased audience, created, ironically, by the misdeeds for which she had just been thoroughly punished. One had to wonder what, if anything, might follow.

Shortly after the close of the scandal, in the spring of 1994, Jeff Gillooly sold an X-rated video of their wedding night to a tabloid TV show. Approximately six months later, stills from the video ended up in the September edition of *Penthouse* magazine, as well as copies of the tape itself. Tonya attempted to defend herself by saying that she had been "drunk as a skunk" at the time.

For the remainder of the 1990s, little more was heard about Tonya, apart from the occasional "human interest story," which usually dealt with strange run-ins with law enforcement agencies. In May 1995, Harding claimed that she was being stalked by professional golfers which somehow resulted in a car chase involving Harding, Gillooly, and the police. In February 1997, during the opening weekend of the US Figure Skating Championships, Tonya claimed that she had been abducted at knifepoint by an unknown assailant, and had escaped by crashing her truck into a tree and running into the nearby woods. Oddly though, the most poetically just incident occurred on 6 January 2000, when, six years exactly after the attack on Nancy Kerrigan, Tonya lost control of her truck, landing in a ditch. She and an unidentified male companion were then alleged to have threatened a press photographer who had been summoned to the scene of the crash to cover the story.

Such incidents may well have prompted Tonya to take the bold decision in 2002 to fight against Paula Jones in a Fox TV Celebrity Boxing Match, which she won easily. Her victory must have struck a chord within her, as, in 2003, she officially became a professional female boxer. Despite losing a fourth-round split decision to Samantha Browning as part of a warm-up bout at the Tyson–Etienne fight that year, Tonya soldiered on, winning her next three bouts by unanimous decisions. But after a first-round TKO loss to Melissa Yanas in August 2003, she began to get up to her old tricks, canceling a fight six months later due to "death threats." Her last known fight was on 25 June 2004 against Amy Johnson, who beat her in the third round with a TKO, though Tonya protested the decision.

After this brief stint in the world of professional pugilism, Tonya chose to retire, blaming her asthma. One can't help but wonder if, with suitable medication, she would be willing to consider taking part in professional wrestling, where insane levels of aggression, treachery, and erratic, lowbrow behavior are not only welcomed, but celebrated. Failing that, there is always the Roller Derby. KD

Vince McMahon Jr

Winner Stays Employed

The "sport" of professional wrestling, due to its heavy dependence on television ratings, and the carefully drafted plotlines that guarantee victory or defeat, is at least as much about theater and spectacle as it is about any kind of athletic contest. As a result, the unique "sports entertainment" genre is dependent on aggressive media promotion of its "championship matches," and the ongoing feuds between "babyfaces" (heroes) and "heels" (villains) that build the audience anticipation for such pay-per-view cable television contests. These are often based on escalating, outrageous behavior on the part of the combatants, leading up to their well-publicized "day of reckoning." Though hated by many wrestling fans and industry competitors, nobody understands this formula better than so-called World Wrestling Entertainment Chairman, Vince McMahon Jr.

Vince Jr grew up in North Carolina, living with his mother and a series of stepfathers. Vince McMahon Sr had divorced Vince's mother when his son was still a baby, and moved north to start a wrestling "territory." The younger McMahon later claimed in interviews that his upbringing was marked by serial episodes of child abuse and domestic violence that left him with some powerful grudges against the men responsible. When later reunited with his father around the age of 12, it is likely that Vince Jr directed much of his accumulated anger into following his father's footsteps into the world of professional wrestling.

While Vince Jr graduated from East Carolina University with a business degree in 1968, he made no serious attempt at any other career, and soon assumed a managerial role in his father's wrestling "territory," the World Wide Wrestling Federation. The sport was divided into regional territories in those days, and the McMahons owned the "promotion" that covered New England and New York State, supported by a series of touring matches, with major "plot points" being saved for weekly televised matches. After sending Vince Jr to work as a ring announcer for a smaller "farm league" territory in

Maine, the elder McMahon put him to work later that year as the lead ring announcer for the entire franchise in 1971.

During the 1970s, Vince Jr became a powerful behind-the-scenes player within his father's company, first renaming it the World Wrestling Federation (WWF), and then taking aggressive steps to secure ever greater broadcast media exposure, and equally aggressively recruiting "talent" to justify such exposure. By the time of Vince Sr's retirement in 1979, his son had purchased the Cape Cod Coliseum as a permanent venue for the company. With the purchase of the senior McMahon's unaffiliated Capitol Wrestling Company in 1982, Vince Jr, along with his wife Linda, turned the WWF into one of the most popular and profitable professional sports "brands" of the 1980s.

One of Vince's first acts as Chairman of the WWF was to secede from the National Wrestling Alliance (NWA), a longstanding governing body that oversaw all the various regional territories and promotions throughout the United States, and tried to ensure professional and fair standards of conduct between them. Following secession, McMahon wasted no time in luring popular performers away from smaller pro-motions using the promise of greater media exposure and better salaries. These shrewd business moves together with a promotional style that focused more on characters, back story, and plot lines and which was less dependant on sensationally violent acts than many other franchises of that time. This combination produced a markedly more family-friendly product which lead to phenomenal commercial and media success, creating what many within the WWF organization would later call the "Golden Age of Wrestling."

The two factors which probably had the most to do with the runaway success of the WWF at that time were its association with the fledgling MTV cable TV channel, which linked the sport with pop music, and the use of pay-per-view cable to hold "championship" events within the increasingly popular "sport." The popularity of the new "national territory" within pop culture seemed to peak in 1987, when Wrestlemania III drew 100,000 people to the Pontiac Silverdome, setting a World Record for attendance at an indoor sporting event. The much anticipated main event was a fight between "Hollywood" Hulk Hogan and Andre the Giant, which offered seemingly irresistible viewing to millions of couch-dwelling Americans. In 1988, however, Vince made the controversial decision to admit that pro wrestling was "fake," as entertainment events are taxed less heavily than sporting events, and coined the term "sports entertainment" to describe the WWF's unique form of public spectacle. The result was a mass defection by many of its established performers, to the recently created World Championship Wrestling (WCW) franchise of Turner Broadcasting. These included wrestlers with any kind of grievance against WWF management, or who wanted to preserve the publicly espoused myth that professional wrestling was in any sense "real."

As a result, the 1990s were a period of turmoil and transition for the WWF, and its increasingly embattled chairman. The low point was probably 1994, when McMahon battled allegations that he was encouraging the use of steroids, and distributing them to WWF performers, having already been publicly accused of sexual harassment by a female former referee, Rita Chatterton, in 1992. It seemed unlikely at the time that the formerly family-friendly WWF could continue to maintain a squeaky-clean public image in the light of such increasingly negative publicity, and attendant dwindling ratings. Rather than denying the controversy, McMahon instead embraced it, bringing about the birth of what came to be called "WWF attitude."

In 1996, the new, harsher promotional style truly began to make its presence felt, through the WWF's acquisition of controversial new performers, increasingly violent matches, and more elaborate and sordid plot lines to drive the action. McMahon himself altered his public persona, from mild-mannered ring announcer and com-mentator, to the Machiavellian "Mr McMahon," a particularly unscrupulous adversary for rising redneck icon, and WWF "superstar," "Stone Cold" Steve Austin. The feud between the two, together with burgeoning numbers of scantily clad women, and increasingly violent pay-per-view matches, translated into even greater commercial success than the "Golden Age" of family-friendly fare, in the form of the highest television ratings the sport had ever seen, and the steady erosion of WCW fans, who were defecting from a promotion which was seen as increasingly outdated and stale.

The drip-feed of defection came to an end in March 2001, when McMahon purchased the beleaguered WCW for a mere $5 million, and promptly liquidated it, swelling the ranks of WWF performers to previously unheard of levels for a pro wrestling franchise. This was understandable given that the WWF had become the only game in town for that kind of performer. McMahon used the summer season following his acquisition to stage a kind of WWF "civil war" between loyal members of the WWF, led, naturally enough, by their Chairman, and members of the so-called WCW/ECW Alliance, which comprised disgruntled members of both defunct promotions, now supposedly bent on revenge. The drama peaked at that year's WWF Survivor Series pay-per-view, in a series of "winner stays employed" matches. Following each match, the loser would be publicly ridiculed and degraded by McMahon in follow-up episodes of regular WWF broadcasts, in exchange for keeping their jobs, especially if they were very popular with the public, and/or an attractive female performer. As if the public didn't already know, Vince seemed keen to tell them that it was indeed good to be Mr McMahon.

This success was substantially altered, but not immediately diminished by two events that occurred shortly afterwards. The first was the terrorist attacks of 9/11, which directed the overtly macho fan base of the WWF in a rabidly patriotic and pro-war direction, which resulted in United Service Organizations (USO) appearances by WWF superstars, and the creation of pro-military and pro-American performers in response to public demand. The second was the company's name itself, when it lost a trademark infringement suit brought by the World Wildlife Federation, which had laid public claim to the WWF initials at the beginning of 2002. The newly rebranded World Wrestling Entertainment, however, was largely undeterred by these developments, having been zealously embraced by flag-waving supporters of the recently declared "War on Terror."

As the new millennium wore on, however, wrestling itself saw its dominance of ratings in combat sports increasingly eroded by the rise of so-called Mixed Martial Arts competitions, which were full-contact, unscripted hand-to-hand combats, with very few rules to restrict the combatants. By 2005, the Ultimate Fighting Championship franchise was routinely "outdrawing" WWE viewing figures by a margin of almost two to one, despite increasingly "shocking" plotlines in the wrestling format.

McMahon attempted to combat this ratings slide by re-releasing a "rebranded" Extreme Championship Wrestling (a small franchise noted for its ultraviolent "hardcore" matches before it was taken over by the WWF). He further entangled himself in plot lines involving both a paternity suit, and an assassination attempt, and invited Donald Trump to make a guest appearance at Wrestlemania 23, for a Hair vs Hair match, after the two had feuded on air for a few weeks over who had trademarked the phrase "You're fired!" The results have not been impressive: an increase in WWE-related banner ads on MySpace; the rise of octagonal-ring sporting wrestling franchise Total Nonstop Action (TNA) Impact on Spike TV; and a bald, embarrassed-looking "Mr McMahon." KD

Performance-Enhancing Drug Cheats

Stanozolol, Dianabol, Cypionate, and Furzabol

While the use of substances to enhance athletic performance used to be a relatively rare phenomenon, conjuring up, for example, images of suspiciously masculine Eastern European female Olympians in the minds of many, there has been a significant increase in the use of such chemicals, as shown by scandals in just about every form of organized professional or international sport. While numerous regulating bodies and policies have been put in place to screen for the use of drugs in general, only 78 of 797 known instances of athletes testing positive for controlled substances were for illicit recreational drugs, such as marijuana, cocaine, heroin, or ecstasy. The remaining 719 cases were all related to the use of chemicals, the sole purpose of which was to give their user an unfair competitive edge in world championship events, or to aid them in setting world records of dubious merit, in order to win lucrative professional contracts or celebrity endorsement deals by means of these questionable accomplishments. An overview of some of the more notable scandals provides disturbing proof of such deliberate misconduct.

• Testosterone injections are suspected by many of having been a significant factor in the World Weightlifting Championships of

1954, in which Soviet athletes won the majority of the gold medals on offer for different weight classes, and broke numerous world records.

- Dr John Ziegler, US team coach for the 1954 World Weightlifting Championships, began to administer Dianabol steroid tablets to his team in the early 1960s, which resulted in the US team dominating the 1962 World Championships.

- In 1967, cyclist Tom Simpson collapsed during the Tour de France, and died en route to the hospital. Two tubes of amphetamines were found in his racing jersey.

- Canadian sprinter Ben Johnson was stripped of his medal and his world record in the 1988 Summer Olympic Games in Seoul, South Korea, when his urine tested positive for Stanozolol. He later admitted to using Dianabol, Cypionate, Furzabol, and human growth hormone as part of his "training regimen."

- In 1998, the entire Festina cycling team was excluded from the Tour de France, following the discovery of large amounts of various performance-enhancing drugs in a team car by race officials. When the team's director admitted to routinely giving his team these kinds of chemicals as part of their "conditioning," six other teams pulled out in protest, including the Dutch TVM team, which was still being questioned by the French police. Tour winner Marco Pantini was later stripped of his title for failing a drug test.

- It was later admitted that four members of Lance Armstrong's 1999 Tour de France team had used the so-called "blood doping" drug EPO, to improve their cardiovascular performance in the endurance-oriented race. While Armstrong himself was never implicated by the four team members in question, these kinds of allegations about many of his team mates have lead to widespread speculation about whether or not the record-setting, seven-times Tour winner may have used similar substances in achieving his victories. So far, however, he has never been officially implicated in any wrongdoing.

- In 2001, six members of the Finnish Cross-Country Skiing Team were disqualified for having taken a blood plasma expander at the FIS Nordic World Ski Championships in Lahti, Finland.

- At the 2002 Winter Olympic Games in Salt Lake City, Johann Muhlegg of Spain, and Olga Danilova and Larisa Lazutina were all stripped of their medals when they tested positive for banned substances.

- The 2003 World Track and Field Championships were marred by numerous contestants testing positive for Modafinil including Kelli White, Sandra Glover, Eric Thomas, Calvin Harrison, Chris Phillips, and Chryste Gaines, many of whom had been medalists at the 2000 Olympic Summer Games on behalf of the United States. Several more, including Regina Jacobs, Kevin Toth, and John McEwan tested positive for the steroid THG.

- Four members of the Oakland Raiders 2003 team, Bill Romanowski, Dana Stubblefield, Chris Cooper, and Barrett Robbins all tested positive for Tetrohydrogestrinone (THG) without any major disciplinary action being taken by the National Football League, even though the team made it all the way to the Superbowl that year. It is probably due to the fact that they did not win the critical championship game that there has been no official League action in this case.

- Also in 2003, Oakland Giants home-run slugger Barry Bonds testified before a federal grand jury, having been granted full immunity from prosecution, concerning allegations that he had used steroids, and was connected to alleged steroid manufacturer Bay Area Laboratory Co-operative (BALCO) through his trainer, Greg Anderson. But Bonds's testimony was evasive, or carefully worded, and he denied that he had ever knowingly accepted, used, or been treated with steroids by Anderson. This testimony later formed the basis of a federal indictment for perjury and obstruction of justice in November 2007.

- In July 2005, the founders of BALCO pleaded guilty to steroid distribution and money-laundering charges, implicating former clients Dwain Chambers, Marion Jones, Tim Montgomery, C. J. Hunter,

Barry Bonds, Jason Giambi, Gary Sheffield and numerous Oakland Raiders in exchange for leniency in their own sentencing.

- In April 2006, US Olympic and World 100-meter champion Justin Gatlin tested positive for the first known instance of the use of a topical steroid cream, rather than the previously more widespread use of injections, which, according to scientific experts, explained why his use of steroids had previously gone undetected.

- In the summer of 2006, Spanish police arrested five people with links to the Liberty Seguros cycling team, on charges that they were orchestrating a massive blood-doping scheme to ensure a team victory in the upcoming Tour de France. Several other cyclists connected with the the team dropped out of the upcoming Tour as a result.

- Less than a week after the 2006 Tour de France, the winner, Floyd Landis, tested positive for elevated levels of testosterone consistent with steroid use, after his stunning stage 17 victory. While secondary testing also concluded that there was evidence of steroid use, Landis was not immediately stripped of his title.

- On 25 May 2007, the 1996 Tour de France winner, Bjarne Riis of Denmark admitted to using Erythropoietin (EPO) from 1993 until 1998, including the period spanning his winning tour. He also admitted using human growth hormone, following similar admissions by four former team mates the previous day. To his credit, Riis offered to "return" his 1996 victory.

- The 2007 Tour de France seemed to set new records for "doping" charges during an international sporting event, with the following multiple scandals:

  - German rider Patrik Sinkewitz pulled out after a stage 8 crash, shortly after it was discovered that he had tested positive for elevated testosterone consistent with steroid use, prompting a criminal investigation of the cyclist in his native Germany.

  - Alexander Vinokourov of Kazakhstan was forced to leave the race after he tested positive for an illegal blood transfusion after winning stage 13.

- Italian cyclist Cristian Moreni tested positive for testosterone after stage 11, and when the results were announced to the press following stage 16, he and his entire Cofidis team left the Tour in protest, though Moreni has never publicly disputed the accuracy of the positive test.

- Michael Rasmussen of Denmark was pulled by his Rabobank team after stage 16, for violating his team rules by lying about his pre-tour training, and missing two preliminary drug-screening tests. He had already been thrown off the Danish National Cycling team because he was suspected of illegal drug use.

- Near the end of the tour, Iban Mayo was the final rider to leave the event in disgrace, having tested positive for EPO.

- In December 2007, the California State Athletic Commission announced that both competitors in Ultimate Fight Championship 73, Sean Sherk and Hermes Franca, had tested positive for banned substances, during routine post-fight testing following their Lightweight Title fight. Both fighters were suspended from competing in the state of California until June 2008, though Sherk filed for an extension to appeal against the charges.

- On 5 October 2007, multiple Olympic and World Championship gold medalist Marion Jones pleaded guilty to lying to federal agents about her use of steroids prior to her record-breaking races at the 2000 Summer Olympic games. She voluntarily returned all her medals from the 2000 games, and the International Association of Athletics Federations (IAAF) voided all Jones' World Championship results from the year 2000.

- In February 2008, veteran Major League Baseball pitcher Roger Clemens appeared before a Senate sub-committee to testify to his use of steroids and human growth hormone. Clemens had been named 82 times in the recently released Mitchell Report on performance-enhancing drugs in Major League Baseball. Despite the contradictory testimony by his former New York Yankees trainer, Brian MacNamee, who had already admitted under oath that he had personally injected Clemens with both kinds of illegal drugs, Clemens flatly and consistently denied ever using either substance, both before and following his questionable public testimony.

While there is no question that such incidents are a blight on organized sport, and there is as little doubt that such incidents are likely to occur more frequently as time goes by. As ever-increasing salaries and commercial endorsement contracts make success as a sports star increasingly lucrative, the pressure for outstanding physical prowess will also increase, from those who provide such funding to the fortunate few in the quest for ever greater corporate profits, and global reach. It is easy to see the taking of performance-enhancing drugs as simply a question of human nature under great pressure, resulting in many otherwise talented and hard-working athletes being willing to risk their health and personal honor as competitors in misguided attempts to guarantee success and acclaim. Meanwhile, great efforts are being made to improve testing procedures, while new forms of cheating continue covertly to evolve, in a technological competition every bit as intense as anything taking place on sportsfields, courses, and tracks around the world, and of infinitely greater importance in determining the true champions of today. A sad, but true, state of affairs. KD

Pete Rose

Gamblin' Rose, Why you Gamble, no one Knows

Pete Rose is probably the "nicest" person in this entire volume. In fact, compared to many of the scandal-prone professional baseball players who are his peers, he seems almost out of place, having, to the best of anyone's knowledge, never used performance-enhancing drugs; never abused alcohol or illegal drugs; never abused or openly cheated on his wife; never been caught driving under the influence; never become involved in random fistfights; never made racially offensive remarks in front of a broadcast audience; and never demanded the equivalent of the national debt of Liberia for a salary. His reputation as a tenacious, adaptable, and, most amazingly by today's standards, *loyal* infielder with the Cincinnati Red Sox had, in fact, all but guaranteed him a place in professional baseball's Hall of Fame. It was a single, but professionally fatal, defect of character, and Rose's inability to be honest about it with the sport's fans that proved to be the undoing of an otherwise exemplary and impressive career, and, to some extent, the man behind it.

Unlike many of today's professional players, Pete Rose was born and raised in the town he later played for. In fact, it was obviously his intention early in his career to stay with the Reds for as long as he possibly could. He joined the team on Opening Day of 1963, following a three-year stint in minor league baseball, and remained with Cincinnati until a free agency in 1979 finally drew him away from his home town, for the remaining five years of his playing career. During that career, he proved himself to be a formidable "contact hitter," with a lifetime batting average of .303, and a quick and determined infielder, who earned the nickname "Charlie Hustle." Rose earned career records for the most "hits" and most "outs" of any professional player at the time. Not content to remain idle following his retirement as a player, he returned to Cincinnati following his 1984 season with the Montreal Expos, as the manager of his much-loved Reds.

Rose's tenure as manager of the Cincinnati team, like his time as a player, was also moderately successful, with his four full seasons as manager coinciding with four second place finishes in the National League's West division. Apart from a dispute with an umpire over an alleged bad call that earned him a 30-day suspension in 1988, Rose was an uncontroversial and hard-working figure during this time. All of this was in total contrast to the allegations about "Mr Baseball" that surfaced during the 1989 off-season.

In February that year, outgoing Baseball Commissioner Peter Uberoth questioned Rose about a number of reports and rumors that he had placed bets on professional baseball games. Given the betting scandals that had occurred during the earliest days of the professional version of the sport, the regulating body of Major League Baseball has a zero-tolerance approach to any coaches, players, or managers being involved in any kind of betting related to the sport, especially through professional bookmakers, whose links to organized crime in the United States were, and are, well established. Still, given Rose's reputation for integrity, and his clear love for both his team and his sport, Uberoth gave him the benefit of the doubt when Pete denied all the allegations.

Uberoth, who retired three days later, did not have the final word on the matter, however. The incoming commissioner, Bart Giamatti, retained private counsel, attorney John Dowd, to investigate the validity of the claims that Rose had bet on baseball. The scandal reached the attention of the public in a *Sports Illustrated* cover story on 21 March.

Dowd's thorough investigation of Rose's known associates, as well as numerous bookies and bet runners, formed the basis of a report presented to the commissioner's office in May. The document alleged that Rose had been an avid sports gambler between 1985 and 1987, placing bets on 52 Reds games, spending as much as $10,000 a day on his activities. While damaging to Rose's reputation, Dowd made the favorable point that Rose had never bet *against* his own team, and as such, had probably never taken any actions to sabotage, or otherwise unduly influence the Reds to do anything but win. This distinction, while significant, did little to neutralize the serious nature of Rose's misdemeanors in the eyes of the commissioner's office.

Meanwhile, Rose, despite well-documented evidence to the contrary, continued flatly to deny all allegations of gambling, and refused to appear at a hearing with Giamatti concerning the charges against him. He even went so far as to file a lawsuit against the commissioner's office, claiming Giamatti had prejudged the case against him, and, as such, he was unable to get a fair hearing. A sympathetic Cincinnati judge aided Rose's efforts by issuing a restraining order to delay any further hearings, but Giamatti successfully fought to have the case moved to the Federal Court, which pushed Rose and his attorneys to settle the case out of court.

On 24 August 1989, it was formally announced that Rose had voluntarily accepted a permanent place on Professional Baseball's ineligibility list, and publicly acknowledged the factual basis for the ban. In return, Major League Baseball agreed not to make any formal finding regarding the gambling allegations against Rose, nor to take other legal action. Rose was immediately replaced as Reds manager by Tommy Helms, and soon began psychiatric therapy for his gambling addiction.

As if Pete Rose did not have enough legal troubles at the time, he soon compounded them, when he pleaded guilty to tax evasion charges the following spring, in 1990. His conviction was based on proven allegations that he had falsified his tax returns by not claiming income he had received from selling autographs and memorabilia, as well as his winnings from horse racing. Following his conviction, he served a five-month federal sentence in the US penitentiary at Marion, Illinois, and paid a $50,000 fine in addition to the $366,041 he owed in unpaid taxes. He received further bad news a month after his release from prison, when on 4 February 1991, the presiding body of the Baseball Hall of Fame voted to formally exclude from induction any individuals who were also on the permanently ineligible list.

The move came as an unwelcome shock to Rose, whose name was the only one on the list, and he had agreed to be listed, partly because he had believed it would *not* effect his eligibility for Hall of Fame status. With the passing of the new bylaw, this most positive aspect of Rose's baseball legacy was denied to him, but he did not accept its loss as final. He applied to newly appointed commissioner Fay Vincent for reinstatement to Major League Baseball in 1992, but Vincent opted to take no action on the application. Rose then applied to Bud Selig on his appointment as commissioner in 1997. So far Selig has concurred with his predecessors and granted Rose no relief.

On the other hand, not all members of the public have taken such an uncompromising stance. When Rose made use of his controversial celebrity to participate in 1998 Wrestlemania XIV as a "guest ring announcer," he received many more cheers than boos during his entrance, and, as a result, found the "fake" professional sport of wrestling a safe haven for future public appearances, in the form of return cameos, during pay-per-view events. Less ludicrously, his was the loudest ovation received during his appearance before Game Two of the 1999 World Series, as a member of the Major League Baseball All-Century Team.

Following this appearance, when asked by NBC Sports's Jim Gray if he was ready to admit to having betted on baseball and to apologize for his actions, Rose remained unrepentant, continuing flatly to deny that he had ever bet on baseball games, and seeming quite annoyed that the questions were marring an otherwise big night for him and the rest of the members of the All-Century Team. In fact, many of that game's players, as well as a lot of the viewing public, stated that the repeated questioning of Gray was far more inappropriate than the appearance of Rose with the All-Century squad. It proved in many respects that the sporting public was far more forgiving of the otherwise great player, than either Major League Baseball or the Sports News Media, who were clearly willing to utilize Rose's controversial presence and popularity to gain television ratings, even as they disparaged him for what were viewed by many as old and minor (if unacknowledged) crimes.

Possibly due to reflection on such matters, Rose released an especially candid autobiography, *My Prison Without Bars*, in January 2004. In the book, Rose seemed to come clean, admitting, in detail, to his former gambling habit, but strongly emphasizing that he only ever bet *on*, and never *against*, the Cincinnati Reds, proof more of a misguided loyalty and a serious gambling addiction, than any kind of intentional blight on the game, or taint of his activities within it. He underscored the book's points in appearances on ABC's *Primetime Live* and ESPN's *Dan Patrick Show*, making his case for reinstatement based on his new candor and the information about the bigger character it allegedly revealed.

Not everyone was happy with this turn of events. Long-time supporters felt that his denials of the past 15 years, which had now been revealed to be false, reflected very poorly on Rose. Others felt that the timing of the book's release and the interviews with Rose were cynical attempts to make a public appeal to the Baseball Hall of Fame, which was announcing that year's inductees shortly after the books publication. In the end, Rose's disclosure only further muddied the waters of an already questionable career, and granted no relief, other than some increased public sympathy for the would-be Hall-of-Famer. Rose is no longer eligible for any kind of standard induction, having bypassed a fairly wide window of opportunity for nomination. Many believe it will take the retirement of commissioner Bud Selig for Rose to have any luck in achieving his cherished goal, and, at the moment, it seems to be "even money" as to whether he will ever gain such relief. KD

O.J. Simpson

Squeezed until the Pips Squeaked

There are few other US sports figures as universally hated as Orenthal James "OJ" Simpson. OJ's likely, but never legally proven, involvement in the brutal double murder of his second ex-wife, Nicole Brown Simpson, and her friend, Ron Goldman, in 1994, and his subsequent high-profile, racially divisive trial over the next year and a half, remains one of the most notorious and shocking episodes in the life of any sports figure in US history. Though never convicted of the gruesome killings, Simpson's questionable post-trial behavior led many to believe the former Heisman Trophy Winner and NFL Hall of Famer may indeed have got away with a double murder, making him a virtual pariah in the world of sports, television, and movies, and inspiring even more erratic and public bad behavior, as his remaining prestige and wealth continued to dwindle.

OJ's earliest years stand in almost complete contrast to the troubling direction taken by the future running back in his later life. Born to middle-class parents in San Francisco, OJ distinguished himself early on as a talented football player at both High School and Junior College levels. His tenure as a running back, while attending the University of Southern California (USC) in the late 1960s, led to the setting of several National Collegiate Athletic Association (NCAA) football records, a Heisman Trophy following his final season with the team, and a cede as a number one draft pick for the National Football League (NFL) in 1969.

That draft pick went to the Buffalo Bills, whose 1–12–1 record in their 1968 season put them in desperate need of a high-powered playmaker if they were ever to have a chance of improving their abysmal win-loss record. OJ was to become the Bills' most valuable offensive asset, but initially, during his first three years, he averaged only around 600 rushed yards a season, seemingly due to weak support from his team. By the 1972 season, however, he had doubled his previous rushing output, running for 1,251 yards that year, then later bettering this with 2,003 yards the following year, setting a record as the first player to rush 2,000 yards in a single season.

In the three years that followed with the Bills, Simpson distinguished himself with consecutive 1,000-yard-plus seasons, before being sidelined, in 1977, by an injury which ended his season. He followed his tenure at Buffalo with two unremarkable years on the San Francisco 49ers, before retiring early, allegedly as a result of injuries having affected his performance following the 1979 season. During his entire career in the NFL, OJ rushed a total of 11,236 yards, placing him at number 16 on the NFL's all-time rushing list, and all but guaranteeing his eventual induction into the NFL Hall of Fame in 1985, the first year in which he was eligible for this honor.

Off the field during his time as an NFL player, OJ's life was far more complex. He raised three children with first wife, Marguerite Whitley – Arnelle, born in 1968; Jason, born in 1970; and Aaren, born in 1977 – but the couple divorced in 1979, following the death of Aaren who drowned in a swimming pool, a month before her second birthday. OJ excelled in the numerous acting roles that his charisma landed him in popular movies and television broadcasts including the miniseries *Roots*, *The Towering Inferno*, *Back to the Beach*, and the *Naked Gun* trilogy of comedies. His most notable role during this time, however, was probably playing himself in advertisements for Hertz Car Rental, in which the former running back utilized his considerable football skills to charge through a teeming gauntlet of fellow travelers in an airport, in a valiant but doomed attempt to secure an expiring reservation with Hertz's competitors.

By 1985, Simpson seemed to have settled into the role of a former athlete turned entertainer, and married his second wife, the youthful, beautiful Nicole Brown. The couple had two children: daughter Sydney, born in 1985, and Justin, born in 1988. By 1989, however, OJ had already pleaded "no contest" to a domestic violence charge laid by Nicole, which led first to a court-ordered separation later that year, followed by a contentious and messy divorce in 1992. Although no one knew it at the time, this troubled relationship was to be the source of most of the controversies which were to define the remainder of OJ's life.

On the evening of 12 June 1994, Nicole Brown Simpson and friend Ron Goldman were found slashed and stabbed to death outside Nicole's Los Angeles condominium. As an ex-husband with a history of domestic violence directed at his ex-wife, Simpson was immediately considered a prime suspect by the Los Angeles Police Department

(LAPD) even while evidence technicians were still continuing their painstaking inspection of the crime scene. When OJ failed to turn himself in to the police, following the issue of a warrant for his arrest on 17 June, an all-points bulletin went out, resulting in the "slow-speed chase" of Simpson and friend Al Cowlings, which was broadcast live on TV, garnering the case immediate, negative media attention. At the same time OJ's friend and initial attorney, Robert Kardashian, read out a poorly written and rambling note written by Simpson himself, which maintained his innocence in spite of the incriminating circumstances. Though he surrendered himself to the authorities hours later, Simpson's initial bad behavior led many to believe that the former running back clearly had something to hide.

All other aspects of the criminal proceedings that followed against OJ received equally high levels of media interest and scrutiny, earning the case the byline "Trial of the Century." The trial surpassed even that of the Manson Family in terms of televised footage of criminal court proceedings, starting with Simpson's arraignment in June 1994, through to the eventual verdict of the jury in October 1995. As a result of extensive exposure on television, the case made temporary, minor celebrities, for good or for ill, of all involved in any significant way, and logged an impressive 134 days of live, televised testimony, and generated numerous articles in just about every newspaper and magazine, making it virtually impossible for any member of the US public to be unaware of the case. It was undoubtedly in response to this attention that Simpson quickly amassed the strongest legal defense team money could buy, and under instruction from them, proceeded with an unwavering plea of not guilty, under the unrelenting glare of the media spotlight.

OJ's six-member defense counsel, the so-called Dream Team, comprised such noteworthy legal scholars and litigators as F. Lee Bailey, Alan Dershowitz, and Johnnie Cochran, who, along with less luminary specialist attorneys such as Barry Scheck and Robert Shapiro, were brought in to support OJ's initial legal counsel, Robert Kardashian. Allegedly amassing a total of $4 million worth of billable hours, the team made numerous shrewd decisions that maximized their legal advantage at every step along the way. They began by having the case moved from the court serving the affluent Brentwood community where the crime occurred, to a more racially diverse, and therefore potentially more sympathetic, venue in the city of Los Angeles.

On 25 January 1995, the trial itself began, with prosecutors Marsha Clarke and Christopher Darden methodically making the State's case against OJ. They established motive by pointing out the legally established history of domestic violence between OJ and Nicole, established opportunity through the testimony of a limo driver who disputed the timeline OJ had given police as an alibi for his movements on the night of the murder, and provided considerable circumstantial proof of his presence at the murder scene with the help of the LAPD Crime Lab. OJ's blood and footprints had been found at the scene of the crime, and a single leather glove soaked in Nicole's blood had been recovered from behind OJ's house. The Dream Team sought to defend Simpson primarily by calling into question the competence and integrity of the LAPD, which was still viewed with suspicion following the notorious videotaped beating of a black man, Rodney King. The defense team contended that the LAPD was prosecuting Simpson as a result of pervasive, institutionalized racism.

The defense team's success in doing so was primarily the result of suppressing almost all the circumstantial evidence, which, it was argued, had been tainted or compromised by improper handling procedures. They then destroyed the professional credibility of the primary LAPD investigating homicide detective, Mark Fuhrman, by alleging that, as a known bigot, he was too biased to conduct a sufficiently thorough, or even competent, investigation. The defense was able to plant plenty of seeds of reasonable doubt in the minds of the carefully selected black-majority jury, chosen before the trial began, to produce their desired verdict of not guilty. "The Juice," as OJ was known by many fans, was finally free, and the accompanying celebrations of many in the black community, further helped to cement a racial divide which had opened up as a result of OJ's alleged victim being white, and the racially divisive tactics of OJ's defense Dream Team.

Simpson's life following his trial quickly proved how few people outside the black community believed in his innocence. With no new celebrity endorsement offers, or acting roles, OJ's earning power all but disappeared overnight. Furthermore, Fred Goldman, Ron Goldman's father, announced his intention to sue Simpson for the wrongful death of his son, alleging that Simpson was certainly involved with whichever parties had murdered his son, and was thus civilly liable. By early 1997, Goldman's suit had succeeded and OJ was ordered to pay $33.5 million in compensatory and punitive damages. With no other source of income apart from his legally protected NFL pension, in 1999, Simpson auctioned off all his most valued possessions from his glory days as a football star, including his Heisman Trophy, but managed to net a mere $500,000. This, together with a close to $1.5 million tax lien filed by the State of California for unpaid taxes, forced Simpson, later that year, to move to the Florida, where the law states that one's home cannot be seized to pay outstanding debts.

Since then, OJ has cut a distinctly low profile, deriving his income largely from his pension and from signing autographs, their value enhanced, in all likelihood, by his notoriety. This period came to an end when it emerged, in the spring of 2006, that OJ had signed a deal to write a book, tentatively entitled *If I Did It*, in which he would detail how he would have committed the crime if he had, in fact, murdered Nicole. By September that year, Fred Goldman had successfully petitioned the court to obtain control of the "right to publicity" for the proposed book, effectively preventing its marketing. He had also succeeded in getting a federal restraining order to prevent Simpson from spending any of the advance paid for the book, which had by then been canceled, and a TV special intended to coincide with its release. While the case was ultimately dropped due to a lack of jurisdiction at the federal level, a California court later restricted Simpson from spending anything but "ordinary and necessary living expenses" from the now contested advance money, pending further litigation in 2007.

Goldman again prevailed in that court case, held in March 2007, when further court rulings prevented Simpson from receiving any of the proceeds from the book and TV deals, awarding them instead to Goldman, and ordered the bundled rights to be sold at auction, as part of the ongoing restitution from Goldman's original civil suit. The rights were later won, in a Florida bankruptcy court, in August that year, by representatives of the Goldman family, who partially applied the purchased rights, to the unsatisfied portion of Simpson's outstanding debt. The title of the book was changed to *If I Did It: Confessions of the Killer*, and it was released after the addition of commentary from the Goldmans and noted journalist Dominick Dunne, whose *Vanity Fair* articles, which had appeared during OJ's original trial, had been among the most detailed and insightful of the entire, sordid period of the case.

At that time, following the turn of events it seemed that Simpson would return to his previous low-profile, and increasingly low-budget existence . Yet less than a month later, OJ was in the news again, this time as an armed robbery suspect in Las Vegas, Nevada. According to the police investigation, Simpson was alleged to have robbed a group of men auctioning sports memorabilia at gunpoint and with the assistance of several accomplices, claiming to those present that he was recovering property that had been stolen from him. When confronted by investigating officers, OJ initially denied any involvement in the robbery, before admitting that he had been present at the auction, but only in order to retrieve his allegedly stolen property.

After the arrest and interrogation of one of his alleged accomplices, Simpson himself was arrested and held in solitary confinement while police continued to track down the remaining conspirators, retrieve weapons used in the crime, and question witnesses in detail as to the order and manner of events. Simpson was subsequently freed on $125,000 bail, conditional on his having no contact with any of his co-defendants, and that he surrender his passport. Two of his co-defendants, Walter Alexander and Charles H. Cashmore, have reportedly already accepted plea bargain agreements with the Clark County District Attorney's office, in exchange for reduced sentences. On 29 November 2007, OJ officially pleaded not guilty, but, at time of writing, it remains to be seen if he will manage to prove his innocence as he faces a tough jury, his co-defendants are clearly unreliable, and his ability to pay for top legal counsel is considerably diminished. He faces a prison sentence of 60 years if convicted of all the charges he faces, and while OJ may very well decide to take the case to trial, he is extremely unlikely to win. It is probably even less likely that anyone, apart from himself, would be very happy if he did go to trial. KD

Mike Tyson

Freak Show

While it could be argued that there have been better heavyweight boxers than Mike Tyson, few have been as feared and hated, or the subject of as much controversy and well-deserved criticism. While he bears the distinction of being the youngest ever World Heavyweight Champion, as well as being the holder of many impressive professional records, his reputation for brutal, bizarre, and erratic behavior, both in and out of the ring are what the general public tends to know him for. And while it remains to be seen what the retired former World Champion will do with the rest of his life, the course it has taken up to this point has made him one of the most notorious figures in professional sport.

Tyson's childhood, spent in the infamous Brownsville neighborhood of Brooklyn, was both difficult and troubled by any standard. Born to a single mother who could barely provide for him, young Michael was physically imposing, fighting other children at an early age, usually for having made fun of his oddly high-pitched and lisping voice. By the age of 13, he had been arrested 38 times for fighting and mugging offenses, expelled from Junior High School, and rotated through several juvenile detention centers. At this point, the delinquent youngster was placed in the Tryon School for Boys, and for the first time, showed a potential to channel his obvious anger, and violent nature, in a more productive direction.

At Tryon, Tyson was introduced to boxing by counselor and former boxer, Bobby Stewart, who was impressed by his pupil's natural talent and impressive physical power. After a few months' training, Stewart introduced Mike to Cus D'Amato, a well-known boxing trainer whose former charges had included Floyd Patterson and José Torres. While a strict disciplinarian and rigorous taskmaster, D'Amato also showed Tyson considerable love and respect, even becoming his legal guardian when his mother died, in an attempt to further cement his positive influence on the young man. The end results of their successful collaboration were considerable.

As an amateur, Tyson held an impressive record of 24–3, and narrowly missed being chosen for the 1984 Olympic Boxing Team on the basis of two consecutive losses to Henry Tillman. Mike became National Golden Gloves Heavyweight Champion that very same year, and, having also turned 18, it was obvious that he would soon become a professional fighter. His rookie year, as it turned out, formed the basis of his legend.

Tyson won his professional debut against Hector Mercedes, in March 1985, with a first-round knock-out. This was to prove far from atypical, as Tyson won 19 of his first 22 fights with knock-outs, 14 of them in the first round. Though the quality of his opponents, indifferent to begin with, had steadily improved, Mike was undeterred and kept winning – decisively. A media buzz that he might become the "next great Heavyweight Champion" gained momentum.

It was unlikely that such public praise would have been allowed to go to Tyson's head at the time, as Cus was a firm believer in a constant training regimen, regardless of his protégé's win–loss record. Unfortunately, Cus D'Amato died, suddenly and unexpectedly, in November 1985, leaving Mike without a humble, grounded, and tough mentor and friend, someone who might have been able to guide him further in his promising career. However, Cus had also taught his pupil always to persevere, even in the face of fear, uncertainty, and pain. If nothing else, Mike certainly attempted to advance his career with these notions in mind.

Tyson's first televised fight a few months later, in early 1986, ended in victory, due to a sixth-round technical knock-out (TKO), despite questionable behavior by his opponent. By the time Mike faced his first Heavyweight Title Championship seven months later, he had nine further victories to show for himself, with only two of them the result of unanimous decisions, and the rest of them from technical or actual knock-outs. When he beat Trevor Berbick decisively for an actual Heavyweight Championship title, with a second-round TKO, he became, at the age of only 20, the youngest Heavyweight Champion in the sport's history.

But just because Tyson had won *that* World Heavyweight Championship, did not make him the actual, *undisputed* World Heavyweight Champion, as professional boxing has three different "governing organizations" which "officially recognize" "World Championships" or "Champions," and Tyson held the Championship belt of only *one* of these, the World Boxing Council. Almost immediately, though, in March 1987, he rectified this situation with a twelfth-round unanimous decision victory over World Boxing Association Champion James "Bonecrusher" Smith. He defended his "combined" title two months later with a TKO win over Pinklon Thomas, and then settled in to train for the most critical fight of his career, the remaining "disputed" World Heavyweight Championship Belt of the International Boxing Federation's Tony Tucker. Three months and 12 rounds later, Tyson once again emerged the winner by unanimous decision, making him the true and absolutely undisputed Heavyweight World Champion, and "Tyson Mania" achieved critical mass.

By contrast, in 1988, Tyson had only three fights, none of which lasted longer than four rounds, and all of which ended in some kind of knock-out. Out of the ring, however, Mike took two actions which would more drastically affect his career and reputation than he might have guessed at the time. The first was to marry sit-com actress Robin Givens at the beginning of the year, and the other was to fire his long-time trainer Kevin Rooney, the sole remaining influence of Cus D'Amato on his life, just before the end of the year.

The announcement of Tyson's marriage to Givens was considered quite strange by many who knew them, largely due to the obvious differences in background and personality between Givens, the polished, college-educated "beauty," and Tyson, the formerly delinquent, and often inarticulate "beast." These suspicions concerning their compatibility seemed to have been justified when, in a joint interview with Barbara Walters, Robin described life with Mike as, "torture, pure hell," and "worse than anything I can possibly imagine," as the Champ looked on, calmly mute. She later "clarified her remarks," by divorcing Tyson on the grounds of spousal abuse and mental instability, on Valentine's Day 1989.

Since there are few staunch feminists who are also boxing fans, little thought was given in the boxing community to the grounds for Tyson's divorce. He was perceived by many young African-American males as being the victim of Givens, who they felt had only married him for his money, and divorced him at the first opportunity. The divorce was even used by some as an excuse for Mike having fought only twice in 1989, even though he'd easily won both fights. And while Tyson was likely to have experienced some emotional distraction as a result of his divorce, the absence of a demanding, focused trainer like Kevin

Rooney was the more likely explanation for an insufficiently robust title
defense, and increasing sloppiness in the ring.

That sloppiness, together with Tyson's opponent's size and desire to
win, cost Tyson his undisputed Championship when he lost to 42–1
long shot, James "Buster" Douglas, on 11 February 1990. The ten-
round fight destroyed the myth of Mike's "unstoppable power" and
"invulnerability" as Douglas withstood his opponent's best shots, and
used a 12-inch reach advantage to deliver a series of unanswered jabs
and other blows from behind a defense which Tyson never really
penetrated. Finally, 35 seconds into the tenth round, Douglas
unleashed a combination of punches which achieved the "unthink-
able," and knocked out Mike Tyson, ending the fight.

Given that the victory was widely perceived as a fluke, most
observers expected Tyson to make a swift and convincing comeback.
But while Mike easily beat his next two opponents in 1990, Douglas lost
the "Undisputed Title" to Evander Holyfield, setting the stage for an
inevitable meeting between Tyson and "Number Two Contender,"
Donovan "Razor" Ruddock, in March 1991. As that fight ended in a
controversial and heavily contested seventh-round TKO victory for
Tyson, a rematch was fought in June. Tyson was again victorious, this
time by a twelfth-round unanimous decision. Immediately, a
September match with Holyfield was scheduled, but it never took
place, for reasons unrelated to boxing, its Championships, or even the
"politics" said to surround both.

The fight never took place because Tyson was arrested, in late
July, for allegedly having raped then Miss Black Rhode Island,
Desiree Washington, in his Indianapolis hotel room, on 19 July.
With no eye-witnesses to the attack, and no compelling forensic
evidence, the case came down to the credibility of the testimonies
of the victim and the accused. The jury sided with Washington
and convicted Tyson of the charge of rape, and the judge imposed
a sentence of six years.

The verdict was greeted with a chorus of, "I told you so!" from
Tyson detractors and supporters alike. His detractors claimed that the
conviction underscored Tyson's obvious and festering misogyny,
alluded to during his divorce from Robin Givens, while his supporters
claimed the verdict was proof that a black man couldn't get an honest
trial, especially when the charge was rape, no matter how rich or
successful he might be. These opinions seemed to have little impact on

Tyson, at least not publicly. He served his time without commenting on the incident, even following his release on parole in 1995.

In fact, the only noticeable difference in Tyson, following his time in prison, was his conversion to Islam. He adopted the name Malik Abdul Aziz, and surrounded himself with representatives of the Nation of Islam. After a couple of initial easy wins in the second half of 1995, "Malik" returned to his quest to reclaim his undisputed title. After recapturing the WBC and WBA within a year of re-initiating his quest, it seemed likely that he might actually pull off a comeback.

Also on the comeback trail, however, was Evander Holyfield, who had lost the "Undisputed Championship" while Tyson was in prison, only to regain it, and lose it again. Although Holyfield was viewed as largely washed up, the Holyfield-Tyson fight was eagerly awaited as the two had never actually fought each for the title, despite the planned fight years before. While Holyfield ultimately won the November 1996 fight with an eleventh-round TKO, his victory was marred by allegations from the Tyson camp that he had used illegal head butts to secure his victory, even though judges had ruled the moves accidental.

The 1997 rematch between the two fighters was even more hotly anticipated than the original bout, as the rivalry between the two men had been further fueled by the controversy. The result was a $100-million gross on the event, and cable TV pay-per-view purchases by almost two million households to watch the fight, both of which stood as boxing records until the 2007 De La Hoya–Mayweather fight. The big rematch ended in even greater controversy, though, when Tyson was disqualified in the third round, for biting both of Holyfield's ears. In the confusion that followed the end of the event, a near riot erupted in which several people were injured.

As a result of the fiasco, Tyson was fined three million dollars (out of his $30 million-dollar purse for the event), and he appeared in public two days afterwards to apologize to Holyfield personally for the incident, and to appeal to the Nevada State Athletic Commission not to ban him for life from the sport of boxing. The Commission was unmoved by the appeal, and voted unanimously to revoke Mike's licence indefinitely, as well as making him pay all legal costs associated with the hearing. While the Commission reversed its decision a little over a year later, irreparable damage seemed to have been done to Tyson's career and reputation, which had been transformed into that of a semi-permanent media "freak show."

The years that followed saw a decrease in both the quantity and quality of Tyson's bouts. He had only one more title fight in his career, a 2002 defeat at the hands of defending champion Lennox Lewis. He continued to have brushes with the law, too, ranging from a 1999 assault conviction, plea-bargained down to fines and probation, an unrelated (and unfounded) allegation of sexual assault that same year, and, most recently, a 2007 plea-bargain conviction for felony drug possession and driving under the influence. He also declared bankruptcy, in 2003, as a result of dwindling earnings and poor money management, having squandered an estimated $300 million dollars, based on his taxable earnings. He finally retired from boxing in 2005, when he refused to continue in the seventh round of his fight against Danny Williams, later stating that he no longer had "the fighting guts or heart any more."

In attempting to sum up a career which showed so much initial promise, but went so brutally and bizarrely wrong, one can't really do better than to quote Tyson's own words, taken from a June 2005 article in *USA Today*: "My whole life has been a waste – I've been a failure. I just want to escape. I'm really embarrassed with myself and my life. I want to be a missionary. I think I could do that while keeping my dignity without letting people know they chased me out of the country. I want to get this part of my life over as soon as possible. In this country nothing good is going to come of me. People put me up so high; I wanted to tear that image down."

Who could argue with such candid criticism, especially from the man himself? KD

Michael Vick

Bad Newz

A professional athlete committing crimes is a far from unusual phenomenon. In the last 100 years or so, there have been over 70 recorded cases in the English-speaking world alone, and it is likely that there will be many more such incidents in the future. However, while most of these cases have been career-related, concerning, for example, performance-enhancing drugs, match-fixing, gambling, or even physical assaults on professional rivals, some are more overtly criminal, for example, armed robbery, assault, rape, or even murder. No crime, however, has been perceived by the public as being as capricious or cruel as the 2007 dog-fighting conviction of Atlanta Falcon's quarter-back, Michael Vick.

The second of four children, born to unmarried, working-class parents in the slum area of Newport News, Virginia – known locally as "Bad Newz" – in June 1980, the young Michael showed a marked interest in, and natural talent for, football, from as young an age as three. Strongly encouraged by his father, as well as by school athletic programs, Vick distinguished himself as a quarterback with a strong running game, who was unafraid to rush for yardage if he saw no open receivers during heavily defended plays. With considerable accomplishments, such as passing for almost 5,000 yards and 43 touchdowns in three years with the Warwick High School Raiders, Vick was hailed as an example of a local boy made good by Bad Newz residents. He later attended Virginia Tech, across the state from his supportive home town, near Roanoke.

He attended Virginia Tech for only three years and two seasons, taking the Hokies first to a tightly contested defeat in the 2000 Nokia Sugar Bowl, and then to a Gator Bowl victory over Clemson in 2001. During his brief time with the Hokies, Michael set collegiate records, both for pass efficiency and for yards rushed by a freshman quarter-back. He was also voted Most Valuable Player for both bowl game showings on behalf of the team. With the obvious talent and potential to begin a very lucrative National Football League (NFL) career, Vick left school following the 2001 season, as the number one NFL draft pick, and, through complicated trade negotiations with the San Diego Chargers, he headed to Atlanta to try to bring his winning ways to the struggling Falcons franchise.

Michael's debut season was promising, but somewhat limited by the fact that he only started eight games, and the team failed to make the playoffs, seemingly as a result of the coach's decision to keep Vick on the bench, as the rookie quarterback had proved that he was an emerging talent to be reckoned with, in terms of both passing and rushing. In 2002 he "arrived" as an NFL superstar, passing for almost

3,000 yards, and personally rushing 777 yards, sending him to the Pro Bowl, before the Falcon's season came to an end in a hard-fought game against the Philadelphia Eagles for the National Football Conference (NFC) divisional championship. The 2003 season was marred by Vick having to sit most of it out, having fractured his fibula in a pre-season game against the Baltimore Ravens, leaving him on the sidelines until the thirteenth game of the season. Despite his late start, however, he still managed to chalk up 585 passing yards and 255 rushing yards in a mere five appearances. In 2004, Michael seemed to return to form, starting all 15 regular season games, passing for 2,313 yards, rushing for 902 yards, and earning a second Pro Bowl appearance, while the team had a record 11–5 season. Vick was rewarded with a ten-year, $130-million contract with the Falcons, the highest such pay award in professional sports history at the time.

The 2005 and 2006 seasons were moderately successful for Vick and the Falcons, as the by now superstar quarterback passed consistently for close to 2,500 yards and rushed for above 500 both years. Nevertheless, Vick's public image became tarnished around this time, firstly for settling out of court with a young woman who alleged that Michael had given her genital herpes while aware that he was infected, and secondly for raising both middle fingers in an obscene gesture to booing New Orleans Saints fans during a November home game, which resulted in a $10,000 fine from the NFL, and in all likelihood cost him a Pro Bowl appearance that year, which would otherwise have been as automatic as his other three appearances, based on merit. When he was later confronted by Transportation Security Administration (TSA) employees at Miami International Airport, in January 2007, for carrying a water bottle with a secret compartment in it, allegedly designed for smuggling drugs (though none were found on Vick at the time), many fans were left to wonder if the talented young quarterback was going too far with "thug athlete" posturing, increasingly popular among young African-American professional athletes at the time.

The answer came about four months later, on 25 April the same year, when it was widely reported that local Virginia police had broken up an alleged dog-fighting ring, supposedly operating out of Vick's Surrey County mansion, with the quarterback's knowledge, consent, full participation, and financial backing, according to those arrested at the scene. By July, the full details concerning "Bad Newz Kennels" had been disclosed to a shocked and disgusted public, as Michael and three co-defendants were charged with federal dog-fighting offences. In exchange for lenient sentences and other plea bargain considerations, the co-defendants unanimously testified that the operation had been bankrolled, promoted, and overseen by Vick, who also co-ordinated betting on the fights, and even executed "underperforming" animals by shooting or drowning them. On 20 August, Michael opted to follow his codefendants' example, agreeing to plead guilty in the face of a possible penalty of one to five years. He formally filed his plea with the court on 24 August, admitting to all aspects of his co-defendants' testimony, with the exception of betting on the matches himself, or executing any of the dogs.

On 27 August, presiding federal Judge Henry Hudson accepted the terms of the plea agreement, and scheduled a sentencing date of 10 December 2007. While still free on bail, Michael failed a random drug test on 13 September, violating the conditions of his pre-sentencing release. As a result, he was ordered to be confined to his Hampton, Virginia, home, and subjected to electronic monitoring. In the face of public disappointment and disgust, and his indefinite suspension from the NFL, Vick showed some character and maturity, reporting early to prison, several weeks before his actual court sentencing, to start accruing time served.

In the end, Vick was sentenced to 23 months in federal prison for his role in the interstate dog-fighting operation. Judge Hudson said that he was convinced that the ring was not a momentary lapse of judgment, and took into account Michael's recent failed drug test when determining his sentence. In the meantime, Vick and his co-defendants took up residence in the Surrey County jail, while awaiting trial by the county court for separate, local dog-fighting charges, which were scheduled to begin in the spring of 2008.

Aside from the legal penalties related to the federal conviction, and the negative publicity it brought Michael, the well-publicized and protracted scandal also had disastrous financial implications for the once popular quarterback. Multimillion-dollar endorsement deals with companies including Nike, which canceled the Michael Vick running shoe line, EA Sports, a top manufacturer of sports video games, Coca-Cola, PowerAde, Kraft Foods, Rawlings, Hasbro, and Air Tran had all been immediately canceled, even before Vick had entered a plea agreement, let alone been formally sentenced. Faced with the $19.9-million settlement he had been ordered to repay the Atlanta Falcons from his

$37-million signing bonus, for having knowingly engaged in criminal activity detrimental to the team, and the low likelihood of his being able to earn a comparable amount any time soon, the embattled former superstar had no choice but to start selling off his high-end property holdings in Virginia, Georgia, and Miami. To further complicate matters, he was also sued by three different banks for outstanding multimillion dollar debts, left unpaid when his football earnings halted due to the scandal.

The case also impacted negatively on people not directly financially linked to Vick. Many residents of the "Bad Newz" neighborhood where Michael had been born and raised, have said publicly that they are both disappointed in him, and angered by the suggestions made by some commentators that dog-fighting must have been part of their community, for the NFL superstar to engage in the activity so readily. Leaders of the area's Boys' and Girls' Club, saw Vick's experience as a sobering lesson about how important moral guidance is to those who come from humble beginnings, and later achieve great success.

However, if any living creatures have felt the full implications and impact of Michael Vick's actions, it is the 49 pit bull terriers seized by animal control officials during the initial raid on Vick's mansion. According to the officials' reports, after attempting to care for the mistreated and abused animals, one particularly tormented and aggressive dog had to be put down for behavioral reasons, and several more will require special medical and behavioral treatment for the rest of their lives. To that end, the court ordered Vick to pay into a $1-million escrow fund for such long-term care. The only thing more fitting might have been to select the former denizens of "Bad Newz Kennels" to sit in judgment on their former owner. They could have been guaranteed to be far less lenient than even the toughest of professional jurists, and far swifter in executing sentence. KD

Music Business Assholes

50 Cent

Small Change

Prize former boxer preaching the greatness of guns, violence, and misogyny, Curtis Jackson chose the nickname 50 Cent as a metaphor for "change." The name was a tribute to Kelvin Martin, a 1980s' Brooklyn robber also known as "50 Cent." Jackson appropriated the name "because it says everything I want it to say. I'm the same kind of person 50 Cent was. I provide for myself by any means." But this isn't the political "by any means necessary" of Malcolm X; 50 Cent's version of any means necessary is far more selfish and self-serving.

50 Cent's popularity started to increase after the successful but controversial underground single, "How to Rob," which he apparently wrote in thirty minutes on the way to a studio in a car. The track explains how he would rob many other famous artists. It's a comical idea, but it degenerates into being an example of the self-obsession with which 50 Cent approaches life, and its success was somewhat inexplicable.

The birth of his son to a "former girlfriend" in 1997 apparently changed his outlook on life. "When my son came into my life, my priorities changed, because I wanted to have the relationship with him that I didn't have with my father." He credited his fatherhood with inspiring his career and giving him the "motivation to go in a different direction." 50 Cent has a tattoo of "Marquise" with an axe on his right bicep. "The axe is 'cause I'm a warrior. I don't want him to be one, though," he explained to *Blender*'s Jonah Weiner, in April 2005. He also has "50," "Southside," and "Cold World" on his back because "I'm a product of that environment. It's on my back, though, so it's all behind me." However, it is unclear whether he has really been able to put his gangland ways behind him even though he is clearly a great deal more financially stable than when he started out. Gangsterism is still present in his lyrical approach if not in actuality.

A gunman attacked 50 Cent in 2000 outside his grandmother's home in Queens, New York. He was shot an incredible nine times – in the hand (one round hit his right thumb and came out of his little finger), arm, hip, both legs, chest, and left cheek. The face wound meant that he had a swollen tongue, lost a wisdom tooth, and ended up with slightly slurred speech. A friend who was with him at the time also sustained a gunshot wound to the hand. They were both taken to the hospital where 50 Cent spent 13 days. The alleged shooter, Darryl "Hommo" Baum, was killed three weeks later. Although there remain doubts as to whether Baum was the real culprit or merely provided a convenient cover story. Jackson refused to co-operate with the authorities so the full truth may never be known. Such a nice man. DL

G.G. Allin

Hated

One of the biggest misperceptions of the widely misunderstood Punk movement, at least during its inception and "heyday," is that Punks in general, whether performers or merely members of that subculture, are inherently violent, destructive, hateful, and foul individuals, who delight in wreaking as much havoc as humanly possible, for the sheer ugly thrill of it. Still, since one of the strongest cultural imperatives among Punks has always been a staunch belief in the right of an individual to think, speak, dress, and act as he or she pleases, without interference from society's institutions, such as the government, organized religion, and business corporations, it seems logical that Punk would eventually produce an individual who would take this ideal to its basest, ugliest extreme. And if one were trying to be as deliberately and aggressively offensive a performer as possible, one would be hard-pushed to surpass the life's work of G.G. Allin.

G.G. was actually born Jesus Christ Allin, in Lancaster, New Hampshire. His father was a mentally unstable religious fanatic, married to a significantly younger woman. G.G.'s young life was chaotic and unpleasant. His father, who kept the family secluded in a log cabin without utilities, was convinced that his newborn son would be a great man, because he had been told so by an angel shortly before the boy's birth, hence the messianic moniker. Why he would later beat and molest his child, especially given his sensational belief, is probably beyond the understanding of a rational mind. Whatever the reason, the effect of such a dangerous and disturbing home life soon became apparent, when the young Allin entered school.

Arleta, his mother, had tried to smooth the transition to some extent by changing his legal name to Kevin Michael when he was in first grade, but such a simple and cosmetic fix was not nearly enough to keep her son out of trouble. By junior high school, he was in "special ed" classes, despite having already been held back a year. He was also known as a trouble-maker, given to acts of vandalism, petty crime, and even coming to school in drag. As G.G. himself observed, "[that] time was very chaotic. Full of chances and dangers. We sold drugs, stole, broke into houses, et cetera. We did whatever we wanted for the most part – including all the bands we played in. People hated us back then."

If this was true, even in his early days as a front man, the feeling was clearly mutual. Allin, who had taken to calling himself G.G., based on a childhood nickname given to him by an older brother who could not pronounce Jesus Christ properly, modeled his stage persona on pioneering Punks who courted controversy like Iggy Pop and Stiv Bators. Due to a reputation for being uncontrollable, violent, uncom-promising, and drug-addled during performances, G.G. burned through close to a half a dozen bands between 1977 and 1987. While not even approaching commercial success, G.G.'s antics did slowly garner him notoriety as something between a cult and a novelty act on the national Punk scene.

Around this time, G.G. "stepped up" his act considerably, ingesting laxatives before shows in order to be able to defecate on stage. He would then either immediately consume his excrement, daub himself with it, and/or fling it at the audience. For this "refinement," together with his existing antics – exposing himself, and/or attacking audience members on the flimsiest of pretexts – he was hailed as the ultimate rebel and transgressor against a rock 'n' roll culture which had grown unthreatening and stale. His Reach Out International Records' cassette, *Hated in the Nation*, released in 1987, added to the "buzz," helping to make him a figure of genuine controversy in the late 1980s. Even so, G.G. continued to try to find new boundaries to cross.

In 1988, he wrote to the famous Punk publication *Maximum Rock 'n' Roll* to let people know that he would commit suicide on stage on Halloween night, 1989. In the interim, he went on the talkshow circuit, wreaking predictable havoc in the form of foul language and other "TV-friendly" forms of belligerence for equally hollow sensationalists such as Morton Downey Jr, Geraldo Rivera, and Jerry Springer. When All Hallow's Eve, 1989, did fall, however, G.G. failed to make good on his promise, or threat, to "end it all" – and for one of the worst possible reasons.

In the late summer/early fall of 1989 he traveled to Ann Arbor, Michigan – allegedly to escape a Chicago assault warrant – where he had been promised "sanctuary" by sympathetic fans. A few weeks after his arrival, which had touched off a wave of fistfights and petty vandalism associated with the local Punk scene, Allin was arrested and charged with the rape and torture of a female fan. As a result of being in jail awaiting trial, he was therefore unable to kill himself on stage as he had promised.

G.G. denied the charges outright, claiming that the woman had been a willing participant in violent and degrading sexual acts with him, and had only later changed her account of events. He also pointed out to the police numerous inconsistencies in the woman's story, which even the presiding judge was forced to acknowledge. In the end, however, Allin entered a plea bargain with the court, to the reduced charge of felony assault. Ultimately, he served a little over two years in prison for his crime, spending some of his time writing *The G.G. Allin Manifesto*, which was published in 1990.

Following his stint in prison, G.G.'s career prospects dwindled considerably. Few venues were willing to assume liability for damage likely to be done by Allin and his fans in the course of a show. Allin's track record for making albums had always been somewhere between shaky and mediocre, and his felony conviction seemed to have delivered him a career-ending blow. However, as was often the case with the unpredictable Mr Allin, there were yet further lows to plumb.

On 28 June 1993, he performed his last show, at a club called The Gas Station, in New York City. Even though G.G. was being video-taped for a concert DVD, which was eventually released under the title *Hated*, he went berserk after the venue lost power part way through the second song of his set. After trashing the club to the best of his well-honed ability, Allin wandered the streets of New York, naked and covered in blood and feces, surrounded by die-hard fans whom he embraced. Music Television Channel VH1 later ranked these goings on, with some justification, as the fourth "Freakiest Concert Moment" of all time.

Eventually, he ended up at the apartment of a friend for a post-concert party, where he died, rather quietly, of a heroin overdose. Several of the partygoers posed for pictures with G.G. on the couch where he had expired, unaware that he was already dead. It is only because he was in the same position on that couch the following morning that anyone realized anything was wrong, and called an ambulance. Paramedics pronounced him dead at the scene.

If his career was viewed as shocking and controversial, and his final concert performance as freakish, G.G.'s funeral proved equally sensa-tional and grotesque. As per the instructions in his song "When I Die," Allin was placed in his coffin unwashed, smeared with his own feces, without make-up, in his black leather jacket and a jockstrap, a bottle of Jim Beam beside him. Friends posed with the corpse, putting drugs and whiskey into Allin's mouth, before attaching headphones connected to a portable cassette player which was playing a copy of his album, *The Suicide Sessions*. Footage from the funeral was included as an unantici-pated "bonus feature" on the *Hated* DVD, a fitting footnote to a career that had produced songs such as "Fuck the Dead," "Expose Yourself to Little Kids," "I Kill Everything I Fuck," and "Kill Thy Father, Rape Thy Mother." A final "good riddance" to very bad rubbish indeed. KD

Annoying Rock Stars

Bono, Chris, Johnny, Fred etc.

Rock stars can be irritating at the best of times. They are hugely wealthy, do very little work, and are adored by millions. This alone would probably be enough to make us dislike them, but the real cherry on the cake comes when a rock star starts to believe in his or her own greatness and becomes either a pompous, preaching idiot, or a virtual self-parody of a self-centered star. One could easily come up with enough infuriating examples to fill a whole book, but, instead, let's focus on a hand-picked few of the most infuriating rock stars ever to have strutted their way across the stages of stadiums around the world.

First prize has to go to U2's Bono, not because he is a bad man, or even a bad musician, but for the sheer enormity of his Messiah complex, and the intensity of his preaching, which would earn him a special place in any pomposity contest. Bono is a man who truly believes that he, single-handedly, can save the world. If it weren't for Bono's extraordinary endeavors, Chris Martin of Coldplay might have taken the prize for the most sanctimonious singer, but, as it is, he can manage only an honorable mention for his twee use of sticky tape and felt-tipped messages on his hands and forehead to convey his own, peculiar brand of smug, middle-class psychobabble.

The prize for the worst singer, in the worst band, ever to declare his own genius to the world goes to Razorlight's Johnny Borrell, a man so in love with himself that he still hasn't noticed that his band's best efforts sound like inferior Boomtown Rats B-sides, while the worst have been known to reduce radio stations' listening figures to zero, as listeners around the world lunge for their off-switches. Borrell exudes desperation to be famous, but seems to have forgotten that most bands achieve fame by making music that people can bear to listen to.

Finally, Fred Durst of Limp Bizkit deserves a prize of his own. From his homophobic outbursts, to encouraging crowd disorder at Woodstock 1999, and from dissing other, better musicians to his unseemly interview with Howard Stern in which he revealed unpleasant details of his time with Britney Spears, he is a definite contender for the title of most annoying rock star ever.

And that's without even mentioning the internet sex tape, which most people would prefer not to be reminded of. Durst was almost certainly annoying before he found fame, but, having been given a platform, he has managed to attain a whole new level of being profoundly dislikeable. Future contenders for the prize will have to aim low, and then lower still, if they really want to outdo Durst. DL

Boy Bands

Not to Be Confused with Talented People

Take That, Westlife, Boyzone, 'N Sync, 5ive, New Kids on the Block, Busted, A1, Blazin' Squad, McFly, Backstreet Boys, East 17, MN8, Boyz II Men, etc. . . . this one's for you.

Boy bands are the latest version of an old music business stereotype: musical performers put together like singing, dancing puppets by a mysterious manager in the background. Traditionally the manager is an overweight, older man, suspected by some of looking to sate pedophilic tendencies. Manufactured bands have come in a variety of forms over the years, from the dancing puppets of the 1950s through to bubblegum and disco performers who mimed to the backing of superior musicians. The modern boy band has jettisoned the pretence of being any kind of real band. They never play instruments, choosing instead to perform some kind of new formation dancing while miming to songs clearly aimed at the ears of 13-year-old girls. Curiously (or not so curiously, depending on your interpretation), some boy bands have a strong crossover appeal to young (or lecherous and old) gay men. Perhaps because they have the appearance of homosexual young lads in random gangs of four or five. This is especially true of Take That, whose early videos and costumes were visualizations of gay fantasy, although not so true of East 17, who were so ugly that not even myopic twelve-year-olds fancied them.

What's the purpose of boy bands? It's hard to know, but they do provide a certain amount of comedy, especially on late-night music channels showing hilariously dated music videos. Boy band members generally have very specific haircuts, without which cosmetic enhancement they would be revealed as merely the bunch of caterwauling barrow boys that they truly are. Most English boy bands can only sing with a strong American accent. This makes it all the more painful to witness their attempts to sound tough while pirouetting in pink jackets, flouncy hair, and sparkly jewelry.

Do not confuse them with talented people. DL

DMX

Gangster of the Ghetto

Following the deaths of Tupac Shakur and Christopher Wallace, aka The Notorious B.I.G. or "Biggie Smalls" in late 1996 and early 1997 respectively, the musical sub-genre of Gangsta Rap was experiencing more than just a "talent vacuum." While still required by fans to appear as "streetwise" and "hard" as ever, many performers were understandably less willing to state their readiness to engage in violence over perceived disrespect, as prescribed by their alleged, and often alluded to, "code of the streets." Now that there was a possibility that they might be taken at their well-publicized word, by rivals, or other "actual" criminals, and end up the victims of a homicide, instead of the swaggering and gloating perpetrators, few wanted to maintain their reputation with that kind of talk. As a result, many chose instead to emphasize the lavishness of their current lifestyle with videos which looked like "ghetto editions" of *Life Styles of the Rich and Famous*, which tried to underscore the credibility of the claim that their subjects were now somehow "elevated," or "evolved," above simple street criminality. And, if anything, the music and misdeeds of emerging "talent" Earl Simmons, aka DMX, might ultimately prove their point.

"Projects raised" in Yonkers, New York, during the 1970s and 1980s, Earl had started rapping at the age of 13, eventually "beat boxing" for local rapper "Just Ice." He took the stage name DMX from the Oberheim DMX drum machine, a favorite instrument of some rap DJs, though he would later claim it stood for Dark Man X. He also claims to have honed those skills during a stint in a Juvenile Group Home that formed part of a pattern of petty crime during his teenage years. This mixture of the right "street pedigree," combined with a nominal ability for simple, in-your-face rhymes, and an inarguably *intense* personal presence, all but assured rapid success in his future "career."

In the early 1990s DMX established himself mostly through participation in the Yonkers "underground" rap scene with a group called Gangsters of the Ghetto (or G.O.G.). While the three-man crew released several "mix" CDs, it was DMX who was singled out for praise by *The Source* magazine's "Unsigned Hype" section in 1991. This led to a solo career which made several false starts, both for him and his affiliated crew the Ruff Ryders, before Earl ultimately signed both to subsidiaries of Island Records, choosing the highly respected rap label Def Jam Records for himself.

His initial tenure there was as a "featured" artist, making cameo appearances of several verses on LL Cool J's "4,3,2,1" single in 1997, as well as Ma$e's "24 Hours to Live," and The LOX's "Money, Power, and Respect." In early 1998, he released his first solo single for Def Jam, the gold-selling "Get At Me Dog," which earned him comparisons with Tupac, probably due more to his shaved head and similarities of vocal pitch, than anything else, and despite an original version of the song (later leaked to the internet), which contained a direct "dis" of the slain rapper. Capitalizing on this initial success, DMX released his first full album, *It's Dark and Hell is Hot* a short while later that same year.

While the album sold five million copies, and debuted at number one, there was little that was innovative about the release. Instead of trying for any kind of novelty, DMX seemed to have picked up where other Gangsta Rappers had recently decided to leave off, in a now familiar lyrical mixture of aggressive posturing, sexual boasts, positive depictions of drug and alcohol use, and cautionary threats of immediate and brutal retaliation, including the murder of spouses and the rape of female children, against any and all who might "dis" him in any way. He was, as a result, openly embraced by those who felt Gangsta Rap had been losing its machismo, even as he was scorned for his addle-minded aggression and juvenile sexism by numerous music critics.

DMX's follow-up album, *Flesh of My Flesh, Blood of My Blood*, was "rush released" in December 1998 to satisfy final obligations in the Island Records buy-out of Def Jam. The rush did not seem to affect his fans' appetite for DMX's brand of cartoonish material in any way; in fact, it increased it, especially after a "performance" in a Hype Williams "hood movie" *Belly* which seemed to give visual "life" to this persona. In fact, it almost guaranteed that the album would debut at a record-setting number one position in the charts, and achieve multi-platinum sales, both of which it did, effortlessly. Simmons seemed to celebrate this success by embarking on the Hard Knock Life Tour with fellow Gangster Rappers Jay-Z, Method Man, and Redman.

As DMX finally met his newly acquired public, he rapidly became involved in numerous incidents involving the police, and, initially, they were the all too familiar antics of a typical Gangsta Rapper. His first run-in was on a Denver tour stop in early 1999, when he was arrested for allegedly stabbing and shooting a fan after a concert. While that incident was quickly cleared up, Earl was arrested again, in May, for assaulting a man who had stabbed his wife in the neck, but, again, the charges were dropped, this time due to the incident being an obvious case of self-defense. Later that same year, more comically, Trinidadian authorities fined him for using obscene language in public, but by fall, arrests by the police ceased to be the result of "misunderstandings," and the charges were far from a laughing matter.

After Earl's uncle (who also acted as his manager) was mysteriously shot and injured in the neck while on tour, Yonkers police raided Earl's home, believing the weapon involved to be his. While the search failed to produce the weapon used in the shooting, thus clearing DMX of that particular charge, the police did find numerous other weapons, as well as marijuana, and several pit bulls kept in cramped conditions, and in obvious poor health. Charged with multiple counts of cruelty to animals, and with illegal possession of weapons and drugs, DMX managed, through plea-bargaining, to get away with a fine, probation, and community service.

Astoundingly, only weeks later, DMX assaulted a police officer while drunk and high, and was sentenced to two months in prison in exchange for a guilty plea. While such a scandal might have damaged or even destroyed the careers of other types of entertainers, it only added to

DMX's street cred, which "authenticated" his image, and reinforced sales. When the album *And Then There was X* was conveniently released mere weeks after Earl's most recent clash with the law, it, too, debuted at number one, selling almost 700,000 copies its first week, and going multiplatinum. He also had a cameo role in the Jet Li film, *Romeo Must Die,* along with noted R&B Diva Aaliyah, bringing that same street cred to a martial arts genre long known to be popular with urban, black audiences. Released in March 2000, the film did $55 million in US box office receipts, and remains Jet Li's highest grossing film in the United States to date.

Despite this success, only days after the film's release, DMX was once again entangled with the law, pulled over by the police following a Buffalo concert. He was cited for speeding, driving without a licence, aggravated unlicensed operation of a motor vehicle, failure to notify the DMV of a change of address, and possession of marijuana, cocaine, MDMA (ecstasy), and percosets. When he failed to make a scheduled court appearance later that month, a bench warrant was issued for his arrest, and Earl turned himself in. The case was pleaded down to a simple conviction for driving without a licence, earning DMX a $400 fine and 15 days in jail. Incredibly, DMX was also convicted at the time for an *additional* marijuana possession charge, stemming from a small quantity of the drug found inside a cigarette pack on his person at the time of his surrender and booking.

By comparison, 2001 was an almost uneventful year for the increasingly troubled Mr Simmons, most notable for the spring release of *Exit Wounds*, a Steven Seagal vehicle with a co-starring slot for DMX, and the fall release of his fourth album, *The Great Depression*. As part of the promotional effort, the "Dark Man" granted a remarkably candid interview with BET TV channel, where he spoke openly about his grief over the recent death of his grandmother, his profound love and respect for dogs, and his diagnosis with bi-polar disorder as a teenager. He also performed a brief, prayer-like rap, flanked by assembled Rough Ryders, at the MTV Video Music awards later that summer, imploring both God, and presumably the viewing public, to bear with him while he struggled to learn how to live "positively." The softer, or, in some cases, almost confessional tone evident in several tracks on *The Great Depression* earned it a fourth number-one debut and platinum sales, but it did noticeably less well than DMX's earlier, more "negative" material.

For the next couple of years DMX cut a lower than usual profile, partly due to the gangster rap market having been infiltrated by younger, fresher talent, and having grown increasingly more crowded, while remaining geared, as ever, to paying the most attention to only the freshest, fiercest, and flashiest of MCs. Compared to the off-microphone antics of emerging fellow "gangsters" like 50 Cent or The Game, another arrest for cruelty to animals in 2002 just seemed lame – and kind of weird. And while his 2003 movie with Jet Li enjoyed modest but respectable box office success, his 2003 album, *Grand Champ*, was both his last number one debut, and his last platinum album.

Since then, many have taken to claiming that DMX now stands for Dumb Man X, as the number of viable recording and other musical projects for Earl Simmons has dwindled considerably. With multiple arrests for everything ranging from vehicle-related misdemeanors (usually driving while drunk, on drugs, or without a licence) to impersonating a federal agent while carjacking a baffled motorist outside JFK airport (again, under the influence of drugs), it seems unlikely that his career will see much of a turnaround.

More likely, gangster rapping, like being an actual gangster, is probably a young man's game, due to the sheer Darwinian nature of the work environment. Still, a recent BET reality show, *DMX: Soul of a Man*, as well as more film projects, will probably ensure the survival of Mr Simmons's career in the short term. However, his obvious lack of impulse control, his defiant attitude towards overt authority figures, and his inability to obey simple rules of social conduct, make it unlikely that he will ever progress beyond a stereotypical state of arrested development, common to juvenile delinquents of all ages. KD

Charles Manson

Cease to Exist

Yes, *that* Charles Manson. Manson's other crimes are well enough known, but he was also a wannabe musician and charismatic hoodlum who finished a jail term, then landed on the streets of Haight-Ashbury.

There he became the leader of a gang of followers who became known as the Family. He had found his way to San Francisco when the 1960s' drug culture was at its height. By late in the decade, he and several members of his Family were living on borrowed land outside of Los Angeles. Manson wanted to succeed in the music business, and hang around on its fringes, but when that didn't work out, his criminal personality developed further and he, together with some of his followers, became involved in torture and murder.

Believing he was an incarnation of Jesus Christ, and that he would come to the fore during racial strife in the United States, Manson persuaded his followers to embark on a 1969 murder spree, during which they murdered seven people. Their most famous victim was actress Sharon Tate, eight months pregnant and the wife of film director Roman Polanski. The subsequent trial lasted seven months (at the time, the most lengthy and expensive in US history), and resulted in guilty verdicts and death sentences for Manson and his followers. However, in 1972, California outlawed the death penalty, and Manson's sentence was commuted to life in prison.

Bizarrely, it was during this period, in 1970, that Manson released an album called *Lie: The Love & Terror Cult* – partly to help finance his defense in the trial for the Tate–LaBianca murders. Released by ESP Records, it included "Cease to Exist," which, as "Never Learn Not to Love," had also been recorded by the Beach Boys. In 1970, the Charles Manson Family recorded an album entitled *The Family Jams* which featured songs written by Manson, although he didn't personally appear on the album. Here was a deranged murderer singing hippy folk songs.

Manson deserves to be in any list of the most appalling people, but we include him in the list of music business assholes because, like others before him, (including a number of rappers) he believed that his life of crime made him special, or important rather than simply a despicable criminal. Before he released any music at all he had been in prison for half of his life.

Music fans. You want gritty authenticity? A bad man, singing songs that glorify his own existence? Look no further. DL

Milli Vanilli

The Lip-Synch Duo

Love it or hate it, one could very easily argue that MTV and its "music video" format drastically and permanently changed the nature of pop music and how it is marketed, and will continue to have an impact for decades to come. Before the advent of MTV, musical performers, especially rock musicians, were frequently considered good-looking by their fans because of their musical talent and/or personal style, even when this was not, strictly speaking, aesthetically true. In the more strongly visual realm of the music video, however, the tendency for photogenic performers to sell well, developed quickly from a noticeable trend at the start of 1980s and the early days of MTV into an almost unwritten rule for commercial success by the end of that decade. It was under these circumstances that the rapid rise and fall of the dance pop duo Milli Vanilli occurred.

The "mastermind" behind the group was German pop producer Frank Farian, who had recorded several Top 40-style dance tracks by artists like Charles Shaw, John Davis, and Brad Howell, who, while vocally talented, were not young enough or photogenic enough for a video music world in thrall to adolescents. So Farian enlisted the help of two models and dancers, Fab Morvan and Rob Pilatus, whom he had met in a Berlin club, to "front" the project, and give it a more striking and youthful "face." Farian appropriated a name for the "group" from a Turkish billboard, and Milli Vanilli was born.

Milli Vanilli's debut album, *All or Nothing*, was released in Europe in the summer of 1988, with Rob and Fab squarely out in front of the project, with no mention of the actual singers. The success of the album caught the attention of Arista Records in the United States, which quickly signed the duo to distribute their records in the United States. Arista remixed several tracks, added a few more, and released the result under the title *Girl You Know It's True* at the beginning of 1989.

The group's initial single, and the album's title track, peaked at number two in the Billboard Hot 100 chart, based on platinum sales of the single and a corresponding amount of radio airplay. Even greater success followed, as the pair's next three singles all reached number one during the course of the year. A fifth and final single from the album made the Top Five at the start of 1990, and given the duo's meteoric rise, they were even "rewarded" with a Grammy for Best New Artist in February 1990.

This is not to say that the duo had no detractors. While their fair-skinned and "metrosexual" good looks endeared them to early adolescent girls of all races, many black adolescent males viewed them as "not black enough," "fake," or "sell outs." Many music critics were equally disparaging of the group, as prime examples of the "style over substance" type of act, perceived more and more to be the mainstay of an increasingly hyper-commercial MTV.

There was also the matter of a July 1989 live performance, captured by MTV, when the recording "Girl You Know It's True" started to skip, continuing to repeat the line "Girl, you know it's . . ." before it was abruptly cut off. Many of the fans present didn't seem to notice or care, and the incident was explained as the malfunction of what was admitted to be a pre-recorded track, which had been necessary due to the constant dancing in the group's act. While this explanation allayed the suspicions of some, especially in the light of similar admissions by other MTV-friendly performers such as Madonna, Janet Jackson, and Paula Abdul, something still seemed "off" to many of the more skeptical members of the music press.

More savvy musical journalists checked the liner notes of Milli Vanilli's European version of the album, which credited the original vocalists, and noted the discrepancy with the Arista release, which put producer Farian under pressure to come up with an explanation. Farian was also under pressure from Rob and Fab, who, puffed up with their recent sham "success," were demanding to do all the vocals on their follow-up album, despite lacking the basic vocal ability to do so. The combined pressure proved too much, and, on 12 November 1990, Farian admitted that Rob and Fab were not in any way responsible for the vocal tracks on their album.

The backlash was immediate and powerful. Milli Vanilli's Grammy was withdrawn within four days of Farian's announcement. Arista dropped the group from their roster and deleted "their" album from the company's catalog, refusing to allow retailers to return any unsold, and now largely worthless, albums. This led to numerous consumer fraud class action and individual lawsuits, against Pilatus, Morvan, and

Arista Records that were not finally settled until late August 1992, when all parties agreed to refund all concert ticket and recording sales to anyone who had purchased them.

Probably due to mounting legal bills before this settlement was reached, Farian tried to keep busy, recording a "Real Milli Vanilli" album for European release in 1991, and an album by a related act, Try 'N B, in 1992. Neither did particularly well – nor did Rob and Fab's eponymously titled 1993 release. Having been "deceived" by all involved in the past, the public wanted no part of any of their futures, except, perhaps, as a source of amusement.

Four years passed, until, in 1997, Rob, Fab, and Farian agreed to put aside any previous differences and focus on working together to produce a comeback album, tentatively called *Back and in Attack*. While Farian and Fab made a solid, if ultimately uneven, effort, Rob Pilatus was distracted during the recording sessions by a recently developed drug habit, and the petty criminal activities he had begun to engage in to support it. Following a three-month jail term, Farian agreed to pay for drug rehabilitation treatment for Pilatus, as well as a plane ticket back to Germany. On the eve of what was to have been a tour to promote the new album, however, Pilatus was found dead in a Frankfurt hotel room, having ingested a mixture of unidentified pills and alcohol, on 2 April 1998.

To his credit, Fab chose to continue moving in a more positive direction, working as a DJ for Los Angeles radio station KIIS FM, while also working on new musical projects. In 2000, Milli Vanilli and their rise and fall were the subject of the inaugural episode of VH1's *Behind the Music* series. In 2007, Universal Pictures announced development plans for a film of the Milli Vanilli story, with *Catch Me If You Can* screenwriter, Jeff Nathanson, slated to both write and direct.

And while music videos no longer drive music sales in quite the same way that they did in the 1980s, a new breed of media-friendly, coiffed and choreographed Top 40-style pop star is selling as strongly as ever. The public may seem no more concerned than before about the quality of this new music – at least compared with the performers' prerequisite good looks, but they are still sensitive to anything resembling lip-synching vocal fraud. If you doubt this, all you need do is talk to a young woman named Ashlee Simpson about a malfunctioning pre-recorded vocal track on her 2004 appearance on *Saturday Night Live*. KD

Mötley Crüe

Hair-Metal Heroes

As the performers and fans associated with the Glam Metal genre themselves might tell you, nothing exceeds like excess. The popular 1980s subculture seemed to be one where the old cliché of "sex, drugs, and rock 'n' roll," was adhered to not as a mere general lifestyle guide-line, but as an important, on-going set of "life goals." Often derided by the media and general public for being superficial, materialistic, sexist, drug-addicted, and cartoonish, the "Hair Metal" bands, as they were sometimes called, nevertheless generated multi-million album sales, sold out world tours, and achieved rock radio and music video airplay dominance for most of the decade, no matter what anyone else thought about them. If one band in particular could be said to have embodied the thrill-seeking , ego-driven ethos inherent in Glam Metal's "live fast, die young, and leave a good-looking corpse" posturing, it is probably Los Angeles band, Mötley Crüe.

One of the reasons, for better or for worse, is that they were one of the genre's "originators," having formed in the LA area in 1980. At the time, the local rock scene was largely dominated by Punk, New Wave, and Power Pop acts, influenced by the fledging MTV cable television channel, all vying to help define what was considered new or cutting edge in the genre of rock as a whole. Whereas the members of the fledg-ling Crüe were more interested in a "tried and true" approach to rock stardom, seemingly left over from the all but deceased "Stadium Rock" culture of the 1970s, when success was defined in terms of loud and enormous stage shows, legions of groupies, endless supplies of drugs and alcohol, and piles of cash to keep it all going. With similarly focused and equally outdated attitudes, the original members of the group – Tommy Lee, Nikki Sixx, Mick Mars, and Vince Neil – saw in each other kindred spirits, as they found each other through LA-area music-oriented classified ads. They immediately directed their thoughts and actions to the task of achieving nothing less than world dominance.

From the beginning, the four approached the band as a "profes-sional" operation, going as far as to hire a manager, Allan Coffman, who was apparently professional enough himself to secure an "investor," to support their initial efforts to gain broader notice. They self-released both a single ("Stick to Your Guns/Toast of the Town") and later a full-length LP, *Too Fast for Love*, on their own label, Leathur Records, in 1981, which sold about 20,000 copies. Helped by club performances, known as much for the band's leather- and spandex-clad appearance and home-made pyrotechnics, as for their Blues-meets-Eurometal sound, the band turned a strong initial buzz and a highly marketable image into a contract with Electra Records, in late May 1982.

The record company insisted on remixing their LP, and re-releasing it in August of the same year, under the same title, to coincide with a brief Canadian tour. That tour generated more publicity from the band's brushes with the law and other offstage antics, than it did from anything which happened on stage. After being arrested for their spiked wardrobe, and the possession of vast quantities of pornography, the Crüe's newfound notoriety peaked with nothing less than a bomb threat, allegedly made by phone to an Edmonton disco, where the band had been booked to play. When the threat was later determined to be an ill-advised publicity stunt, made by the Crüe's manager, he was fired at Electra's insistence, and replaced by veteran Hard Rock managers Doug Thaler and Doc McGhee. Ultimately, their public bad behavior caused the boys to prematurely cancel later tour dates, having allegedly earned the dubious distinction of being "banned for life" from the city of Edmonton. Still, the misadventures in Canada had helped build the rookie band's reputation as devil-may-care rebels, with obvious disdain for authority and its conventions.

Mötley Crüe's appearance at the so-called "Us Festival" in the Spring of 1983, marked a "breaking out" point for both the band and the burgeoning Glam Metal scene, as the largely southern Californian musical style (and thus the band) gained newfound national exposure from the concert. This was rapidly followed by the release of the band's second album, *Shout at the Devil*, in the fall of the same year, supported by a couple of provocative music videos, both featuring flocks of scantily clad young women, and an obligatory tour. While critics were completely unimpressed with the sophomore album, and the generally sophomoric image and antics, both onstage and off, of these rebels without a point, the Metal public clearly disagreed. Fans provided the group with a sufficiently steady stream of sales for them to channel conspicuously back into living out the most debauched expectations of the rock star fantasy lifestyle.

Hotel rooms were trashed as a matter of course, hard drug use and binge drinking were obvious and constant, and nearly automatic sex with groupies was alleged to be frequently degrading and/or abusive, often for no other obvious reason than the group member's admitted boredom and his ability to behave in such a way. The band members also made high-profile purchases of extravagant homes, fast cars, and loud motorcycles, which, when combined with the rest of their trappings, constituted Mötley Crüe's "arrival" at the endless party which they, and their fans, defined as "the good life."

In 1984 though, the party almost came to an abrupt end when lead singer Vince Neal collided head-on with a passing motorist while driving drunk with a friend to a nearby liquor store. Having seriously injured both occupants in the on-coming vehicle and killing his passenger, Hanoi Rocks' drummer, Nicholas "Razzle" Dingley, Neal was charged with DUI (driving under the influence) and Vehicular Manslaughter, underscoring the sobering consequences of such deliberately reckless behavior. After a protracted and costly court battle, however, a plea bargain by the singer succeeded in limiting the charge to DUI, and he was sentenced to 30 days in prison, five years of probation, $2.6 million in restitution payments to the victims' families, and 200 hours of community service. To underscore his supposed remorse for the incident and respect for its consequences, Vince went so far as to be featured in anti-drunk driving Public Service Announcements, and the band dedicated its 1985 release, *Theatre of Pain* to the late "Razzle."

That album and its follow-up, *Girls, Girls, Girls*, saw the band finally reach platinum sales and international stardom, both supported by protracted world tours. The Crüe men were all married by then to centerfolds or pin-ups – most notably drummer Tommy Lee to "jiggle TV" star, Heather Locklear – and when touring, traveled in a tightly secured and very private world, designed to minimize any potential negative publicity. In spite of such precautions, however, bassist Nikki Sixx, by then a full-blown junkie, still nearly managed to overdose on heroin. After he was declared clinically dead for a couple of tense moments, management forced an "intervention" on behalf of the entire band, who were deemed too self-destructive to continue touring. The entire band, with the exception of Mick Mars, who was able to quit drinking (his only known vice) on his own, entered intensive bouts of rehab and therapy.

When the group re-emerged, in 1989, allegedly clean and sober, they named their resulting album, *Dr Feelgood*, after the intravenous concoction frequently given to energize and satisfy the cravings of former cocaine addicts. The album debuted at number one and stayed on the chart for 109 weeks, buoyed by the professed zeal for recovery of the Crüe, rather than by over-the-top efforts to prove themselves the reigning rebels in a deliberately controversial genre. The only incident which came close to being a controversy at this time was the firing of Doc McGhee, when he promised, and then failed to deliver, a slot for the boys in that year's Moscow Music Peace Festival. For a moment it seemed like the band had – gasp! – *matured*, or at least become more civilized.

The 1990s proved to be a far more difficult decade for Mötley Crüe and its members as individuals. In the two years between the release of *Dr Feelgood* and Mötley Crüe's 1991 follow-up greatest hits volume, *Decade of Decadence*, rock fans had largely drifted away from Glam Metal, which was perceived as being too shallow, fake, egotistical, and insincere. Many fans had switched to the Grunge sub-genre, which utilized much of the same classic rock-style riffs as Glam Metal, but comprised groups more concerned with "intangibles" like sincere personal expression, or creative freedom, than chart-topping sales and the material rewards that went with them. As a result, the disk made it only to number two on the charts, before sliding back into obscurity after only a few weeks.

This lack of success baffled the band, and provoked a lot of infighting, both with regard to what had happened with the sales of their most recent album, and which direction the band should take for an upcoming studio effort, scheduled for later in the year. The infighting peaked in February 1992, when Vince Neil was either fired, or quit, depending on who was asked about the controversy, leaving the band to scramble to find a suitable replacement. By the time one was found, in the form of the little known vocalist John Corabi, and Mötley Crüe had released its eponymously titled 1994 album, the genre of Glam Metal as well as the group, were largely considered to be "over," leaving the remaining Crüe members baffled as to what to do next.

Privately, the ageing rockers spent much of their time having a go at family life, but with sluggish or downright ugly results. Vince Neil lost a daughter to cancer, before divorcing his second wife, allegedly as a result of her depression thought to stem from the loss of her daughter. Tommy Lee was jailed for battering his second wife, the mother of his children, *Playboy* centerfold and *Baywatch* star, Pamela Anderson, which resulted in their divorce. In fact, by 1997, the finances and careers of all the band's founding members were in sufficiently bad shape that they agreed to collaborate on a new album, *Generation of Swine*, with the condition, demanded by Sixx, that they check their egos at the door.

The new album debuted at number four, but sank quickly thereafter, largely due to Electra doing little to promote what was viewed as the outdated product of has-beens. In response, the Crüe fired the surviving members of their original management, and started their own label, Mötley Records, in 1998. While working on the new album, Vince Neal and Tommy Lee fell out, with the result that Lee left the group in 1999 to pursue solo projects, and to try to counter his "troubled" image.

Since then, there has been little new activity. *The Dirt*, an autobiography detailing the band's excesses and transgressions during their 1980s heyday, was released in the summer of 2002, eventually reaching a position in the top ten of the *New York Times'* bestseller list, and sparking some talk of a film adaptation. There have also been various Mötley Crüe recording projects, with various drummers, which have not done well, truncated but profitable tours, and endless infighting. Ousted band member Tommy Lee has starred in an NBC TV reality show, in which he attempted to get through a semester as a college freshman. Nikki Sixx has released *The Heroin Diaries*, his more candid and precise take on his 1980s heroin dependence, with an accompanying "soundtrack" album. And Vince Neil has been claiming in radio and other interviews that there will be a new album, with the same title as their band biography and upcoming film adaptation, *The Dirt*, which he claims will feature Tommy Lee, despite assertions by Nikki Sixx to the contrary. Perhaps the listening public will get "lucky," and one of the band members will "relapse," sparing us the monotony of those who seem never to know when their party is really, and finally, *over*. DL

MTV

"Edgy"

MTV (Music Television) has been the premier purveyor of bad music across the planet for years, but amazingly, people are still watching. The main MTV channel doesn't even play much music any more. Most of the evening shows are some sort of soap opera or reality television, seemingly designed to appeal to a lobotomized sheep. There is now more music *between* the shows than there is *in* them. MTV seems to dislike its audience, and to be contemptuous both of music, and its viewers. The main concern is the commercial exploitation of a niche in the market.

At its beginning back in the 1980s, MTV was designed as an alternative, edgy channel showing "groundbreaking" music and video. Sometimes it even seemed momentarily to be living up to the hype. But gradually it has become an awful men's magazine cliché of half-naked, miming strippers, and permatan boys with bad haircuts jumping around to music that sounds like it has been programed by a faulty computer. Yet MTV can safely assume that many of its viewers are so brain-washed by now that they they won't turn off! They surely have to be brain-washed. Why else watch the same five music videos 15,000 times in one day.

MTV, which promised to be ground-breaking, is actually grinding down creativity. "It's not MTV enough" means "It doesn't have the latest yodeling princess wiggling her way across the screen boasting minimal clothing, less talent and a song she didn't even write . . . and even worse it's not nice enough to look at!" Don't mention swearing; MTV is so "edgy" that swearing was banished long ago. Swearwords even have to be blanked out of the songs which is one of the factors that has fed into the rather odd moments in modern songs when blanks and bleeps are used to imply edginess, while the audience is left trying to work out the missing words by a process of elimination.

Imagine the typical MTV audience member, sitting there staring at the endless parade of inanity, each moment further eroding their ability to understand the point of music, with their money dripping away into a huge vat that further enriches the corporate gods of MTV. Now imagine them finally getting up the gumption to stand up turning the television off.

Listen to the silence. Isn't that better? DL

Prince

Cease and Desist

Prince, The Artist Formerly Known as . . . and Unpronoucable Squiggle apparently hates his fans. It seems he now has an issue with photographs of himself being posted online. Prince's lawyers sent a "cease and desist" letter to a number of fan sites requesting that they immediately remove any photographs of the singer, including official photographs, fan-submitted concert photos, and, most absurdly, even pictures of people adorned by Prince tattoos. Prince's lawyers also insisted the sites had to provide "substantive details of the means by which you [fan sites] propose to compensate our clients."

Like so many music business stories, this is a tale that started off promising so much and ended up dragged into the gutter by the artist's runaway ego. Prince started well in the 1980s. His early albums were well reviewed and Prince became a prolific and fascinating artist, releasing several hundred songs, both under his own name and with other artists. Well known as a perfectionist, Prince is highly protective of his music, to the point where the adjective "precious" comes to mind. He produces, composes, arranges, and performs almost every song on his albums. The problem is that after his most successful albums (*Parade*, *Sign of the Times* etc.), he seemed increasingly to be turning into a prize asshole. His public pronouncements and, most absurdly, name changes increasingly sent the message that the ego had not only landed but had grown into a monster. In spite of all this, he continued to make the occasional decent record. Although the good ones were more and more infrequent, and interspersed with an increasing amount of howlers –

mostly irritating fusions of progressive rock's complexity with the self-indulgence of jazz-funk work-outs. But he retained enough popularity to be inducted into the Rock and Roll Hall of Fame in 2004.

Still, you don't have to be the greatest of marketing geniuses to spot that attacking your fans isn't a great idea. Perhaps Prince felt that his fame and genius had reached the level where he didn't need his fans any more. Or perhaps he thought he could go on and on making records that no one wants to hear any longer because they can't remember what he's called, or even what he looks like because of the ludicrous embargo on this photographs. Who is this man anyway? What does he look like now?

Send your pictures anonymously and confidentially to . . . DL

Axl Rose

?!*@

In the late 1980s, the so-called Glam or Hair Metal musical sub-genre could not have been more popular in the United States, particularly among white, suburban teenagers. While extremely derivative, both in terms of musical style and structure, as well as in the appearance of its performers, the genre was nevertheless quite successful, largely due to its hedonistic lyrical content, and its aggressive use of music videos as marketing tools. These were often used to underscore the "endless party" lifestyle of its conveniently photogenic purveyors. Its detractors, however, felt the sub-genre was too pretty, watered down, user-friendly, and weak, desperately needing an infusion of "true" rock 'n' roll rebelliousness to regain any sense of authentic Metal Attitude. As if on cue, to fill this "attitude vacuum," appeared one W. Axl Rose, the deliberately controversial front man of the now notorious LA band, Guns 'N Roses.

Born William Bruce Rose Jr, in Lafayette, Indiana, the younger Rose was allegedly sexually abused by his biological father, who abandoned the family when his namesake was only two years old. His mother remarried, to William Bailey, shortly thereafter, changing her first-born's last name to that of his stepfather. Any hope that the young Axl Rose's home life would improve were quickly dashed, however, both for Axl and his two later half-siblings, as Mr Bailey was a both a devout Pentecostal and a firm believer in corporal punishment. A further complication was that Bailey raised Axl to believe that he was Axl's biological father, in all likelihood to enforce the boy's obedience to him and his religious beliefs.

Church attendance, as it happened, had a very different effect on young Axl to that hoped for by William Bailey. Forced to attend church between three and eight times a week, Axl sought refuge from the constant preaching and proselytizing in the church choir, singing before the congregation for the first time at the age of five. His rebelliousness first found expression in this forum, too, as Axl would often sing in changing voices of varying pitch, usually inappropriate for the song, and often irritating the choir master. His interest in music proved sincere, however, as he continued to study the piano throughout his lifetime, and later became a member of his high school chorus.

It was during his years at high school that William Bailey Jr began his transformation into W. Axl Rose. It started when he was thrown out of the family home aged sixteen, for refusing to cut his hair. This initiated a spree of "acting out," characterized by over 20 arrests for fighting and public drunkenness. At the age of 17, while rifling through hidden papers in his parents' home, William Bailey Jr discovered the truth about his biological father, his mother's divorce, and his true identity, if only in terms of his name. From that time on, he took to calling himself W. Rose, both acknowledging and rejecting the identity of his long-lost father.

Shortly afterwards, the newly renamed W. Rose left Lafayette on the advice of his attorneys, who were concerned that the local authorities would make good on their threat to incarcerate him as a habitual criminal if they charged him with any further felonies. In December 1982, Axl set out for Los Angeles, hoping to track down his friend and fellow Lafayette troublemaker, Izzy Stradlin, who had moved out to the city a few months beforehand. Upon reuniting, their misadventures in Los Angeles served as a basis for the controversies and mayhem which were to follow them, and even propel them, to international notoriety.

For three years the pair drifted through several Glam Metal bands, and contented themselves during their free time with binge-drinking, hard-drug use, and promiscuous sex with seemingly interchangeable partners. They barely paid their bills through minimum-wage jobs and "quick money" arrangements, such as smoking cigarettes for a UCLA scientific study. In March 1985, they allied themselves with guitarist Tracii Guns, and Guns 'N Roses was born.

They made their debut at The Troubadour in Hollywood. The venue was part of an established Los Angeles Metal scene which had spawned a large number of acts, thanks more to their proximity to numerous LA-based record companies and their easily marketed "images," than the originality of their musical "visions," or even their basic musical talent. For almost two years the band was a fixture on this scene, while undergoing various changes of personnel and engaging in stereotypical rock 'n' roll decadence, garnering themselves a reputation as emerging bad boys in an equally rebellious genre. By 1986, the band had released the independently produced *Live ?!*@ Like a Suicide* EP, and signed to major label, Geffen Records.

Appetite for Destruction, Guns 'N Roses's debut album, was released in the summer of 1987, but it took almost a year for the band to receive any real attention for it, or, more importantly, any significant sales. This changed with the release of the single "Sweet Child O' Mine," and the subsequent music video, which shot the band to the number one spot on the Billboard Charts by the fall of 1988. When this success finally combined with the band's aggressive touring schedule, opening for established acts such as Gene Loves Jezebel, Poison, and Aerosmith, commercial success became almost a given, and the band duly sold 15 million copies of their album, making it the fourth bestselling debut of all time.

In retrospect, the album's success probably came from combining a darker take on typical Glam Metal "sex, drugs, and rock 'n' roll" lyrics, with crisply attacked but well-worn Classic Rock-style music. The latter garnered them a certain amount of critical praise for bringing some melodic musicianship back to Metal, which practically guaranteed a certain amount of airplay by album-oriented rock radio stations. But it was the darker take on Glam Metal, combined with erratic public behavior, increasingly in the spotlight, which made Axl Rose more than a mere hard-rocking miscreant.

It all began in late 1988, with the release of the Guns 'N Roses stop-gap EP, *Lies*. Since the band was exhausted from touring, but did not want to lose momentum, before they retired to the studio to start work on what would be a make-or-break second album, they attached a couple of their more recent studio tracks to their previously released *Live ?!*@ Like a Suicide* EP, and distributed the "new" album to the public. Even though the song had been around for over two years, suddenly everyone was aware of "One in a Million," which the band had recorded when they were nobodies.

The song relates the experience of a presumed young, white, middle-American male as he attempts to navigate life in LA at "street level." Ultimately, its narrator (Rose himself?) rants about the police, "niggers," "faggots," and immigrants, before "turning around" and demanding that "radicals and racists" not judge him for his views as a "small-town white boy, just trying to make ends meet." Given both the basically "liberal" attitudes of the commercial rock business and the widespread commercial attention Guns 'N Roses had attracted up to that point, such material had them instantly branded as racists and homophobes, almost literally overnight.

For someone at the center of such an ugly controversy, Rose did little to convince detractors that he was not a racist and homophobe. He made incoherent remarks about how the word "nigger" didn't necessarily mean a black person, and how he had said he merely didn't understand "faggots," but ultimately meant them no harm. Apparently, the Gay Men's Health Crisis charity was unconvinced, and threw the band off a 1989 benefit concert performers' list, and neither was Vernon Reid of the African-American Metal group Living Color, who alluded to the song while onstage at a Rolling Stones concert date shortly thereafter, where both bands were opening acts. While both incidents were never entirely addressed by the frequently dismissive and combative Rose, his mounting difficulties made the controversy merely one of an ever-growing list of troubles.

It was public knowledge at this time that Axl was romantically involved with Erin Everly, the daughter of the singer Don Everly. Allegedly the inspiration for the band's first hit, "Sweet Child O' Mine," Erin appeared in the video, and her face even ended up tattooed on Axl's arm. Devoted though he may have seemed, it is unlikely that she expected him to show up, as he did in April 1989, armed with a gun, demanding that she elope to Las Vegas with him and marry him. While Ms Everly agreed to marriage in the end, the couple separated on a number of occasions before the marriage was eventually annulled in 1991. While it lasted it served as the basis for a civil lawsuit involving charges of physical and emotional domestic violence, which was settled out of court in 1994.

The year 1990 was make or break for Axl and Guns 'N Roses. Having recently been forced to replace their drummer on account of his substance abuse problems, and with the controversies which had resulted from the *Lies* EP still festering in the background, the group was under considerable pressure to produce nothing less than another classic, or face being relegated to flash-in-the-pan status. Anyone other than Axl might have tried to play it as safe as possible.

Instead, it was announced that the project, provisionally called *Use Your Illusion*, would be a double album, released as two separate CDs or cassettes, and available by the spring of 1991. As the anticipation grew, so did the stories of bickering and infighting, the number of tracks involved, and the number of delays before it was finally slated for release. Even as final adjustments were being made in the studio, the band started a 28-month long tour to coincide with the intended release date.

Early reports from the road were not encouraging. The new material was drawing mixed reviews from fans, and many were annoyed at delayed starts to shows, frequently due to Axl's tardiness. A Saint Louis show that summer saw Axl attempt to jump off stage to attack a pirate videographer, and when frustrated in doing so by the size and demeanor of the crowd, he stormed off stage, sparking a riot. As the date for the album's release continued to be pushed back, many fans began to question whether the band was worth the trouble.

When *Use Your Illusion I* and *II*, debuted at numbers two and one respectively in September 1991, sales were driven almost more by a frenzy of curiosity than anything else, but the response was less than warm. Critics, for the most part, found the whole project bloated, inconsistent, and often lacking in either sincerity or good taste. Most of the lyrics seemed like an endless whine about how hard it was to be Guns 'N Roses, or, specifically, Axl Rose. And while diehard fans kept the albums on the charts for over 100 weeks following its release, the albums did not enjoy the sustained popularity of *Appetite for Destruction*.

The rest of the *Use Your Illusion* tour did little to offset these problems. In fact, two months after the actual album release date, founding member Izzy Stradlin quit the group, citing irreconcilable differences with Rose, and increasing discontent with the tour, and the album it was intended to support. At this point, Axl demanded and received sole ownership of the name Guns 'N Roses from the remaining founding members, McKagan and Slash, though both retain song-writing credits and royalties on all relevant material.

In 1992, the band attempted to attract wavering public attention back by devising a grand finale for their troubled tour. They attempted a co-headlining tour with equally popular metal group, Metallica, who had just started a tour performing material from their enormously popular "black album." This nearly came to a premature end in August, when Metallica's vocalist was injured by a pyrotechnic display gone awry, and Guns 'N Roses were asked to take the stage early.

The result was a troubled Guns 'N Roses set, in which Axl stated, after seven less than enthusiastically received songs, that it would be their "last show for a long time." On concluding the track "Civil War," which turned out to be their final number of the evening, Rose told the crowd, which was by now quite agitated, "Thank you, your money will be refunded," and left the stage. This led to a riot, which the Montreal police were barely able to suppress.

By this time, the public had grown tired of Rose's self absorption, his big mouth, temper tantrums, and endless excuses for everything. Though Guns 'N Roses later released an album of covers, *The Spaghetti Incident*, most noteworthy for its inclusion of a Charles Manson song, it never again toured with its original line-up. In fact, by 1995, Rose was the only founding member still in the group, which was apparently fine by him. Lawsuits involving charges laid by former girlfriends came to use up increasing amounts of his time and wealth, to the extent that, by 1996, he had become an infamous Malibu recluse, largely invisible to the public, save for the occasional sighting. It was almost as if Axl had *finally* gotten the public's memo letting him know that his 15 minutes of fame had expired. As far as many were concerned, they had expired a *long* time ago.

Almost, but not quite, however. Until the spring of 2006, when Rose resurfaced in a rare *Rolling Stone* interview, claiming that he had been hard at work on a newly revamped Guns 'N Roses album, tentatively titled, *Chinese Democracy*. The project, in typical Axl style, was supposed to comprise 32 tracks in total, and was due to be finished "soon." After a few live appearances, which attracted mixed reviews, Axl revised his release date, promising whatever fans he might still have a fall release date. By the time of his appearance at the 2006 MTV Video Music

Awards, Rose had issued a third revision of the release date, claiming that a tour would begin in late October, and that the album would be out by the end of the year. Guns 'N Roses's few live appearances since have met with mostly mixed reviews, but the long-promised album has yet to materialize. We can only live in hope that Axl will finally realize that *no one cares any more.* KD

Britney Spears and Kevin Federline

It Takes Two to Tango

Britney's first two albums sold more than 30 million copies worldwide, but her overall power transcended her success as a singer. She was young, cute, had an apparently wholesome personality, and, as the record industry put it, "an ability to cross the boundaries of age, sex, and class." Her marketing power could be harnessed to anything from soft drinks to face cream. By the age of 22, she had been named by *Forbes* magazine as the "World's Most Powerful Celebrity." However it would be a long road down from there.

In 2004, she married Kevin Federline, a 28-year-old sometime rapper and actor with whom she subsequently had two children, Sean Preston and Jayden James. The pair divorced in 2006, citing irreconcilable differences, but, by then, Britney's life had become a painful merry-go-round of embarrassment, humiliation, and rehab. She attempted a "comeback" at the 2007 MTV awards but even that ended in farce as she took to the stage, looking pale, and squeezed into an ill-fitting sparkly bikini, seemingly having forgotten the words to her songs.

When he got engaged to Britney, Kevin Federline already had a pregnant girlfriend, Sher Jackson. Sher Jackson and Federline also had a five-year-old daughter Kori. Someone with more sense might have been able to see Federline was going to be trouble, but Britney didn't.

Since being with, and subsequently splitting from Federline, Britney has been through a series of mishaps, most of them self-inflicted. She was seen driving her car with her son, Sean Preston, on her lap, she partied without her knickers on, entered rehab for drug and alcohol addiction, shaved her head on impulse, attacked a paparazzo and his car with a large umbrella, was seen dazed and confused at the wheel of her car, seemingly unable to locate her home, despite being in LA. Subsequently she entered rehab again, lost custody of her children, lost visiting rights to her children, was admitted to hospital after being intoxicated on an "unknown" substance, and was eventually sectioned under the mental health act for her own good. She has been photographed in all of the above moments, which does, in the end, make one wonder whether or not the root of Britney's problems lie in her need for attention.

To observe such self-destructive behavior is always uncomfortable. However, given that most of Britney's behavior eventually results in some "comment" or "action" from her ex-husband, it makes you seriously wish that he had the sense to stop sticking his oar in and simply try his best to sort out his family wrangles in private. More than anything this would seem to make sense for the sake of the children involved. To date, Britney's career seems to be shot, her looks are fading, her marriage is over, and her children have been taken away from her, while Federline's fame has increased. The worst of all possible outcomes. DL

Phil Spector

Not Worth the Aggravation

Phil Spector was a pioneer of the 1960s' girl-group sound, responsible for over 25 Top 40 hits between 1960 and 1965. He went on to work with various artists, including Ike and Tina Turner, John Lennon, and the Ramones, with similar success. In 1989, Spector was one of the first non-performers to be inducted into the Rock and Roll Hall of Fame. If you've ever been shopping during the holiday season, it's impossible not to have heard his *A Christmas Gift for You* with some of the classic seasonal pop tunes keeping you upbeat as you shop.

However, in later years, Spector became increasingly noted for his eccentricity, reclusive temperament, and obsessive behavior. As a result, Spector can be seen as an asshole, who has had many conflicts, sometimes bizarre, with the artists, songwriters, and promoters with whom he has worked. Describing the collapse of their Philles Records partnership, Lester Sill said, "I sold out for a pittance. It was shit, ridiculous, around $60,000. I didn't want to, but I had to. Let me tell you, I couldn't live with Phillip . . . I just wanted the fuck out of there. If I wouldn't have, I would have killed him. It wasn't worth the aggravation."

Spector's odd behavior came to a peak when he was put on trial for second-degree murder. On 3 February 2003, he was arrested on suspicion of murder after the body of a 40-year-old nightclub hostess and B-movie actress, Lana Clarkson, of Los Angeles, was found at his mansion, Pyrenees Castle, in Alhambra, California. Police answered to a 911 phone call from Spector's driver and found Clarkson, who had been shot. She was pronounced dead at the scene. On 20 November 2003, Spector was indicted for Clarkson's murder.

Spector's bizarre defence was that Clarkson's death was an accidental suicide. However, on 28 October 2005, a judge ruled that potentially damning statements that Spector had allegedly made to police could be used by the prosecution in his trial. Spector's lawyers had tried to suppress a statement which Spector was supposed to have made after Clarkson was found. He is alleged to have said, "I think I killed somebody." His lawyer argued that comments attributed to the music producer shouldn't be heard in court because he had been suffering from prescription-drug withdrawal symptoms. Two months previously, Spector had said in an interview with UK newspaper the *Daily Telegraph* that he suffered from bipolar disorder and that he considered himself "relatively insane." The judge also ruled that transcripts from a deposition Spector made months before Clarkson's death could be introduced by the prosecution at trial.

During the preparation period and the actual trial, Spector went through at least three sets of attorneys, firing each one in turn. As soon as he felt that things weren't going his way, the attorney was the scape-goat. He even tried to sue former attorney Robert Shapiro for a

$1-million retainer paid prior to the first trial, although he eventually gave up on that – for the time being, at any rate. Spector remained free on $1-million bail while awaiting trial.

Not surprisingly, given Spector's eccentricity, the trial was controversial from the start. Famous forensic expert, Henry Lee, who had also provided key evidence in the O. J. Simpson trial, was accused of hiding crucial evidence, which the District Attorney's office claimed could prove Spector's guilt. In addition, a coroner who examined Clarkson's body concluded that bruising on her tongue indicated that the gun used to kill her had been shoved in her mouth. Despite these setbacks, Spector's defense team had a breakthrough when the Los Angeles Sheriff's expert stated that only Clarkson's DNA had been found on the handgun, which was a boost for Spector's defense that she had shot herself. The DNA expert also found none of Spector's DNA on Clarkson's fingernails, which weakened the prosecution's argument that Clarkson had struggled with Spector.

The jury eventually "reached an impasse," and Judge Fidler adjourned the case for attorneys to review the situation. The jury was split 7–5; but no indication was given as to which side was which. Fidler said that he would consider whether or not the charge of involuntary manslaughter would fit the profile of the case. The charge in the case against Spector was second-degree murder. If he had been convicted, Spector could have served a jail term of anything from 15 years to life, with a further ten years automatically added because the crime had involved a gun.

The jury could not reach a verdict, announcing a deadlock of ten for guilty, and two for not guilty. Judge Fidler declared a mistrial in the murder case against Phil Spector.

At time of writing, it has been confirmed that Phil Spector is to be retried, with preparations being made for a 2008 court date. Clearly, Spector is difficult to work with. Only one of Spector's initial defense team remains. All of the remaining members of his previous defense team have either resigned, or been dismissed following the mistrial. Also, in the same month, Spector decided to go back and sue former attorney Robert Shapiro for the retainer paid before the first trial. Spector's claim was that Shapiro had prepared inadequately for the trial, and may have been responsible for the prosecution filing charges at all. In typical asshole fashion he is determined to prove that everyone else is guilty, except himself. DL

The Spice Girls

Skinny, Tubby, Nutty, Stupid, and Baby-Jane

"The Spice Girls are something of an anachronism – after all, if anyone wants to be entertained by five not especially pretty women clumping around a stage like a gang of age-worn hookers now, they can just go and see The Pussycat Dolls" – Stuart Heritage, *Heckler Spray*, 29 June 2007.

Skinny Spice, Tubby Spice, Nutty Spice, Stupid Spice, and Baby-Jane Spice (sorry, Posh, Scary, Sporty, Ginger, and Baby), seemed to be having a successful comeback until it dawned on them that it was just as rubbish as before and they canceled a substantial part of their "World" tour almost before they'd begun. Reportedly this was due to disappointing audiences, as some of the earlier shows were only half-full, with many ticket-holders failing to turn up, perhaps because on sober reflection they were simply embarrassed to be seen at the event. A planned three-month stint became a four-week dabble, and they sensibly chose to hang up their sparkly mini-skirts and go back to their vacuous *Hello!*-sponsored lives.

On Tuesday, 5 February 2008, free London newspaper *Metro* reported, "Angry Spice Girl fans have started a vicious Internet hate campaign after the girls canceled the rest of their world tour after bitch fighting. Outrage is so widespread, hate groups have been set up on Facebook and devoted fan sites closed down, branding the five singers 'liars.'" The girls themselves stuck to the official line that they had canceled because of family commitments. Still, it's no surprise that journalists speculated on the real story.

Not quite miming strippers, the Spice Girls first bounced onto the music scene back in 1997, shouting randomly about "girl power" and Margaret Thatcher, and whatever else they thought might gain them attention. Clueless about how to do anything other than promote themselves, the girls quickly became an embarrassment to thinking women everywhere with their confused political messages, peculiarly awful clothes, and increasingly strange body shapes. They slowly morphed into five silly girls who had been given too much money to spend on themselves, and too many articles and interviews in which to air their pointless views. That's not to mention the music. It's kindest not to, and instead to let it die a slow death in the bargain bins of thrift stores around the world.

One, and not the one you might think, has admitted to anorexia and eating disorders during the Spice Girls' heyday; another has since become the poster girl for pro-anorexia websites, but hasn't chosen to step up and put the record straight. Maybe she's too busy trying on all her frocks at home.

It's hard looking back to understand what the fuss was about. They weren't great singers or dancers. According to some reports, their shows were always mimed, and it is alleged that they employed some musical software which matched their out-of-tune on-stage voices with a perfect pitch recorded voice to deliver an enhanced vocal that somehow managed to sound in tune. However, if you've experienced their live performances you might be doubtful about this information.

So what are we left with? Bad singing, bad clothes, bad ideology, bad make-up, and bad advice; it's no wonder there are so many articles speculating about cat fights – if they were true it would be the most amusing thing they've ever done. DL

Self-Test: Are *you* an Asshole?

Perhaps you have reason to suspect that you're an asshole, but you're not quite sure if you are, or if you're not. Are you *really* an asshole? And, if so, what *kind* of asshole are you? The "Are *you* an Asshole?" self-test is the surefire way to find out. Simply mark the course of action that you would take in each case, then tot up your score at the end.

Good luck!

Childhood

1. To test the power of your new BB gun you shoot and kill a small defenseless animal of some kind. Do you:

   a) run home crying, swearing to God you will never do anything so cruel again?

   b) acknowledge the sinking feeling in your stomach, and bury the poor creature?

   c) mumble "Cool!" and go looking for more "targets"?

   d) garnish the carcass with fireworks and enjoy the "show"?

2. You have just watched a TV ad for the coolest toy you have ever seen. Do you:

   a) remind yourself you can't have everything, then turn off the TV and do your homework?

   b) politely suggest to your parents that it would make a fine birthday or Christmas present?

   c) pester your parents incessantly, until they simply can't take it any more and they buy it for you simply to shut you up?

   d) study the security features of the local toy shop and just go get the damn thing?

3. While playing with friends in the house, you break your mother's favorite vase. Do you:

   a) tell her immediately, apologize sincerely, and offer to fix or replace it, out of your allowance if necessary?

   b) see if it can be fixed with a covert gluing, and, if not, reluctantly inform your mother of the mishap?

   c) pretend you don't know how it happened, and deflect blame onto any siblings who might have been home at the time?

   d) smash all the matching accessories, and laugh about it when confronted?

4. Upon arriving at the corner store to buy candy, you discover you don't have enough money, but the shopkeeper is busy with other customers, and paying no attention. Do you:

   a) sigh with disappointment and head home, knowing that when you finally *do* buy the candy, it will be sweeter for having had to wait for it?

   b) ask other customers at random for the spare change you need to buy the candy?

   c) slip the candy into your pocket and exit the store quickly, savoring the thrill of not having had to pay for it?

   d) slip as much candy as will fit into your pockets, and make a mental note to return to the store in search of further opportunities for pilfering?

5. A new, unusual-looking, and weird-acting kid moves into your neighborhood from somewhere you've never heard of. Do you:

   a) try to make him feel welcome and ask him if he needs a friend?

b) study him somewhat suspiciously, and maybe ask a couple of blunt questions about his appearance and behavior?

c) make fun of everything about him, from the way he talks to the way he dresses, as well anything else you can find out about him, or where he comes from?

d) make him the neighborhood pariah based on his being different, even making up stories about him, if it will encourage the other kids to shun and humiliate him?

School

1. You haven't done the assigned homework for a subject you really dislike. Do you:

a) frantically try to complete the assignment on the bus the next day, hoping your guesses will be good enough?

b) shrug and try not to think about it – since you hate that class, you could care less about your grade in it?

c) make up a plausible and reasonable excuse for the teacher as to why it wasn't completed, and hope that he or she believes you?

d) threaten someone smaller than you who excels at the subject, so you can copy down her answers for the assignment?

2. You are presented with a pop quiz for an assignment you haven't bothered to read. Do you:

a) take the bad grade, and accept the teacher's offer of further help on the topic?

b) take the bad grade and hope you improve before the report cards come out?

c) copy the answers off the kid sitting closest to you and hope for the best?

d) excuse yourself to use the bathroom before the quiz can be given, pull the fire alarm, and hope that the ensuing chaos will postpone the quiz until at least a day later?

3. While standing in line for lunch, another kid cuts in front of you. Do you:

a) immediately inform the nearest teacher or lunch monitor of the infraction of the rules?

b) loudly complain about the situation with the rest of your friends, hoping to make the kid who cut in look bad?

c) immediately pound them without hesitation or mercy – the kid should have known better than to do that to *you*?

d) threaten to pound the kid unmercifully unless he agrees to let *you* cut in front of *him*, not just then and there, but for the whole school year?

4. It is a beautiful spring day in your senior year of high school. Your course work comprises completely meaningless electives, and you've been accepted into the college of your choice. Do you:

a) promise yourself you will make the most of the day during your non-school hours?

b) take longer at lunch than you should, but otherwise bide your time until spring break?

c) abruptly skip a class or two and lie convincingly when confronted?

    d) pursue absenteeism as a new hobby, and encourage other students to join you?

5. Your regular teacher has been replaced by a substitute who doesn't seem to know much about the subject, or even how to follow the teacher's lesson plan. Do you:

    a) remain seated and wait patiently while the substitute attempts to figure it all out, attempting to aid her when possible?

    b) wonder to yourself, "Where do they find these people?" and wish the class would end soon?

    c) use the substitute's obvious distraction to haze, and pull various pranks on, the other members of the class in a bid to foment chaos and establish your dominance over the substitute?

    d) use the substitute's obvious distraction to pull various pranks on him or her to see if you can force him or her to quit?

Love

1. Your romantic partner has just put on a particularly unflattering outfit, that he/she is clearly enjoying wearing, and asks, "How do I look?" Do you:

    a) attempt diplomatically to explain that what he/she is wearing might not be the best "look" for him/her?

    b) notice how happy your partner is, say that he/she looks fine, and hope that no one else notices?

    c) tell your partner that he/she looks fine, even though you know you're lying, and hope the ridicule of others will deter him/her from dressing that way again?

   d) tell your partner in no uncertain terms how terrible he/she looks, and suggest that perhaps you should dress him/her in the future?

2. Your partner engages in a constant, compulsive, but harmless habit that you find very annoying. Do you:

   a) keep quiet about it and try to accept the one you love, flaws and all?

   b) politely explain how much the habit bothers you and hope to find a compromise as a way of dealing with the problem?

   c) tell him/her in no uncertain terms how annoying you find the habit, and how engaging in it proves how compulsive and weak he/she is?

   d) let your partner know that he/she has to stop engaging in the habit immediately, or the relationship is over?

3. Your partner is very friendly with a person you find extremely annoying. Do you:

   a) accept the friendship as part of your partner's life, and work on being more tolerant of his/her friend?

   b) politely inform your partner of how you feel about his/her friend, and try to find a mutually satisfying solution for dealing with him/her?

   c) make fun of and belittle the person whenever possible, in an attempt to show your partner how worthless you think his/her friend really is?

   d) demand that your partner immediately sever all ties with the friend, or you're dumping him/her, simple as that?

4. You suspect that your partner may be cheating on you, but have no direct evidence of your suspicions. Do you:

a) assume that you're being paranoid, and try to work on being less distrustful?

b) quietly look for proof of your suspicions, being careful not to speak about them with your partner until you are *certain* that your suspicions are well founded?

c) read his/her diary, hack his/her e-mail account, and do anything else that might yield quick, reliable intelligence – if your suspicions are proved correct, punish him/her as harshly as possible for his/her misdeeds?

d) use your suspicions as an excuse to sleep with whoever you've been interested in, or can hook up with easily, outside the relationship; then, when you're finally bored, arrange for your partner to find out all about it?

5. Your relationship is in serious trouble and is probably heading towards a particularly messy and/or ugly break-up. Do you:

a) end it as quickly and cleanly as possible, knowing that whatever abuse you will be subjected to is simply a reflection of how hard it is to be rejected?

b) break things off cleanly, while refusing to tolerate any insults or misbehavior from your now ex-partner while doing so?

c) quit returning all phone calls and e-mails, block him/her from your social networking site, and hope he/she goes away?

d) explain to him/her in no uncertain terms what a worthless person you think he/she is, and how it would be a mercy to the world at large if he/she fell off the face of the earth?

Work

1. You wake up not feeling like going in to work. Do you:

    a) remind yourself of how much you are needed there, and go in anyway?

    b) go in anyway, but make request vacation time – *soon?*

    c) call in sick, and use the much needed day off to catch up on soap operas and internet porn?

    d) go in anyway, fake an "on-the-job injury," and spend the next couple months collecting disability payments?

2. You find that a universally used piece of work equipment, such as the photocopier, is broken, but no one has called for it to be repaired. Do you:

    a) immediately call the service company, figuring the person who broke it was too busy to do so themselves?

    b) call the service company, leaving an anonymous note on the machine, detailing the situation you encountered, and politely requesting the first person to find the machine not working to call for it to be repaired, *THANK YOU?*

    c) look for a functioning machine, figuring that if you didn't create the situation, you don't have to fix it either – it's not *your* company, *right?*

    d) vandalize the machine further, figuring if that's how people are going to be, you'll go one better; besides, it might give you the excuse you need not to have to work for a while?

3. In reviewing a co-worker's recently completed project, you find numerous errors and mistakes. Do you:

a) correct the errors yourself while making a mental note to politely discuss the project with him/her?

b) politely point out the errors to the co-worker, and offer to help them fix them?

c) let the errors stand in the project, as it was your co-worker's responsibility to do a good job, and you're not his/her baby-sitter?

d) immediately point out the mistakes to your supervisor, and suggest that the co-worker should be fired immediately for such incompetence?

4. In reviewing the project of a superior, you find numerous cases of questionable accounting that seem to benefit him/her at the expense of the company. Do you:

a) immediately inform your superior of the perceived problem, and hope that it is resolved as quickly and cleanly as possible?

b) anonymously report the discrepancies to your superior's immediate superior, and let *him/her* sort it out?

c) mind your own business and hope no one else notices either; it was getting boring around there anyway?

d) inform your superior of what you have found, and say that you want a cut of whatever he/she is up to, or you'll turn him/her in?

5. You have consumed entirely too much spiked eggnog at the company Christmas party. Do you:

a) switch to bottled water, before calling a cab, or getting a ride home?

b) slow down on the "nog," but hang around to see what craziness others might get into?

c) keep drinking, and later take the opportunity to let others know just what you've always thought of them, using plenty of four-letter words to underscore your "points"?

d) keep drinking and see how many ill-advised stunts you can pull (after all, company Christmas parties are *made* for regrets, so no slacking!)?

Marriage

1. Your spouse is wildly devoted to a hobby or pastime you couldn't care less about. Do you:

a) hope your spouse enjoys himself/herself anyway, as his/her happiness is your happiness?

b) accept the difference in your interests, but let your spouse know when he/she is boring you with needless trivia, or if he/she is spending too much time pursuing the hobby?

c) constantly mock or disparage your spouse's interest, in the hope that this will convince him/her to quit?

d) actively sabotage or interfere with his/her interest in the hope that he/she will quit in frustration?

2. Your spouse hasn't been doing his/her share of household chores. Do you:

a) assume that something has been preventing him/her from getting the work done, and do it yourself?

b) ask your spouse if there is something preventing him/her from getting the work done, and gently remind him/her of his/her responsibility, if there isn't?

c) loudly complain and criticize your spouse's obvious laziness, and insensitivity to your comfort in the hope that this will motivate him/her to get their act together?

d) quit doing your share of the chores as well; why should you be a sucker too?

3. You find one of your in-laws especially annoying and difficult to get along with, despite the fact that your spouse adores them. Do you:

a) remind yourself of the importance of family unity and tranquility, and silently suffer through the in-law's occasional visits?

b) remain polite, but tactfully assert any problems you might have with his/her actions or speech?

c) openly mock and criticize the in-law as he/she isn't *your* family, so who cares?

d) tell your spouse straight out that it's either the in-law or you – if your spouse loves you, he/she will know what to do?

4. Upon pulling up to your home you realize that you have completely forgotten that it's your wedding anniversary. Do you:

a) admit to your spouse that you forgot, beg his/her forgiveness, and try to take them out somewhere special anyway?

b) admit nothing, telling your spouse that dinner is a "surprise," after having secured a restaurant reservation on your cellphone, while still in the car?

c) act surprised, say you forgot, and offer no consolation whatsoever for this lapse in memory and conduct; why is this such a big deal anyway?

d) laugh, and respond only by saying, "So?"

5. At a party, you are hit on by someone who is very cute, but clearly not your spouse. Do you:

   a) tell them immediately that you're married, and then seek out your spouse so you can tell them what happened, and apologize for being so attractive to others?

   b) flirt guiltily until your discomfort peaks, then excuse yourself to get another drink?

   c) flirt right back, enthusiastically, but cautiously, so as not to draw attention to yourself, while seeing if you can get the person's number for a possible fling?

   d) use the flirtation as an open invitation to solicit an adulterous affair; it's not *your* fault you're so irresistible, and it would be a shame to keep such innate sexiness to yourself?

Sex

1. While having sex with your partner, you reach orgasm before he/she does. Do you:

   a) continue to pleasure him/her through alternate means until he/she climaxes as well?

   b) apologize and promise to make it up to him/her some other way?

   c) ask your partner what his/her problem is, and harangue him/her about whether or not he/she finds you attractive any more?

   d) shrug, roll over, and try to get some sleep?

2. You are feeling quite aroused, but your partner is not. Do you:

a) tell your partner that you completely understand, and tactfully change the subject so as not to make him/her uncomfortable, or feel too much pressure?

b) tell your partner you completely understand, but should he/she feel like changing his/her mind, you're willing to make it worth his/her while?

c) tell your partner that he/she would do what makes you happy if he/she really cared about you and your relationship?

d) hold your partner down, muffle any protests, and proceed as planned; he/she should not have turned you on if he/she didn't want it?

3. While having sex, you want to engage in behavior your partner says it too kinky, messy, or disgusting. Do you:

a) apologize for suggesting something he/she found so objectionable, and never broach the subject again?

b) ask your partner why he/she objects, and if there is any way to change his/her mind about trying it?

c) drop the subject, and make a mental note to find someone who appreciates your idea of fun?

d) hold your partner down, muffle any protests, and proceed as planned; you know he/she really wants it anyway?

4. While having sex, your partner does something unusual, though not painful or disgusting, which is distracting you from taking any pleasure in what you're otherwise doing. Do you:

a) let your partner continue, because you love him/her and don't want him/her to think he/she doesn't turn you on?

b) tactfully stop him/her, and explain the problem?

    c) ask him/her where the hell he/she got the idea to do something as stupid as that?

    d) break up with your partner on the spot, and tell everyone you know how lousy he/she is in bed?

5. You discover nude pictures of your partner while surfing the internet. Do you:

    a) pretend you never saw them, and hope such wild behavior has been worked out of his/her system by now?

    b) confess your discovery, emphasizing that you would like to know his/her side of the story?

    c) break up with your partner on the spot, and tell everyone what a sleazebag he/she is?

    d) use this as an opportunity to suggest a new career for him/her in adult entertainment, with you as his/her manager?

Parenting

1. Your child breaks a favorite toy while engaged in overly rough play. Do you:

    a) replace the toy immediately, as it wasn't your child's fault it was so easily broken?

    b) explain that such accidents are part of playing too rough, and while very distressing, are often the natural consequence of such behavior?

    c) laugh and say that's what he/she gets for being so clumsy and stupid?

d) confiscate all his/her toys, and tell your child that he/she can have them back when he/she knows how to play with them the "right" way?

2. Your child is behaving badly while shopping at a local mall. Do you:

a) attempt to calm him/her down, and leave the mall, so as not to cause any further disturbance?

b) explain that you understand his/her boredom or discomfort, but that you need to get this bit of shopping done, and will reward him/her for better behavior, if he/she co-operates?

c) smack your child immediately and tell him/her that he/she will get more of the same if he/she continues to behave badly?

d) smack your child immediately, and then proceed to tell him/her how typical his/her behavior is for such a rotten child as him/her?

3. Your child has taken a strong interest in an unusual, though not inappropriate, subject. Do you:

a) encourage him/her to follow his/her interest, regardless of how unseemly or odd it may appear to others?

b) acknowledge that you understand your child's interest, but that others might not be so understanding?

c) tell your child how weird and wrong his/her interest is, attempting to discourage it rapidly, so no one will know what a weirdo you have for a kid?

d) force your child into mandatory therapy and put him/her on behavior-modifying drugs if possible – you will *not* raise a freak?

4. Your child has brought you a report card with much lower grades than you had anticipated. Do you:

a) ask your child if he/she is having trouble with his/her school work, and, if so, help him/her when he/she gets stuck?

b) get the name of a good tutor from your child's teacher, and arrange for extra help?

c) ground your child until his/her grades improve, and let him/her know you will not tolerate his/her obvious stupidity, or else?

d) beat your child, ground him/her, put him/her on behavior-modifying drugs, and threaten him/her with being sent to a military academy if he/she doesn't shape up?

5. Another parent knocks on the door of your home, and says your child has been misbehaving around the neighborhood. Do you:

a) apologize profusely, and promise to give your child a stern talking-to when he/she gets home?

b) promise the complainant that you'll handle it, and talk to your child about the allegations to see what, if any, defense he/she has for his/her actions, before punishing him/her, if necessary?

c) tell the other parent to mind his/her own fucking business, and start devising suitable punishments for the little brat when he/she returns home?

d) immediately have your child declared incorrigible and have him/her locked into a juvenile detention facility, or shipped to the nearest military academy?

Politics

1. You discover a friend holds an opposing political view to your own. Do you:

   a) use this as an opportunity to learn more about his/her point of view, and let him/her speak at length about it, without criticism or interruption?

   b) let him/her know your views are in conflict with his/hers, but that you respect his/her opinion, and agree to disagree?

   c) criticize your friend's party's position on numerous issues, and ask your friend how he/she could be so stupid as to agree with such idiotic notions?

   d) break off the friendship on the spot, and make a point of harassing him/her about his/her views whenever you encounter them socially from that point on?

2. A campaign worker for a candidate who opposes yours in an upcoming election knocks on your door one weekend morning. Do you:

   a) let him/her make his/her pitch, using it as an opportunity to learn more about the opposition, before politely explaining your own political loyalties, and wishing him/her good luck in the upcoming election?

   b) cut them off gently, mid-pitch, explaining you have no interest in his/her candidate and why?

   c) tell him/her to get off your property before he/she gets hurt?

   d) make an anonymous call to the police, telling them a man fitting the campaign worker's description is exposing himself to children in the neighborhood?

3. A news story reveals credible evidence of your candidate behaving in a scandalous, though not criminal, manner. Do you:

a) use the information to consider whether or not your candidate truly deserves your vote?

b) assume that the story is controversy for its own sake, fueled by the need of the media for better ratings, but is, nevertheless, something to really think about?

c) assume that the story is the work of your candidate's opponent, and immediately send a large contribution to him/her so as not to let such treachery go unanswered?

d) assume that the story is evidence of the bias of the entire news media against your candidate and his party, and immediately start a media watchdog group to expose the sham?

4. A news story reveals credible evidence that your candidate has taken illegal contributions from lobby groups in exchange for his/her vote on active legislation. Do you:

a) sever all ties with the candidate, and hope your party puts up a suitable replacement in good time?

b) wait to see which other politicians are also caught up in the scandal, so you can decide if your whole party is on the take, or just your candidate?

c) remain loyal to your candidate regardless of where the investigation leads – after all, which politician isn't at least a little corrupt, right?

d) swear eternal vengeance against the media, the opposition party, and anyone else who *dares* breathe a word of criticism against your candidate, especially based on such an obvious smear job campaign?

5. You have been asked to run as your party's candidate for an upcoming election, but you know that you have numerous skeletons in your closet. Do you:

   a) tell your party you're flattered, but you feel that you are a totally inappropriate choice, and explain why?

   b) tell the party you're flattered, but have other things you want or need to do with your life at the time?

   c) admit nothing, accept the nomination, and hope no one finds you out?

   d) admit nothing, accept the nomination, and hire numerous people to bury all the evidence, as well as a few potential witnesses, of your previous indiscretions?

Money

1. You find a lost wallet, containing $300 cash, multiple credit cards, and current ID in the back of a bus. Do you:

   a) go to whatever lengths necessary to find the owner, and return the wallet, exactly as you found it?

   b) turn it in to the police, so you won't have to worry about it, and it will be returned to its owner by an "unquestionable" source?

   c) keep the cash, but give the wallet to the bus driver and let him figure out what to do with the damn thing?

   d) keep the cash, use the credit cards to go on a spending spree, and ditch the rest – what a jackpot!

2. You desperately need to borrow money from someone, and the only

one who will lend it to you, is an old and dear friend who is also struggling to get by. Do you:

a) look for the money from some other source, as it would be wrong to impose on an old friend in such a way?

b) ask for the loan, but be prepared to be rejected, and willing to do whatever has to be done to repay it, should your friend be so kind as to help you out?

c) ask for the loan with confidence, because if you don't get it, you will never speak to your friend again; after all, this is *you* he/she is helping out?

d) ask for the loan, get the money, never pay it back, and when your friend brings it up more than once, never talk to him/her again; it serves him/her right for being such a sucker?

3. You are offered the opportunity to invest in products which will definitely harm, or even kill, people, but are completely legal. Do you:

a) categorically refuse the offer, and alert the media to these vile new products being developed?

b) categorically refuse, but know that there isn't really anything you can do; sick people will always find disgusting new ways to make money?

c) make a minor initial investment, and after ensuring that no controversy breaks out, invest even *more* money; better safe than sorry, right?

d) put everything you have into it, and fuck everyone; this is how fortunes are made?

4. You hit the lottery, and win $1 million of pre-taxed cash. Do you:

a) give as much away to charity and the needy as possible, just to try to make the world a better place; you'll content yourself with whatever's left?

b) settle your debts, buy gifts for your loved ones, and develop a portfolio of sound, long-term investments; everything else, you donate to charity?

c) do whatever the hell you want, it's your money, dammit?

d) use the money to secure political influence and relative immunity from prosecution, and then get to work with appropriate "investments" – after all, it takes money to make money, right?

5. You are offered a vast fortune to do something you consider to be profoundly distasteful, or even just plain *wrong* (such as sleeping with Robert Redford at his current age, for example.) Do you:

a) tell the person making the indecent proposal that you can't be bought, and walk off in a huff of righteous indignation?

b) think about it, but ultimately reject such an idea, knowing that it would bother you for the rest of your life; lousy *integrity?*

c) accept the proposal, take the money, and spend the rest of your life attempting to put it out of your mind, by whatever means neccessary?

d) accept the proposal, take the money, and use it to have the person who made the proposal abducted, tortured, and killed to show them what such power's *really* about?

Religion

1. As one of its essential tenets, your religion claims to be the only true path to salvation in the afterlife. Do you:

   a) accept the fundamental nature of this assertion and try to lead a life that is worthy of it?

   b) realize that this is something all religions say, but pay lip service to the idea when around others who share your faith?

   c) use this as a motivation to convert all non-believers?

   d) use this as a justification for the extermination of all non-believers unwilling to convert to the one truth faith?

2. You encounter someone whose appearance alone indicates that he/she is of a religious faith other than your own. Do you:

   a) ask him/her sincere and respectful questions about his/her faith; after all, different doesn't have to mean *wrong*, right?

   b) avoid speaking to him/her, at least about religion, as he/she obviously has beliefs of his/her own.

   c) attempt to convert him/her to your own religion, as his/hers is clearly irrational and false?

   d) loudly criticize everything you know about his/her faith, even if you're not entirely sure what you're talking about – no way is it better than *your* faith?

3. You encounter a missionary of an unfamiliar religion, who seems quite emphatic about wanting to share his/her different metaphysical views. Do you:

   a) attempt to find common ground to try to understand his/her different point of view, even accepting some of his/her free literature when you part company?

b) attempt to find common ground, but defend any personal beliefs which are different from his/hers in a mature and tactful fashion, while refusing any literature?

c) take the opportunity for vigorous and partisan debate – if he/she doesn't like it, he/she should not have approached you?

d) get away from him/her as quickly as possible before phoning through a description of him/her to the Department of Homeland Security as a possible "terror threat"?

4. Your local religious leader tells you that you must vote for a specific candidate in an upcoming election because the candidate holds identical values to your religion. Do you:

a) take your religious leader at his word, as obviously a representative of divine power would *never* lie to you?

b) examine the candidate for yourself, and vote for them on the basis of your own judgment?

c) not only vote for the candidate on the basis of your religious leader's endorsement, but campaign for him/her as well?

d) campaign and vote for the candidate and question the faith of anyone in your religion who does not?

5. The highest ranking religious leader of your faith calls for a "Holy War" against any and all non-believers. Do you:

a) protest this immediately as being inappropriate for *any* clergyman, even if it means being executed for doing so?

b) pay lip service to the injunction in public, but ignore it as much as possible?

   c) volunteer immediately for military service in defense of all you
      hold sacred – let the infidels tremble at the very idea!

   d) volunteer immediately for military service, execute all orders
      without question, and volunteer for any mission likely to ensure
      the defeat of the infidels, even if it entails certain martyrdom?

Scoring

Give yourself a score of zero for every time you answer (a), a single
point for every time you answer (b), two points for every time you
answer (c), and three points for every time you answer (d).

Your total score indicates the following:

0–49 **Harmless Victim**
Not only are you highly unlikely ever to be an asshole, you almost as
unlikely to be human. Either you live to suffer, you enjoy disappointment, or you're trying, misguidedly, for some kind of sainthood.

50–99 **Regular Schmuck**
While you have your ugly moments, like everyone else, most of the time
you take actions which are half-assed enough to offend almost no one.
Good luck maintaining your balance with that.

100–149 **Common Asshole**
No question about it, when the term was conceived, you and those like
you were probably the basis for it. Now that you know, do the rest of
us a favor, and just go away. Far away.

150 **Complete Asshole**
You have achieved the perfect score, a full house. Not only does no one
question what you *are*, no one questions you, *period* (except maybe the
local cops when they have no other leads). In fact, you probably only
took this test to see if there was something you might have missed. And

since, clearly, there was nothing you'd missed, please consider this an invitation to kill yourself, as quickly as possible, for the sake of the species. Not that you'll listen, of course. KD

Coping with your Inner Asshole

By now, you probably know more about those we call "assholes" than you had ever hoped to know, and, depending on your test score, perhaps more than you had ever wanted to know about yourself, too. It seems like wherever there is dirty money to be made, lies to be told, power to be seized, violence to dispense, or divisive opinions to be disseminated, there will be assholes, ready, willing, and able to make the world that little bit uglier, and harder to take. And the worst thing about such people is that they all started out just as inherently neutral as anyone else born into this chaotic and imperfect world we all have to live in, no different from ourselves, save for the deliberately selfish ways in which they have chosen to react to the common challenges of human existence.

It is no secret that life's trials and tribulations shape our characters and personalities to a great extent, but what separates most of humanity from the assholes of this world is how we react to events in our lives. While, for example, millions of people selflessly volunteered to do anything they could for the people and institutions of the city of New Orleans following the devastation wreaked by Hurricane Katrina, a few thousand assholes seized the opportunity to indulge in some brazen looting. Similarly, while millions of patriotic Americans volunteered themselves to aid their country in whichever ways they could in the "War on Terror," a small and privileged group saw the national tragedy of the terrorist attacks of 9/11 as an opportunity to grab more power for their political party, to strike back against longstanding ideological foes at home and abroad, and to challenge the patriotism of anyone who asked valid questions about their divisive and nakedly self-serving agenda. If such people don't manage to rise to *such* an occasion, one wonders what occasion they might ever rise to? And if they never do rise to any sort of occasion, why don't they?

The answer, as with non-assholes, is often to be found in some kind of crisis, challenge, or difficulty, experienced by the asshole in question, at a proverbial "young and impressionable age." While non-assholes might experience similar abuse, mistreatment, tragedies, disasters, injuries, or losses to their asshole counterparts, their reaction, attitude, outlook, and behavior are all likely to remain as selfless, reasonable, or compassionate as ever. For future assholes, on the other hand, such experiences serve as a justification for any number of bad acts, all emanating directly from their wounded psyches, but concerned only with the furtherance of their own ambitions and whatever they deem to be of the greatest importance to their future wellbeing, and, sometimes quite literally, to hell with the rest of the world. While mental health professionals have yet to determine the specific psychological basis of this moral X-Factor, nearly all agree that the propagation of compassionate and equitable social systems, cultures, and institutions, based on fair and ethical principles and rules greatly decreases the risk that such "morally fragile" people will be overwhelmed by the challenges they face. In a larger sense, this logic has been the basis for all human civilizations, religions, and ethical philosophies since the beginning of human history. So what, if anything, can be done to improve our so-called human condition, when, as far we know, we're doing pretty much the same as we've always done, which is also about the best we can do at any given moment in time and space?

The answer to this question begins and ends with ourselves, our notions of the kind of world we want to live in, and in constantly asking ourselves how we can make this world more closely resemble our ideal. When we see someone loaded down with shopping approaching a door that we, too, are about to pass through, do we hold it open for them, or enter quickly, rushing past them, and keep going? When we are ordering a meal from a clearly overworked and exhausted fast-food worker do we calmly correct any mistakes he or she might have made in a friendly, non-judgmental manner which takes into account the difficulty of the worker's situation, or do we angrily restate our order in a way which leaves the worker in no doubt that we think he or she has behaved like a perfect idiot in failing to perform a basic task? When we see another driver attempting to join our lane in rush-hour traffic, do we slow down and allow him or her to go in front of us, or do we punch the gas and leave the "pushy" driver to the mercy of whoever the hell's behind us? Our willingness to act in the former way in each case, rather than the latter, is based largely on our ability to conceive of how such incidents might be experienced by the other parties involved, and comparing that to how we might want to be treated in a similar situation. This serves as the logical and empathetic basis for the Christian "golden rule" of doing unto others as we would have others do unto us. As with all the best examples of moral thought, it is firmly based in everyday reality.

In everyday reality, however, sometimes we don't hold the door open, or calmly restate our food order, or allow other drivers to cut in front of us. Sometimes, we tell ourselves we just don't feel like it, or we're running late, or, most frequently, someone has just done something equally rude, thoughtless, or deliberately unkind to us. If we've been in malls and shopping centers all day, encountering equally unco-operative people, we are far more likely reflexively to be just as spiteful about opening a door for an overburdened, fellow shopper. If we've been busy dealing with thousands of irate callers to a customer service hotline all morning, we are much more likely to want to complain and criticize the server who messes up our lunch order. And studies of so-called "road rage" have proved, almost conclusively, that those who drive aggressively and competitively during rush hour all too often encourage others to drive just as badly, leading to stringent new laws against such behavior, and the aggressive enforcement of such legislation by authorities, to make the point stick.

If anything, such instances prove that we must be constantly mindful of our behavior towards others, and remain consciously committed to altering our own behavior as required, regardless of whatever might be troubling us in a particular situation, or in our lives in general. Our needs, and the needs of others, should always consciously be given preference over the passing desires of even our own disturbed egos, but it is naïve to think that such an ideal can ever be lived up to, except through a daily, ongoing, if imperfect, commitment to be mindful of the fragility of the world around us, and the people in it, especially those in our immediate presence. Put another way, this is the "discipline" inherent in "spiritual discipline," which, like all functional disciplines, is a means to something greater than ourselves, rather than an end to the evolution of our thoughts, feelings, and conduct.

This is not to say that the practitioners of even the most conscious and deliberately moral conduct, never suffer lapses, but, with the correct emphasis on larger, more profound, goals, rather than temporary, undesirable circumstances or results, it is far easier to correct ourselves, and move on. This impulse to correct our actions when we feel bad about some aspect of them is, in fact, vitally important to that process, as merely feeling remorse, or asking to be forgiven without offering proof of our desire to change our behavior is often met with incredulity, or even hostility, by those we have harmed, even if inadvertently. This is the basis for acts of atonement and contrition, which, when offered sincerely by transgressors, often have a profoundly healing effect on all concerned, a result far more positive than merely stemming the tide of negative thoughts, feelings, and bad conduct in general. Rather, an act of atonement or contrition is a reminder of the most valued aspects of human potential, which both nourish and encourage all who show the courage to accept its basic challenge to grow and change, both wisely and well, as an ongoing and inescapable aspect of all human evolution. Simply put, as a species, we must either learn, eventually, to live together, in a slowly improving world, or prepare to die alone, on a planet scarred by the steady disintegration of civilized human behavior. The challenge we face is ongoing, complex, and total, and it remains to be seen which choices we make in the course of our collective history. KD